American Brasserie

American Brasserie

*180 Simple, Robust Recipes Inspired by the
Rustic Foods of France, Italy, and America*

GALE GAND AND RICK TRAMONTO

WITH JULIA MOSKIN

WINE NOTES BY MARTY TIERSKY

PHOTOS BY TIM TURNER

Wiley Publishing, Inc.

For general information on our other products and services or to obtain technical support please contact our Customer Care Department within the U.S. at 800-762-2974, outside the U.S. at 317-572-3993 or fax 317-572-4002.

Wiley also publishes its books in a variety of electronic formats. Some content that appears in print may not be available in electronic books.

Library of Congress Cataloging-in-Publication Data:
Gand, Gale.
    American brasserie / Gale Gand and Rick Tramonto with Julia Moskin.
    paperback
            p. cm.
    Includes index.
    ISBN 0-7645-2449-6
    1. Cookery. 2. Cookery, French. 3. Cookery, Italian.
    4. Cookery, American. 5. Brasserie T.I. Tramonto, Rick.
    II. Moskin, Julia. III. Title
TX714.G353   1997   97-21819
641.5—dc21   CIP

Interior Design: Amy Trombat

Manufactured in the United States of America
10 9 8 7 6 5 4 3 2 1

American Brasserie is dedicated to:

A life that began at almost the same time as the book: our son, Giorgio Montana Gand Tramonto. We promise you there will always be stockpots full of love, and that the generous spirit of food and wine will always be present in our home.

Bob Payton, to whom we owe so much and who opened doors for us that have never closed. Thank you for your eccentricity and unlimited energy and for giving us the opportunity to gather these stories and dishes. We miss those three star dinners that began at six, lasted until ten, and ended with chili dogs at midnight! We love you.

Myrna Gand, my sweet, brilliant, artistic, feisty Hungarian mother, who told me I was born under a lucky star—and I believed her. Thank you for giving me the ability to experience joy and beauty, and for your hands of gold that made only the most perfect pie crusts. I wish we had had more time…

Contents

Acknowledgments

Thanks to...

Our families: Frank and Gloria Tramonto for love and support and putting up with our hours; Bob Gand for pointing out that everyone's gotta eat and for always bringing music into our lives; Gary Gand and Joan Burnstein Gand for their good appetites; Lana Rae Goldberg for great *mandelbrot* and being there for us; Grandma Elsie Grossman for giving Gale a love for kitchen alchemy; Aunt Greta and Uncle Robert Pearson for the copper bowl and whisk and for the first good glass of red.

The whole Brasserie T and Vanilla Bean Bakery team, whom we count on every single day for long hours and hard work. We couldn't have done this without you. Special thanks to Muhammad Solaudin, for keeping us sane and keeping the bunnies in the pen while we worked on the book; Mary Mullins, for brains, beauty, handholding during the pregnancy, great computer skills, and the ability to meet our demanding deadlines; and our courageous investors, who somehow believed in our vision when all they could see was plaster dust and scaffolding. To all of our vendors, especially Tom Cornille for produce knowledge; the whole family at European Imports; Vin di Vino; and Giovanni Puatti, for planting the seed for Tramonto wines. Nancy Warren for architectural vision, Dierdre Zimmerman for perfect graphics; Barb Charal for keeping the numbers straight. Kurman Communications, especially Cindy "The Kurmanator" Kurman, for PR wizardry and friendship.

Book people: Jane Dystel, our agent, for taking our appointment and taking us seriously and Jennifer Griffin, for really making it happen. Our deepest, gushiest gratitude goes to Karen Katz, for testing the recipes night after night and to her family, for eating it all. Julia Moskin, for her friendship, talent, and for being the one who holds the guiding light when we ask, "What do we do now?"

Our friends: Larry Binstein, who keeps us laughing and in olive oil, cheese, and chocolate, for expert map reading and driving the "elegante." Marty Tiersky for friendship, intellect, generosity, wardrobe inspiration, and attention to detail, as well as helping us figure out what wine really goes with chocolate cake. Al Friedman and Michael Fox, for helping form this slightly perfect union. Wendy Payton and Peter Weber, Murial Hamon, Moe Brooker, Marthe Hess, Vinnie Rupert and Jimmy Bonnesteel, Brian Bram, Dee DeCarlo, Val Landsburg, and Debbie and Carlos Nieto. Debra Chase, for being an angel on earth until her last day. We miss her.

Chefs, vintners, and food people, for inspiration and guidance: Greg Broman, Albert Kumin, Alfred Portale, Charlie Trotter, Michel Guérard, Anton Mosimann, Raymond Blanc, Nico Ladanis, Pierre Gagnaire, Alain Ducasse, Paul Bocuse, Julia Child, Michael Chiarello, James Haller, Emeril Lagasse, Norman van Aken, Jonathan Waxman, Joachim Splichal, Dave Thomas, Bobby Flay, James Beard, Robert Mondavi, Laura Chenel, Randel Graham, John Mariani, the Chappellet family, and our friends at ChefWare and the TV Food Network for making us feel like stars.

In Chicago: The folks at Lettuce Entertain You Enterprises for taking our phone calls, and a special thanks to Rich Melman for friendship, wisdom, support, and sharing his golden touch. Bill Rice, Pat Bruno, Phil Vettel, and all the other food writers who cared about our food; our customers, who make us proud to be part of the great Chicago food scene.

Gale's Special Thanks

To my husband, Rick, who makes me feel smart and loved and who gave me someone to share this culinary calling with. You are always the driver of this bus, and I feel lucky to be along for the wild ride.

Rick's Special Thanks

To my Lord, Jesus Christ, for keeping me on the right road!

To Myrna Gand, who brought my best friend, Gale, into the world and who was nutty but always supportive of me and my mission. I miss you and thank you.

To Gale, my wife, my partner, and the mother of my son.

Julia's Special Thanks

To Sam Sifton, Jane Dystel, Maron and Nach Waxman, and Carole DeSanti, who all nudged me along the road. To Rick and Gale, for their amazing courage and humor. To Max, for his patience, faith, and wonderful appetite. To Nancy, Anne, Ellen, Susannah, Amy, Lisa, Emily, Shira, Hilary, Steve, Rie, Bruce, Holly, Karl, Christine, Deb, Rosemary, Ali, Pat, Julian, Jeremy, Ava, and Grandma, who kept me laughing and sane. And the Big Thank You: Mom and Dad, for teaching me how to chop parsley and everything that came afterward.

Introduction

In 1994, when we decided the time was right to open a world-class brasserie in Chicago, even our most loyal fans and friends were surprised. At our last restaurant, we had been building a reputation as culinary virtuosos. Our creative French-Japanese-Italian cuisine and innovative presentations were winning international praise, and the restaurant was booked solid for months in advance.

We told them that Brasserie T would be different—that we were creating a casual, French-inspired restaurant with family style and a menu of big-flavored, simple, but satisfying dishes. Instead of fusion food, we would be cooking robust traditional dishes like French onion soup with grainy mustard and melted Gruyère cheese, sautéed salmon with spinach and mashed potatoes, artichoke and wild mushroom risotto, blueberry bread pudding, individual apple tarts, and homemade dark chocolate biscotti, all complemented by great table wines and American microbrewery beers. They were delighted, but the name perplexed them. By now they all knew what a bistro was, but a brasserie? Some of the construction workers on the site were even embarrassed to say the name.

What *is* a brasserie, anyway? We've been asked that a lot. Literally, it's a brewery—a place where *brasser* (French for "to brew") is the main order of business. In France the first brasseries evolved in the northeastern parts of the country, as taverns attached to local breweries and beer-brewing monasteries. Fresh beer foaming from the tap was the star attraction; simple, hearty local foods were supplied free by the owner. It's probably no accident that many of the classic brasserie dishes: onion soup, *choucroute garnie*, platters of smoked fish and *charcuterie*—are salty and savory enough to make you reach again and again for that tall glass of refreshing golden lager! However, brasseries as we know them—the bustling, casual restaurants that capture the essence of French city life—began, like so many other food stories, in Paris.

During our years as professional chefs, we've been lucky enough to spend months eating, cooking, and traveling in Europe. At Stapleford Park Hotel, a luxurious English hotel where we ran the kitchen for two years, our friend Bob Payton, the hotel's owner, encouraged us to explore every dish, every ingredient, every idea we could come up with. It was exciting to be able to stretch our talents and imaginations to the utmost, and whenever we could grab a few days' vacation, we were off to nearby France and Italy to learn more. We prowled through Paris's phenomenal food wholesale market, Tuscany's mozzarella factories, wineries, and olive oil mills, witnessing the tradition and craftsmanship that go into the products that we used to take for granted. We ate in countless restaurants, comparing notes and tastes, trying to understand the choices the chefs made and the methods used for each dish. But some of the places we loved the most were the places where we, and everyone else, could just relax and enjoy: the brasseries of Paris, Lyons, and Nice.

When we began our search for brasserie tradition, we headed first for Alsace in northeastern France, a region running along the Rhine River that has been traded back and forth between France and Germany for centuries. Thanks to this history, the land evolved its own combination of French and German culture, language, and food. In the nineteenth century Alsace was also the center of the French lager beer industry (see "A Short History of Beer and Brasseries"). When the German annexation of 1870 forced thousands of Alsatians to flee to other French cities, many made new lives crafting beer and other regional Alsatian specialties for their compatriots. This became the common thread tying the great French brasseries together. Most still continue the Alsatian tradition of generous, hearty food served in an easygoing atmosphere, although few brasseries today make their own beer. In fact, at the moment there are more real "brasseries" (we call them brewpubs) in Chicago than there are in Paris or in Strasbourg, the Alsatian capital!

In Paris today a brasserie is any restaurant where the beer is on tap and the menu is large and flexible. But the term has come to mean much more that. In our visits to France, we discovered brasseries to be casual but stylish restaurant-cafés, open all day, where you can order anything from an omelet and a glass of wine to mid-afternoon coffee and pastries to a satisfying dinner of oysters, chicory salad, with warm bacon vinaigrette, and roast chicken. We immediately loved their warm welcome, their bustle, their casual chic.

The beer-soaked heritage of brasseries doesn't mean that you don't drink wine at a brasserie— everyone does. In fact, you can eat and drink just about anything you want at a brasserie. That's what we like about them. It's no accident that brasseries are city restaurants; like cities themselves, brasseries absorb a huge diversity of influences and turn them into something unique and energetic, fun and flexible. In the same way we were convinced from the start that brasseries are perfectly suited to America, with its busy schedules, diversity of tastes, and tremendous appetite for hearty home cooking.

One thing we know that a brasserie most definitely is *not* is a bistro. French bistros serve their inspired, exalted home cooking in cozy, intimate surroundings. A bistro can have as few as five or six tables, while a brasserie needs lots of elbow room. Traditional bistros are often what we would call "mom and pop" establishments, with small wait staffs and leisurely service, while brasseries are manned by armies of waiters in white aprons, skimming efficiently through the room.

So what is brasserie cooking? At a bistro you are generally expected to choose from a set menu of several courses; at a brasserie you can have a dinner of two dozen oysters followed by profiteroles with chocolate sauce, or a 2 A.M. snack of pork chops, sauerkraut, and chocolate mousse, and no one will bat an eye.

Since many trendsetting Paris brasseries were founded and are still run by Alsatian expatriates, there are certain dishes of that region that often turn up on brasserie menus: *choucroute garnie* (see our Chicago Choucroute, pages 148–49), *tarte à l'oignon* (see our Caramelized Onion Tart, pages 18–19), *coq au riesling* with spaetzle (see our Coq au Riesling, pages 142–43 and our Mustard Spaetzle, pages 204–5), and *tarte aux mirabelles* (see our Plum Crostata, pages 238–39). Waverly Root, in his classic work *The Food of France,* says (rather Francocentrically, of course) that the genius of Alsatian cooking is that "the Alsatians have added a French subtlety to the often rather unimaginative heaviness of German food." Whether these dishes are German, French, or utterly American, we know from experience that they please anyone who likes good food.

Brasserie cuisine has always been both hearty and inexpensive, so you will often see filling, full-flavored, but not necessarily elegant dishes like onion soup with croutons and melted cheese, garlic sausage with lentils, and calf's liver (see our version with balsamic vinegar sauce, pages 144–45) on brasserie menus. And the classic dishes of French bourgeois cuisine that have become popular in every part of the country—snails with garlic and parsley, chicken braised in red wine, expertly boiled beef with vegetables—are all regular features of a brasserie kitchen, often revolving on and off the menu as the seasons change.

When we set out to create our own brasserie right in the heart of the American Midwest, we knew we wanted to bring all of these elements together. We just didn't yet know how. It didn't take long for us to realize that in an American context, our brasserie would have to reflect local tastes, traditions, and products—or to admit to each other that we didn't want to cook only classic French brasserie food. After years in prestigious fine-dining kitchens, Rick wanted to revisit the home-style Italian dishes he grew up on: spaghetti with tomato sauce and escarole, sausage, and white bean stew. He had recently returned to Italy to study its food traditions and was eager to put all he'd learned about cooking polenta, making pizza, and saucing pasta to work. For Gale the same urge for rustic home cooking kept leading her thoughts toward classic all-American desserts like rice pudding, chocolate cream pie, and baked apples. For both of us, the strong flavors and redolent spices of the Mediterranean that we discovered in Provence, Italy, and Spain had become an integral part of our cooking. Clearly, our brasserie would be very much our own—and very American in its combination of cuisine and ideas.

We were lucky that circumstances and choice landed us in Chicago. With its booming restaurant scene, cold winters, tradition of hearty eating, and strong German-American and Italian-American food influences, the response to our robust French-German-Italian-American menu was immediate and overwhelming. When Brasserie T opened its doors in July of 1995, even we were shocked by the enthusiastic response. We were delighted to find that our vision of a friendly, French-inspired restaurant where anyone could feel comfortable, eat well, and leave nourished in body and soul struck a chord in the community. And the first time we drove up to find a party of six sitting in the bar sipping a Provençal pastis and sharing a bowl of *moules marinières,* with the French doors open to the late afternoon sun and warm summer breeze, we knew we really were on to something.

As far as we were concerned, the American microbrewery boom couldn't have come at a better time. The only difficulty was in choosing which of the many wonderful new beers and ales to serve on tap. We finally narrowed it down to twelve, with an additional eighteen available in the bottle. Lagers, ales, stouts, porters, German wheat beers, and English bitters can all be beautifully matched with our dishes and are rapidly becoming available across the country. You'll find many recommendations on the following pages (turn to "On Wine, Beer, and Food" for more ideas about beer with food). In our home-grown American tradition, beer is often paired with big-flavored food like hearty sandwiches, chili, and pizza. Our flavorful, inspired versions include Roasted Vegetable–White Bean Chili (pages 120–21); Skirt Steak Sandwiches with Roasted Shallots and Horseradish Mayonnaise (page 89); and Tuscan Arugula Pizza (page 65). Gale even brews her own root beer (a distinctively American quaff) for the restaurant.

Our versions of French and Italian classics like *steak frites, salade Niçoise,* osso buco, and apple tart were customer favorites from the start, but as our menu evolved, we found to our surprise that they most loved the dishes we were most uncertain about. We already knew that *we* loved classic, hearty brasserie food, but we wondered: "Would they really order the liver and onions? Would they appreciate our authentic choucroute, or just think 'Why have sauerkraut for dinner?' Would they yawn at the idea of onion soup and rice pudding?" On the contrary. They loved them, demanded more like them, and never stopped asking us for the recipes. We've chosen 180 favorites for this book.

All our dishes, from soups to pastas to roasts to desserts, have something important in common: bold, generous, simple flavors. We like serving (and eating) them at Brasserie T, and they adapt remarkably well to American home kitchens. They use ingredients you don't have to send away for, and techniques that won't eat up your precious free time, and more important, they are truly satisfying family fare. We know that when you've gone to the trouble of cooking, you want a dish whose flavors and textures please and soothe you. Our goal in developing the menu for Brasserie T was to come up with a group of dishes we—and our customers—could choose from *every single day* and always feel happy and satisfied. The same principle applies to this book. Looking for a speedy weeknight pasta? Spaghettini with Quick Tomato-Basil Sauce (pages 94–95) fits the bill, and so does Rick's favorite—Farfalle with Many Mushrooms, Tomatoes, and Fresh Herbs (pages 92–93). An impressive holiday supper? What could be better than Lemon-Sage Roast Chicken with Sausage-Mushroom-Potato Stuffing (pages 166–67)—except perhaps an elegant Hazelnut-Crusted Rack of Lamb (pages 184–85)? Need a comforting dessert? Gale's Blueberry Bread-and-Butter Pudding (pages 248–49) is a simply brilliant take on the American classic, and her fabulous Roasted Fruits with Cinnamon–Red Wine Glaze and Toasted Almonds (pages 232–33) pulls together in minutes.

At Brasserie T we take pleasure in creating unexpectedly simple but appealing dishes that need little or no cooking, in the French brasserie tradition of serving platters of charcuterie and cheese at all hours and for all occasions. Informal, interesting meals of cheese, salad, fruit, and bread, put together from the

"Salads," "Cheese Plates," and "Breads" sections of *American Brasserie*, please all the senses. These plates were also inspired by the English tradition of serving an intensely flavored "savory" after a meal, such as the incomparable combination of Stilton blue cheese, fresh walnuts, and aged Port. They're great with drinks before dinner or as after-dinner savories to linger over while finishing a bottle of wine. Our big Italian-style whole-meal sandwiches are popular throughout the day, and they are especially terrific with cool golden beers. Our pizzas, with savory toppings like asparagus, eggplant, prosciutto, and sausages are easy, healthful, and satisfying for quick family dinners or summer buffets.

We know that when you turn to your cookbook library, it's most often in search of the centerpiece for a meal—so we've included not one but two chapters devoted to main dishes. "Main Courses" is packed with easy dishes that either cook in a flash, can be begun ahead of time, or take very little time to prepare, perfect for weeknight dinners with family and friends. For days when you have more flexibility and may feel like exploring a new ingredient, method, or dish, the "Weekend Cooking" chapter deliciously illustrates what happens when you take time for layering and building flavors. These recipes are not necessarily more challenging but may require some extra patience. All make impressive entrees for special dinners, and most—like Portofino Bouillabaisse (pages 158–60), Osso Buco with Saffron Risotto and Orange Gremolata (pages 178–80), and Cassoulet (pages 168–70)—are based on Old World classics that are very close to our hearts. Many of our main dishes are complete in themselves, such as Pot-au-Feu (pages 186–87) and Spring

Vegetable and Rabbit Fricassee (pages 161–63), but most are rounded out with one of our favorite grain or vegetable side dishes. You'll find suggestions at the top of each main dish recipe, and all the recipes are collected in the "Side Dishes" chapter.

When it's time for dinner at home, we always heat up some water and chop up some onions. We don't always know what we're going to do with them: boil potatoes, cook pasta, make a stew, or flavor a vinaigrette. But it's always an easy way to get started, and that's what we want to offer in this book—an irresistibly easy and appealing way to get back into the kitchen and start cooking. The pleasures of the table abound at Brasserie T, but in *American Brasserie* we also bring you the pleasures of the kitchen. To us no perfume can compete with the smell of onions and garlic cooking on the stove, waiting to be transformed into something wonderful. The fragrance of a simmering stew, a handful of mixed chopped herbs, or a baking pound cake all give intense pleasure that we appreciate as part of the meal.

All of our recipes, especially Rick's classic slow-cooked specialties in the "Weekend Cooking" chapter and Gale's astoundingly delicious desserts, will remind you and your family of how much pleasure a good meal can bring—in the cooking as well as in the eating. Before our son, Gio, was born in August of 1996, we had almost forgotten about home cooking; now cooking for each other and for him is something we look forward to. At home we don't cook like chefs; we cook like our parents, who were our first teachers. Come join us in our home kitchen, our brasserie, our trattoria, our pizzeria, or our bakery—they're all right here in these pages.

A SHORT HISTORY OF BEER AND BRASSERIES

The legendary brasseries of France, like La Coupole, Lipp, and Georges, are the best places in the world for a glass of beer, a *choucroute garnie*, and a session of people-watching. But they're more than restaurants: they're also unique institutions, the end product of a rich brew of ideas about art, industry, architecture, geopolitics, tourism, electricity, feminism, religion, and botany that simmered in nineteenth-century France. All these factors contributed to the evolution of the great brasseries and the bustling spirit they still exude. It was in mid-century Paris that the great lager brewers of Munich and Vienna built large beer halls to promote their product in France, and it was in Paris that French taste quickly transformed the rustic German tavern into a more cosmopolitan and exciting kind of venue. That's how the brasseries we know took their final shape, but their story goes back much, much further.

The Brew of the Ancients

Since the very word *brasserie* simply means brewery, the beer itself is the place to start. Barley, from which most beer is made, was one of the earliest cultivated grains, and the production of barley beer is documented as far back as the Sumerian civilization, which flourished in the Fertile Crescent around 4,000 years ago. The fact that it's almost impossible to make good bread from plain barley probably helped make it the grain of choice for brewing. Until the relatively recent addition of hops and flavoring herbs, around A.D. 900, most beer probably tasted quite nasty as well. Cloudy, sweet, and much lower in alcohol than any modern-day brew, the beer of the ancients really was a nourishment-packed, filling bread substitute more than a thirst-quenching drink.

In the ancient Nordic sagas, frequent references to beer and the goddesses who oversaw its brewing suggest that beer, not bread, was truly the staff of life in most of northern Europe. Beer was food and drink, an inexplicable and generous gift from the gods (no one knew then how or why fermentation took place), and a mild intoxicant that warmed, relieved pain, and nourished. Women brewed at home the beer they needed to feed their own households. Although today we think of beer as a manly drink, it was generally accepted for centuries that brewing, like baking, was the province of the woman of the house.

The Emperor's New Beer

Until the Roman conquest, most of modern France was inhabited by the Celts, tribes who eventually were pushed by the Romans and other invaders all the way back to the British Isles (where, among other accomplishments, they continued to develop their brewing techniques). Winemaking is not easy in the northern reaches of France, with its short summers and long, overcast springs and autumns, and there was virtually no grape cultivation there for centuries. Meanwhile, the grain that was needed for beer and bread grew ever more plentiful as agriculture developed.

In the year 92, the Roman Emperor Domitian abruptly split Europe in two by decreeing winemaking to be illegal in all parts of the empire where grain could be grown. Domitian was determined to protect the Italian vineyards from competition from the north, where advances in agriculture were beginning to make winemaking possible. All the vines in Alsace, Champagne, and elsewhere in France were abruptly ripped out by Roman troops. This drastic measure had the effect of dividing Europe for centuries into southern wine drinkers (think of Italy, Spain, and Portugal) and northern beer drinkers (think of Germany, Belgium, the Netherlands, and northern France). This large and rebellious northern region was known to the Romans as Gaul.

Two hundred years later Domitian's order was rescinded. (As Waverly Root points out in *The Food of France*, restrictions on alcohol were no more popular in Roman times than in our own.) Soon afterward, the birth of Christianity brought wine to the north—with a vengeance. Wine was deeply important to the new religion, since it was identified as the actual blood of the Savior; beer was already intertwined with the ancient pagan rites and the daily life of the people. The early years of Christianity in Gaul pitted wine against beer in a struggle for supremacy that seems to have gotten violent at times. In documents dating back to the fourth century A.D., beer was accused by Christian priests of causing all sorts of medical and spiritual turbulence. In 306 the idea of excommunicating all brewers was seriously discussed, and through the Middle Ages brewing and distilling were persistently associated with sorcery, alchemy, and other dark arts.

Monasteries and Brasseries

Although beer was considered an unholy and distasteful drink by the church fathers in sunny Rome, the new monasteries of northern Europe were forced to brew beer to keep their parishioners alive. The monasteries acted as agricultural and manufacturing centers, with enough technology and resources to store reserves of grain and brew large batches of beer, either from their own crops or as a service to parishioners (a percentage of the finished beer was retained by the monks as the price of brewing). Most northern parishes were far too cold and too poor to consider the long and complicated process of making wine. Grain was more nutritious and always available, whereas ripe grapes were hard to come by, could not be stored through the winter, and could not be substituted for bread.

Most of the important preindustrial developments in beer brewing, including the use of hops and cold fermentation, took place in the monasteries, and their beer culture became extremely sophisticated. The fact that only monks had the ability to read and write undoubtedly had something to do with this: recipes and improvements could be handed from monastery to monastery and from generation to generation. Certain monasteries, like the ones at Orval in Belgium and St. Gall in Switzerland, became (and have remained) celebrated for the quality of their ales. Most had at least three brews available at all times: a special one for the fathers, one for the brothers, and the last and weakest for the poor, pilgrims, and nuns. In the absence of inns and hotels, the monasteries offered travelers and pilgrims a modest meal accompanied by unlimited beer. These taverns were pretty low on amenities—but they seem to have been the very first brasseries.

The Business of Brewing

As towns and cities developed, brewing beer, like milling flour and making cheese, moved away from the monasteries and the housewives to become the province of specialized merchants. In 1259 the first commercial brewery in Strasbourg, now the capital of the French province of Alsace (then an independent state called Elsass) was founded, ensuring a steady supply of beer for the many masons at work on the city's soaring new Gothic cathedral. As competition developed, manufacturers diversified the product: marjoram, bay leaves, juniper berries, mint, coriander seed, and even horseradish were commonly added as flavorings and preservatives, and towns began to develop characteristic styles. Certain brews, especially spicy and sweet ones, were renowned and promoted for their medicinal or aphrodisiac qualities, and ecclesiastical brewers did their best to ban these completely.

The ultimate response to all this creative brewing came not from the church but from the state. In 1516 Bavaria passed the still-in-effect *Rheinheitsgebot*, or Beer Purity Law, ensuring that only malt, water, yeast, and hops could be used to make beer. Paris has similar, though much less stringent, laws dating back to 1268, imposing fines on anyone making and selling adulterated beer. The self-imposed *Rheinheitsgebot* was a sign of the hardheaded business sense that turned brewing into a respectable, thriving industry, complete with apprentices, governing bodies, and inspectors.

The Protestant Reformation of the sixteenth century also strengthened the position of beer through its challenges to the Catholic Church. Although Catholic monks had certainly been deeply connected to the region's brewing traditions, the Reformation seems to have encouraged the commercial brewers to assert their claims on the market for beer. By 1789, the year of the Revolution, French brewing was entirely commercialized, and the industry was stronger and bigger than ever before.

Vive la liberté!

The French Revolution swept away the web of restrictive legislation that had come to surround the making, selling, and drinking of beer. Going back to statutes of 1514, all French brewers had held the exclusive rights to selling their own beer. Most breweries sold their beer directly, bottled or in pitchers and jugs, from a pub on the premises that also offered food as an incentive to buy. In Alsace, these are known as *bierstubs*; they mark another step in the evolution of the brasserie. When the selling of beer was deregulated, new beer taverns quickly sprang up in Paris and the northern provinces—and they multiplied quickly. Through the first half of the nineteenth century, the commercial breweries of Strasbourg, Lille, Munich, Brussels, and Vienna flourished and expanded, and beers like Kronenbourg, Stella Artois, Fischer, Spaten, and Löwenbräu became known throughout France.

Meanwhile, a new phenomenon—the restaurant—was catching on. In 1765 a M. Boulanger opened the first large establishment in Paris. He was promptly sued by the city's guild of *traiteurs*, or caterers, who claimed they held the monopoly on selling cooked meat. But when they were just as promptly defeated, the restaurant was born. Since the titled aristocrats of the French *ancien régime* had no use for restaurants (would not, in fact, have dreamed of eating in a public place), in 1789 there were still fewer than a hundred restaurants in Paris. But by 1800 there were over five hundred restaurants, all competing to feed the new bourgeoisie. The guilds had been abolished altogether in 1791, freeing restaurants to serve anything they liked; thousands of cooks had fled the employ of aristocratic homes; and people were crowding into the capital seeking work. The stage was set for the great nineteenth-century boom.

Different Times, Different Beers

The beer taverns, or brasseries, a word that soon came to mean both a brewery where beer was made and a small pub where it could be drunk, soon rivaled the cafés of Paris in number and popularity, though not in grandeur and elegance. The brasseries were extremely casual establishments, but had one distinct advantage: they served food as well as drink, simple dishes like sausages and potatoes that provided energy for the working class. These *plats brasserie* provided a filling alternative to the food at other cheap eating places available in Paris at the time: the *bouillons* and *gargotes,* or greasy spoons, devoted to serving as many people as possible as cheaply as possible with diluted beef broth and bread.

In 1860 French beer received a strengthening shot in the arm from an unexpected source: French vineyards. The plague of phylloxera swept through the vines of Europe like a flame, sending wine prices through the roof and anyone on a budget into the brasseries. The wine industry would continue to stagger uncertainly for the next two decades before reestablishing itself in the 1890s. In the meantime, Paris experienced an enormous surge in the popularity of beer and brasseries.

The Expositions Universelles, or world's fairs, of the 1800s also played an enormous role in bringing people, restaurants, and brasseries to Paris. The very first fair in Europe was held in Paris's Champ de Mars in 1798 and was so successful that others followed quickly. London's famous Exhibition of the Works of All Nations in London in 1851 was a major international event that spurred the French on to ever more impressive and lavish spectacles.

The Paris fairs of 1855 and 1867 brought a new beer to the capital: the dedicated brewers of Munich and Vienna had developed a markedly different, clear and light, drinkable and flavorful beer. The age of lager beer had begun. Over the protests of the French brewers, Löwenbräu, Spatenbräu, and other lagers were rapturously received throughout Paris, especially in the Latin Quarter, where the students of the Sorbonne often gathered for *chopes*, mugs of beer.

Once the lager beers had established their supremacy, a decisive new step was taken: the German brewing companies opened their own brasseries in the French capital. Designed along the lines of the spacious, festive beer halls of Munich and Vienna, the first large-scale Paris brasseries were decorated in a traditional German style, with tiled walls, wooden tables, and beamed ceilings. In Germany beautiful beer halls were being designed by the same architects who devoted their talents to churches and theaters, but in France dark and dingy taverns had long been the rule. Now beer gardens with music, lights, and flowers became the center of social life for thousands in the French capital. (The German *biergartens* were also the model for the marvelous beer gardens of Chicago, St. Louis, Milwaukee, and Cincinnati, now, alas, gone.) Instead of dark, forbidding places for men to furtively indulge a bad habit, the new brasseries were designed as festive places for eating, dancing, flirting, and relaxing, as well as for drinking beer.

These were heady times of great wealth and expansion, change and ambition in Paris. The Second Empire was underway, as were tremendous construction projects under the supervision of Baron Haussmann: the Champs Élysées, the Arc de Triomphe, the Opéra, and the grand boulevards radiating out from it throughout the Right Bank. Enormous and beautiful railroad stations like the Gare de Lyons and the Gare d'Orsay (now the Musée d'Orsay) were built by the fabulously wealthy new railroad corporations. Parks and department stores, theaters and restaurants were built for the pleasure and amusement of a newly grown middle class with at least a little extra money to spend. The new luxuries and entertainments provided employment for thousands of women: actresses and seamstresses, saleswomen and waitresses multiplied, and women became far more visible in the public life of the capital.

The Great Brasserie Scandal

As Ginette Hell-Girod writes in her 1995 book, *L'Esprit des Brasseries*, the histories of women and beer in nineteenth-century Paris collide in an interesting mid-century phenomenon: the *brasserie à femmes*, or "brasserie of women." Although ancient Nordic cultures had closely associated women with the magical, nourishing power of beer, by the nineteenth century the only reminder of this relationship was the all-female wait staffs traditional at German beer halls, famous for their tight bodices and ability to carry many beer steins at once. When the German-style brasseries began to open in Paris, bringing the traditional costumed wait-

resses with them, there was a ripple of protest from the French, for whom waiting tables was a serious and therefore, of course, masculine business. But that was nothing compared to the outrage to come.

In addition to the usual national pavilions, the Exposition of 1867 featured brasseries where the food and drink of each land was served by young women scantily clad in a version of that country's national dress. Le Tout-Paris came to gape at these new sights: American cowgirls, Circassian shepherdesses, and Spanish *señoritas*. These *brasseries à femmes* were so popular that they outlived the fair, quickly developing into scandalous, extravagant combinations of brasseries, whorehouses, and theme parks. The *filles à brasserie* (waitresses) were required to encourage their customers to drink as much as possible, to "entertain" them in private back rooms, and to give back a portion of their earnings to the brasserie owner. Some had themes, like Brasserie de l'Enfer (Brasserie of Hell), where nearly nude Eves wearing little more than a fig leaf served the clientele, and À la Guillotine!, boasting a French Revolution decor and nightly reproductions of public beheadings. A scandal was inevitable.

Finally, the brand-new women's rights movement took action. In 1892 the radical women began to distribute a pamphlet addressed "To Women Employed in Brasseries," encouraging them to rebel against the exploitation and to form a union to protect themselves. Ultimately, the *brasseries à femme* were prohibited altogether, and a whole network of laws was passed, making it actually illegal in many cases for women to work in brasseries. Even today it is extremely rare to see a waitress in a Paris brasserie.

The Threat from the East

Meanwhile, the popular new German beers were spurring French brewers to improve their product. In Alsace the brewing industry was brought to fever pitch. In addition to the new yeasts and techniques, the most important brewing innovation of this period was the Strasbourg-Paris railroad line, which by 1855 was bringing five shipments of fresh beer to the capital every day. The Alsatian brasserie Bofinger, which opened in Paris in 1864 and is still enormously popular, served that same year the very first *bières pressions*, or draft beers, drawn in the city. (The invention of the tap made this possible; previously all beer had been sold in bottles and jugs.)

But the peaceful cohabitation of French and German beer in the cosmopolitan capital would not last long: Germany invaded France in 1870. The defeat of France at Sedan, the surrender of Napoleon III, and the subsequent seizure of Alsace and Lorraine by the Germans, marking the beginning of the Franco-Prussian war, had two decisive effects. First, thousands of Alsatian refugees fled to Paris, Lyons, and other urban centers rather than become German subjects, bringing with them their regional cuisine and knowledge of brewing. Second, it suddenly became impossible for any patriotic Frenchman to drink German beer. But a challenge remained: to create a French product that would rival the high standard of German beer: light, clear, and long-lasting.

In 1870 Louis Pasteur himself, determined that French beer could equal and even outshine that of Germany, set out to make it happen. His research into the behavior of microorganisms led to a greatly improved understanding of the whole fermentation process. (Before Pasteur, even brewers had no idea of how yeast worked; they were just grateful that it did. An old English term for yeast is *Goddisgoode*.) Only since Pasteur have brewers been able to control and predict the brewing process and make yeast and beer behave in accordance with their wishes. In June of 1871, Pasteur patented his new manufacturing and storing process. But he offered the use of his ideas to any French brewer, provided that the beers made by this new process were clearly labeled with the name Bière de la Revanche, "Beer of Revenge."

The German brewers quickly disappeared from the French capital and were just as quickly replaced by Alsatian patriots, many of whose establishments are still open today: Brasserie Flo, Brasserie Lipp, Chez Jenny, and Bofinger are all named after their Alsatian founders. An 1890 review of a then-new brasserie, the Zimmer, makes the position clear: "If lovers of good beer wish to reconcile their taste with their patriotism, they can go to the brasserie Zimmer." Eating an Alsatian choucroute and drinking Alsatian-style beer in a brasserie could be experienced as an act of patriotism and defiance. The German occupation of Alsace continued for more than forty years, until 1918, more than long enough for Alsatian brasseries to become an established part of the restaurant scene in Paris and other urban centers.

The Art of the Brasserie

This time period, roughly 1870–1930, coincides with some of the most important artistic trends of the modern era. In their time, as in our own, trends in design were often reflected first in new restaurants. First came the brief but glorious life of art nouveau, an international artistic flowering whose legacies include diverse, brilliant works like the "dragonfly" Paris Metro stations designed by Hector Guimard, the textile designs of William Morris, Louis Sullivan's design for Chicago's Carson Pirie Scott department store—and the interiors of France's most beautifully enduring brasseries.

Harking back nostalgically to the handcrafted work of medieval artisans, art nouveau schools were founded throughout Europe to preserve and celebrate skills such as making tiles, blowing glass, stonecarving, and carpentry, which were in danger of being replaced by large-scale machine production. Rejecting the new geometric, squared-off forms in favor of curving, floral, organic lines that were perceived as lush and natural, art nouveau left an indelible stamp on the city of Paris, especially its restaurants. This was art for daily life, not confined to galleries or the apartments of the wealthy; anyone who could afford a mug of beer or a ride on the Metro could enjoy the art as part of the experience.

In addition to this democratic spirit, the most truly *nouveau* idea offered by the movement was of a wholly unified interior, with no artistic hierarchy. The floor tiles were designed to be as beautiful as the paintings, the light switches just as aesthetically pleasing as the chandeliers, the wooden bar carved and polished as carefully as any sculpture. Out of this tradition come the shiny hat racks at Brasserie Flo, the flower-decorated glass panels that filter the room's light at Julien; Lipp's tropical-themed ceramics of palm trees, monkeys, and bananas; Mollard's incredible tiled surfaces with motifs of pine boughs, magnolias, ferns, butterflies, irises, and water lilies. At Chez Jenny hand-carved panels of wood in different shades of brown and blond are inlaid in patterns, creating life-size "paintings" of village life in Alsace.

All of this careful handiwork could be seen and admired only because of the relatively recent miracle of plentiful electric light. Until this phenomenon became widespread in the 1880s, most restaurants and taverns were only dimly lit, and it would hardly have been worth decorating them—the effects could not have been visible. But modern brasseries are characterized by their bustling brightness, and most are literally covered with light fixtures: globes, sconces, chandeliers. The multitude of shiny materials like bronze, brass, and mirrors used by the brasserie designers also shows a delight in the effects of reflected and re-reflected light.

In the 1910s and '20s a drier, more geometric style took shape, clearing away all the leaves, reeds, vines, flowers, and fruit in favor of simple, clean patterns and bold color blocks. This new look—art deco—received its name and its energy at the 1925 international exposition of decorative arts in Paris. Art deco dominated the world of international design in the 1920s and '30s, with machine-age materials like plastic, chrome, and Bakelite taking the place of wood, bronze, and ceramics. Certain brasseries are a triumph of the style: the Terminus Nord, Vaudeville, Balzar, and especially La Coupole, with its clean, airy look, squared-off columns, and the celebrated mosaic floor that unmistakably echoes the shapes of Cubism.

The Brasseries and the Bohemians

The story of La Coupole is truly the story of the brasserie in this century. The devastations of World War I had destroyed the extravagant mood and energy of nineteenth-century Paris. But after the 1918 Armistice, the capital erupted in a frenzy of pleasure seeking and creative energy that quickly made it the undisputed center of the world art scene. The shift was marked by the movement of artists, writers, models, and their inevitable nightlife from the hill of Montmartre down to the relatively peaceful Montparnasse. These new bohemians gathered at large cafés like Le Dôme, Le Sélect, and La Rotonde to see and be seen and to discuss the latest artistic, intellectual, and personal scandals.

In 1927 the owners of Le Dôme announced an ambitious plan to build the largest brasserie in Paris, a single huge room with a ceiling of unprecedented height. Eventually they were convinced to add columns to their design, but many still doubted that the ambitious project would ever materialize. On December 20 the Lafons convened le Tout-Montparnasse to unveil their beautiful masterpiece, complete with elegantly boxy art deco chandeliers and thirty-two tall columns, each decorated by a different painter. The crowd of more than two thousand revelers went wild, and the party went on until dawn.

La Coupole instantly became what it has remained ever since: the most famous brasserie in the world and a meeting place for Parisians from all walks of life—and an appreciative audience of foreigners as well. Among the hundreds of expatriates in Paris in the 1920s, the place and time made famous by Hemingway, Stein, and Fitzgerald, were many professional bartenders forced into exile by the American Prohibition of 1919. They brought the cocktail to Europe with them, and soon many brasseries could boast a "Bar Américain," consecrated to the consumption of martinis, highballs, and other fashionable New World concoctions that were not served at dignified French restaurants or traditional cafés. In the raucous 1920s and '30s, the new and old brasseries of Paris, fueled by Americans, artists, and cocktails, enjoyed a new flush of popularity.

The Worst of Times, the Best of Times

With the Second World War and the devastating occupation of the city by Hitler's forces, the international art scene drifted across the Atlantic to New York. The blithe spirit of Montparnasse and the rest of the city gave way to a grimmer outlook, and the young people had their eyes on America. After the war brasseries were no longer fashionable; instead, *les drugstores*, *les fast-foods*, and *les selfs* were chic and popular. English- and Irish-style pubs became the preferred venues for beer. Many great brasseries disappeared into piles of rubble, and others, like Flo, Terminus Nord, and even La Coupole, were allowed to slide into disrepair.

Not until Jean-Paul Bucher, an Alsatian-born lover of brasseries, acquired the Brasserie Flo in 1968 and restored it to health did Parisians begin to recognize what was being lost. Today Bucher and his Groupe Flo own many of the traditional brasseries in Paris, all expertly restored to their original beauty. Independent brasseries like Balzar and Lipp are as popular and idiosyncratic as ever. A visitor to La Coupole, which now serves about fifteen hundred dinners on an average night, is greeted with a scene of indescribable bustle and activity. Yet somehow the grace of the soaring ceiling, the jewel tones of the paintings on the columns, and the sense of being part of a glorious crowd absorb and soften the chaos.

You could say the same thing about the many brew pubs that dot the American landscape today; they are as close as we have come in a hundred years to re-creating the festive beer gardens that were once found in every American city. In "fancy" restaurants in France, they still simply do not serve beer, and the same is also true of a dwindling number of American restaurants. But we are beginning to be proud of our beer-drinking heritage and to break free of the idea that "serious" food automatically means "serious" wine, appreciated in a "serious" way.

Brasseries are not serious about wine, beer, food, or anything else except the importance of enjoying life, food, drink, and other people. Wine, beer, and food are just equal parts of the same whole: the nourishing of our bodies and our spirits. Sharing these around a table is the root of the brasserie experience, stretching in an unbroken tradition from twelfth-century pilgrims seeking shelter and a mug of beer, through nineteenth-century students at the Sorbonne who greeted a new beer with a joyful parade through the streets of the Latin Quarter, through Hemingway ruminating over a cold lager and hot sausages with *pommes à l'huile* at the Brasserie Lipp, all the way to the person who just yesterday strolled out of Brasserie T after dinner, feeling warm, comforted—and maybe just a little bit full.

ON WINE, BEER, AND FOOD

As chefs, we have always been mystified by the idea that wine has a special, separate identity from food. We rarely enjoy one without the other. To us the two are integral parts of the same thing—a great meal. We are far from experts about wine, but through years of experience and education, tasting and testing, we have developed some of our own ideas. We now have only one ironclad requirement for the wines we serve at Brasserie T: they have to taste wonderful with our food. By our lights an expensively aged French Bordeaux isn't "better" than a young Rosso di Montalcino from Italy or an Oregon Pinot Noir; it all depends on the food and the occasion. At Brasserie T we find that most of our dishes and dinners are casual and copious, and the wines need to flow accordingly.

French brasseries have an energetic ambiance that encourages distraction, conversation, and consumption, not silent contemplation of the qualities of a fine wine. No real brasserie is the kind of place to appreciate a fine Montrachet or Saint Emilion *cru classé*, and you'll rarely see such a grand bottle on a brasserie *carte de vins*. Brasserie wine lists tend to be brief and serviceable, with a few carefully chosen and well-priced wines that can set off a wide variety of dishes. As you would for a homey dinner party of friends, at Brasserie T we look for wines that enhance the flavors of your food and the moods of your companions, without making too many demands on anyone. Those are our favorites, the easygoing wines we return to again and again because they make heavenly pairings with the dishes we love to cook and eat.

We've cooked in many of the world's great food and wine regions and learned a lot about both along the way. One of the first things we learned is that there are people everywhere who absolutely love to talk about wine. At first we listened to all of them. Some told us that Champagne goes with everything; others, that it goes with nothing. We struggled to remember everything they said about the intricacies of French and Italian wine labeling systems, the significant years for Burgundy whites, the grape varietals that go into each Chianti, the subtle distinctions between different vineyards in the same commune and different communes in the same village. At restaurants and vineyards, we tasted countless wines, identifying fragrances and flavors of leather, chocolate, green apple, cedar, and hundreds of others that make wine such a complex and exciting drink.

It was interesting and challenging and also confusing. We learned a lot, but the primary lesson is that tasting wines "blind," out of the context of food and the table as the experts do, is interesting but not very useful when it comes to choosing a wine for dinner every night. You might have all the wine guides in print at your fingertips, but none of the authors will really know what a particular bottle will taste like with *your* food, at *your* dinner table.

Just as every cook has a few highly individual recipes up her sleeve that she can make practically in her sleep, that taste great, and that everyone in the family adores, anyone who enjoys wine can keep a few tried-and-true bottles on hand that will cover most occasions. With two white and two red wines on hand, carefully chosen, your cellar will be able to admirably complement almost anything you might cook at home. Unless you are genuinely curious about wine, there's no need to try a different one every time you sit down to dinner. There's nothing wrong with constantly updating your palate, but it certainly is not required for anyone. In most wine regions of France, for example, people drink virtually the same wine every day for decades; whatever wine is decent and regional will turn up at bistros, at home, and at local wine shops. To do

the same, find drinkable wines you like and feel free to stick to them.

The term *drinkable*, as applied to wine, is much more complimentary than it sounds. It doesn't mean bland and homogenized. In fact, the opposite is true. The magic ingredient in the pairing of wine and food is *acid*. Winemakers and wine merchants will rarely describe a wine as acidic, since to consumers that could suggest an excess of acidity and a sour wine. But good levels of acid are what give wine the ability to complement food and add to the enjoyment of a meal. Imagine that you're beginning a meal with our Caramelized Onion Tart (pages 18–19), a composition of sweet onions, savory custard, buttery crust, and fresh herbs. You take a bite, savor it, and what do you want next? A sip of wine to clear the palate, with the acid in the wine cutting through the richness and sweetness of the food. Now you're ready for another bite. In this case, either a red wine or a white wine could be delicious—as long as it had the right acid balance. Good, strong acidity—balanced by other flavors and textures, as in any well-made wine—is absolutely necessary and can be a more reliable guide to choosing a wine for your meal than the grape, the age of the bottle, or a host of other factors.

Once you put aside the vintage charts, vineyard maps, and wine encyclopedias, you can start to choose wines the same way you choose food—through imagination, experience, and instinct. Imagine that your best friends are coming over for dinner on Saturday night. So—a round of silky Roasted Red Pepper Soup with Herbed Fresh Ricotta (pages 38–39), then Pan-Roasted Salmon with Coriander Seed and Wilted Spinach (pages 128–29), and finally dessert. Where to begin with the wines? Roasted red peppers are sweet, but the ricotta is milky and herbal tasting. Salmon is a rich, fatty fish, so you could choose either a round, jammy red wine to harmonize with it or a full-bodied, astringent white for some contrast. But you would also want to remember that the fish is flavored with orange and coriander seed, strong, bright flavors that might fight with a fruity red. Our second principle for choosing wine is, try to consider how the dish is going to be cooked and what it will be cooked with, as much as the main ingredient. Don't just think "red peppers" or "salmon," but keep in mind the flavors of the whole dish.

There is no fixed principle for putting these factors together. Some say the wine should contrast with the food; others, that it should complement it. Some even suggest alternating these approaches, course by course. *It doesn't have to be that complicated.* Let your palate be your guide, keep an open mind, and feel free to use the suggestions we've supplied as a starting point.

This brings us to another point, the basis of many of our wine choices at Brasserie T and in this book, and the point where our feelings about wine diverge from other American chefs. Many American restaurants have an easygoing, experimental attitude toward wine, enthusiastically matching French wines with Asian foods, California wines with Italian dishes, and so on. It's a lot like the attitude of many great American chefs toward cuisine: you take only what you like from the rigid traditions of older-world cooking and turn it into something new and flexible. We appreciate this spirit, but we also believe that the best wines for a particular dish will usually be those that partake

of the same regional traditions of the food. We respect the ancient winemaking traditions of regions like Burgundy and Tuscany, and we know that the cuisines of those regions have grown right alongside them over the years. There's simply no substitute for that kind of organic process.

For example, when we are cooking and eating a traditional *coq au vin*, a Burgundian dish that has slowly evolved over centuries, we try to use a young red wine of that region, made from Pinot Noir grapes. Now, even if the taste difference between a Burgundy Pinot Noir and one from California were not a factor, we would appreciate the unity that comes from drinking French wine with French cuisine. We feel that this harmony adds to our appreciation of both the food and the wine. It was Marty Tiersky, who chose the wines both for Brasserie T and for this book (and whose discussion of pairing wine and food begins on page 318), who first taught us to appreciate this dimension of wine.

Terroir is a term that wine lovers use to describe the combination of influences that the land brings to wine; the same *terroir* will always help to shape a region's cuisine. We believe this on several levels. So we love to serve big Tuscan reds with our mushroom pastas, and crisp Alsatian whites with onion tarts and choucroute. Our updated all-American chicken pot pie harmonizes best with California Chardonnay. It's certainly not a hard-and-fast rule, but we have found it to be a great place to start, especially for anyone who is just starting to make sense of the world of wine.

Since brasserie cuisine was to some extent invented by Alsatian patriots with a deep loyalty to their region's foods and wines, that rich wine tradition deserves some space here—especially because we feel that Alsatian whites are particularly good wines for our food. Wine has been produced in Alsace since well before the time of Christ, although with many interruptions. The frequent battles for dominance over this tiny piece of land have all too often decimated Alsatian vines and wine production, beginning with the Romans pulling out all the grapevines to eliminate competition for Italian wines. As recently as 1945, the Alsatian wine industry was struggling to survive. And yet the winemaking traditions have thrived. Dry, full-bodied Alsatian white wines like Pinot Blanc, Pinot Gris, and great Rieslings are miraculously good with food, even red meat; the spicy-sweet quality of the best late-harvest Gewurztraminers make them as seductively refined as any Sauternes.

The reputation of the wines of Alsace has not always been as high as it is today, with the effect that marvelous Alsatian wines are available throughout France and, to some extent, in the United States at much lower prices than comparable white Bordeaux and Burgundies. Alsatian wines made from the Riesling, Pinot Blanc, and Pinot Gris grapes are uniquely suited to the dinner table, as many brasserie wine lists would demonstrate. To us nothing could be a better recommendation for a wine than that. Most brasseries with an Alsatian heritage offer a young Riesling as their house white wine, and in Alsace itself, Riesling is considered the ideal accompaniment to everything from pizza to *truite au bleu*.

Alsatian wines are also especially accessible in their labeling system. Unlike the innumerable chateaux of Bordeaux and communes of Burgundy, Alsace follows the American pattern of labeling its wines according to grape. These "varietal" names are the most important indication of an Alsatian wine's character, since within each varietal the styles of individual producers tend to be quite similar. The next thing to know is the producer, sadly few of whom manage to export their wines to the United States. Names like Trimbach, Zind-Humbrecht, Preiss-Zimmer, and Hugel are reasonably well known here, but the extraordinary wines of houses like Beyer, Baumann, Bott Frères, Jean and Louis Sipp, and Becker have yet to be tasted. Behind the producers proudly stand the fifty officially designated *grand cru* vineyards of Alsace, with mellifluous names like Sonnenglanz, Mandelberg, Ollwiller, and Zotzenberg. Do not be fooled by the German-sounding names into thinking that these are German-style wines; above all, do not think that Alsatian Rieslings bear any resemblance to the American or German wines called Johannisberg Riesling. Only by drinking an Alsatian Riesling can you understand how it can be dry and supple, floral and mineral, mellow and crisp all at the same time.

The other Alsatian varietal you are likely to encounter outside Alsace is Gewurztraminer, a complicated and rich wine that has somehow acquired the reputation of being good with spicy food. Perhaps this is because it is itself somewhat spicy, especially if you are lucky enough to be drinking the *vendange tardive*, a late-harvest dessert wine made from grapes that have been left to overripen on the vine and fill with sweetness. But the floral sweetness of the regular Gewurztraminers—some say they taste of red roses—actually makes them difficult to match with food, including the Indian and Asian dishes for which they are most often prescribed. If you have tried a lukewarm

Gewurztraminer in this context and concluded that you do not like Alsatian wine, we urge you to get your hands on another bottle, chill it well, and serve it forth with a firm, ripe, semi-soft cheese. Of course, the best place to experience this celestial combination is Alsace itself, where the hospitable local producers run both a *route du vin* and a *route du fromage*, with plenty of opportunities for tasting, and where visitors also have the opportunity to become deeply familiar with the quintessential brasserie dish, *choucroute garnie*.

Alsace is the only region of France where beer and wine are produced side by side on almost the same small patch of land. Breweries once formed a thick ring around the city of Strasbourg, and even today the city is home to major lager producers like Fischer, Schutzenberger, and Kronenbourg. Some breweries run their own restaurants, from modest canteens for the workers, where sausages, potatoes, and beer are the lunchtime special, to sophisticated Strasbourg restaurants like l'Ami Schutz, where the chefs create an elegant *cuisine de la bière* with dishes like salads of hop shoots and pork shank braised in strong ale, each course served with a different Schutzenberger beer.

That said, today it is relatively rare for a French dinner to be eaten with beer, even in a brasserie and even in beer-producing regions like Alsace. Most brasseries have only one or two beers on tap, and most "serious" restaurants don't serve beer at all. A tall golden lager is popular with a sandwich at lunchtime, after work, or in the afternoon, to while away an hour on the terrace or the sidewalk tables of a café or brasserie. But when the dinner service begins, the wine bottles begin coming up from the cellar, often two or three at a time. The same is true in Italy. The best

cooking of both countries evolved along with the wines, and most of the dishes in this book reflect those traditions.

There are some exceptions to that rule, though, and there are plenty of beer-friendly recipes in the following pages. We follow the southern Italian tradition of drinking beer, not wine, with pizza. German-accented Alsatian dishes like Saucisson with Green Lentils and Potato-Onion Ragoût (pages 150–51) and Chicago Choucroute (pages 148–49) are wonderful with good fresh lager. In Paris at lunchtime, nothing is so refreshing with a Croque Monsieur (page 88) as a tall *pression*, or draft beer. In fact, most of our sandwiches are dense and chewy enough to make a sparkling, citric beer like a Pacific Northwest pale ale or German *hefe-weizen* welcome.

There are so many new beers being imported and crafted in the United States that giving specific recommendations would be pointless. The important thing is to learn to distinguish the flavors and characteristics of different beers, just as you might for wines, and then start to compare and contrast them to the flavors of your food. For example, the basic distinction between wines is between reds and whites. Of course, within those two broad categories lie enormous variations—but that's the fundamental flavor distinction.

Among beers, a similar flavor distinction can be made between top-fermented and bottom-fermented beers. The terms technically refer to the whether the yeast sits on top of the brew, mixing with the wild yeasts in the air, or sinks to the bottom, where it works in a slower, more systematic way to convert the sugars in the brew to alcohol. Both types of beer can be very light to very dark in color, so do not let color be your guide in choosing your beers. There is an enormous range of flavors and aromas to be found in beer, once you start to pay attention to them: floral and citric tastes, as in the popular pale ales we serve at Brasserie T; the banana and caramel notes of some British bitters; the citrus quality of beers made with wheat as well as the usual barley; and the deep, rich chocolate flavors of velvety British stouts.

Top-fermented beers include bitters, ales, porters, stouts, German *weizens* and *hefe-weizens*, *weissbiers*, all the Trappist and monastery brews, and *bières blanches* or *witbiers*. They tend to have at least some sweetness, a smooth texture, and depth and complexity of flavor. Some have the creamy freshness of fine Champagnes, and others are reminiscent of the finest dry Spanish sherry; still others are as yeasty as bread or brewed to the taste and texture of espresso coffee. Their complex character is best appreciated with simple food like cheese and charcuterie (or our very British Fish and Chips in Peppery Amber Beer Batter, pages 164–65), and they should not be served too cold or the flavors will be lost.

The tighter, more acidic beers are the bottom-fermented brews, which include the huge international family of lagers, Pilsners, Dortmunders, bocks, dunkels, and Märzens. *Lager* is simply a German word that means "to lay down," as you would lay down a supply of wine or flour in your cellar. This lagering, or cold storage, of the beer takes place in carefully controlled circumstances and at very cold temperatures, which results in brilliantly clear brews with high alcohol and little sweetness. The dominant flavor in a well-made lager is that of the fresh hops in the mixture, a citric, fresh, almost bitter taste that makes lager an excellent

choice for drinking with many of our favorite dishes. Many of our mass-produced American lagers have had the distinct flavor of hops "smoothed out" to make them blander and more accessible, but the various microbrewed lagers have strong individual characters. It's well worth tasting lots of different microbrews to find your favorites. You can choose among smoky, earthy, lemony, herbal, and a host of other characters to complement your own cooking.

In our beer notes for this book, we've made some choices that provide contrast and some that add harmony, just as we might for wine. For example, the fruity-nutty-cheesy character of our Roquefort and Pear Salad with Grapes and Spiced Pecans (pages 10–11) is accentuated by our beer choice: a British nut-brown ale with a strong malty-grain character. The flavors of the beer continue the themes of the food. But for Escargots with Lots of Garlic, we chose a light, sparkly *gueuze*, a Belgian wheat beer that will cut through the intensity of the garlic and the richness of the butter and provide refreshing contrast. The level of sparkle, or carbonation, in a beer can be a guide to pairing it with food. Carbonation is to beer as acid is to wine: it's what refreshes the palate and keeps you coming back for more, increasing your enjoyment of both the food and the drink.

Now that we can (and do) get fresh beer from nearby breweries like Goose Island, Sprechers, and Flatlanders, we realize that the freshness of beer is a key factor in its taste. Like a lot of people, we grew up thinking of beer as another canned drink, like soda or juice. But fresh beer, like fresh vegetables or fresh bread, is a living food; canning changes it completely, and so does keeping it around too long. If you have access to freshly brewed local beer, you'll find that it makes a much better accompaniment to good food than the pasteurized, homogenized beers at the supermarket. Beer, after all, is a form of food: it deserves the chance to show off its natural flavors at their best.

From our viewpoint at Brasserie T, we have been pleased to watch the Midwest's great brewing traditions revive themselves in recent years. At local brewpubs, chefs and brewmasters are constantly expanding our definition of "beer food"; where customers used to expect nachos and hot dogs, today freshly made potato chips with dipping sauces, platters of house-smoked sausages, and innovative desserts like Flatlanders' Chocolate Stout Float are becoming the rule. And we know, as you probably do, that this is happening not only in Chicago but all over the country. Like America's winemakers and bread bakers, America's brewers are learning more about the traditional, old-world methods of production and becoming more comfortable about adding their own ideas to the mix. At Brasserie T we've been happy to respond to our customers' interest in beer: these days, our twelve beer taps are always flowing with new American brews, and many of our regulars drink beer through dinner. It looks to us as though the future of the brasserie tradition is here—and now!

NOTES ON INGREDIENTS

These are quick notes on some building blocks of our cooking. Just making sure to have key basic ingredients on hand, like good olive oil, frozen stock, fresh herbs, a piece of cheese, and a supply of lemons and oranges, can make an enormous difference in your cooking.

Olive Oil. Extra-virgin olive oil has incomparable flavor, but there are many cooking situations for which it is too overpowering and too expensive. In sautéing, the solids in extra-virgin cause it to burn at a lower temperature than other oils, so a lighter olive oil, such as one marked "pure" or "light," can be a better choice. There are many good olive oils on the market now, from Spain, Morocco, Italy, Greece, France, and California, so let your taste be your guide.

Kosher Salt. We always use kosher salt in cooking. The coarse granules sprinkle more evenly over food, and it's easier to gauge how much you're using. Because of the bigger crystals, a teaspoon of kosher salt actually holds less salt than a teaspoon of table salt, so be careful if you substitute table salt in our recipes.

Stock. Fresh stock is easy to make (see pages 307–11 for recipes) and adds just the right flavor, but if you're caught short, low-sodium canned broth is an acceptable substitute. It not only is less salty but has less of a "canned" taste than regular canned broth. Bouillon cubes have a completely different flavor and cannot be substituted for stock.

Water. Remember that if your water has strong flavors, such as chlorine or rust, they can affect the flavors of your food. As a cooking medium for pasta and vegetables, tap water is fine, but when using water as an ingredient in soups and sauces, you may want to use spring or filtered water instead.

Unsalted Butter. Using unsalted butter guarantees freshness, since even the slightest staleness or rancidity can be tasted. The salt is supposed to act as a preservative, but it also masks the creamy fresh flavor of the butter. Butter and salt have a completely different taste from salted butter—try a taste comparison on bread—and we prefer those flavors to come through in our cooking. Also, using unsalted butter means that you can control the amount of salt yourself.

Fresh Herbs. The basic distinction in cooking herbs is between "soft," fresh-flavored ones like basil, parsley, cilantro, and chives, and "hard," pungent ones like rosemary, sage, and thyme. Hard herbs add flavor to a dish during the cooking; soft ones lose their flavor quickly in a hot pan and must be added at the very last minute. Within those categories, however, feel free to experiment with your favorites and substitute what is available to you. Dried hard herbs can sometimes be substituted for fresh (cut the amount by about one-third), but dried soft herbs are quite useless. We can't say enough how important fresh herbs are, and all you have to do is chop them to release their flavors. Get into the habit of using and storing them so that each recipe doesn't require buying a new bunch of herbs. We always use Italian flat-leaf rather than curly parsley. For parsley and other soft herbs, trim off the ends of the stems and stick them in cold water as you would do for fresh flowers. Refrigerate with a damp paper towel on top.

Oranges and Lemons. As you cook from this book, you'll notice that oranges and lemons are almost as ubiquitous in our kitchen as salt and pepper. Like salt, they add their own flavor to a dish, but they also bring out flavor in the other ingredients. Oranges are less acidic than lemons, so they're great when you want to brighten flavors without adding a sharp lemon or acid taste. We often squeeze an orange over a stew or a lemon over a plate of vegetables as a final touch, but for more concentrated flavor, freshly grated zest is the best choice. Leaving the bitter white pith behind is key:

invest in a zester for the easiest method, or rub the fruit against a handheld grater.

Plum Tomatoes. We often use tomatoes as a garnish as well as an ingredient. Diced small, they add fresh flavor, a note of acid, and bright color. There's no need to peel them for this purpose, but do remove the seeds and gel first with your fingers. Use a sharp knife when cutting them so that the pieces stay firm.

White Beans. We use dried cannellini or great Northern white beans for all our cooking. Canned beans are completely cooked when they come out of the can, so they tend to fall apart when reheated in other recipes. One cup dried beans yields 3 cups of cooked beans. This is the method we use: soak the beans overnight in plenty of cold water. The next day, discard the soaking liquid, cover the beans with unsalted water or chicken stock, and simmer them (do not boil), covered, until cooked through but still firm, adding more boiling water as needed. In most cases the beans will cook a little more in the recipe.

Pasta. The firm texture of well-cooked dried pasta adds immeasurably to our enjoyment of a good pasta dish. Without this firm texture pasta isn't nearly as interesting or satisfying. We find it's easiest to achieve this with a high-quality imported durum-wheat pasta like De Cecco®. Domestic pastas tend to go too quickly from uncooked to over-cooked; a good pasta will remain firm long enough for you to drain and sauce it without collapsing.

Artichokes. Peeling large globe artichokes down to the hearts can be awfully time-consuming: whole fresh baby ones are much easier to work with. Peel off the leaves until you get to the pale green, slice off the top 1/2 an inch, and cut off all but 1 inch of the stems. Cut into quarters, dropping them as you work into a bowl of water combined with the juice of a ¹/₂ lemon. Boil in salted water with the juice from the remaining lemon half until just tender, about 30 minutes, and use in recipes that call for artichoke hearts. Frozen hearts are a fine substitute; brine-packed canned ones slightly less so but still acceptable.

Mozzarella Cheese. Mozzarella that is pressed into blocks and shrink-wrapped is a completely different product from the soft fresh cheese, which has a true fresh-milk flavor and springy texture. Most supermarkets now stock fresh mozzarella packed in brine or milk. Lightly salted mozzarella has the best flavor.

Toasted Nuts. We often use walnuts, pecans, and almonds in cooking, and they are almost always toasted first to release their flavors. This can be done on top of the stove in a heavy skillet over medium heat, tossing the nuts constantly to make sure they do not burn. Or spread them on a baking sheet and bake at 350°F for 10 to 20 minutes, stirring occasionally. Slivered nuts will toast more quickly than whole ones. Sesame and pumpkin seeds can be toasted the same way. See the headnote on page 184 for instructions for hazelnuts, which must be peeled before using.

Egg Yolks. We very occasionally use raw egg yolks in our cooking. There is a slight risk involved, but here's how to minimize it: always buy a fresh carton for the purpose, keep the eggs very cold, and use them straight out of the refrigerator, not at room temperature. Of course, you should never serve a dish with raw egg yolks to anyone who is ill or immune impaired. Never use farm-stand eggs raw.

Vanilla. We use both vanilla beans and vanilla extract in baking. Choose beans that are plump and firm, not too dry, and with plenty of "vanilla caviar" inside. We don't scrape out this flavorful stuff, but just split the beans lengthwise and toss them into the mix for ice cream, compotes, and many other desserts. Vanilla beans can be reused: simply fish them out of the pot at the end of the cooking, rinse them well, and refrigerate, well wrapped, until next time. Always use pure vanilla extract, not imitation; the price difference is negligible, and the flavor difference huge. Don't be concerned about the high alcohol content in vanilla extract: the amount of vanilla used in recipes is small and the alcohol usually evaporates with cooking.

Chocolate. Among the premium chocolates now on the market, Callebaut® is a good choice for the recipes here. Others, like Valrhona, are designed for different uses and may change the recipe too much. We used supermarket baking chocolate to test the recipes. Make sure to use fresh chocolate from a market with good turnover. Store it in a cool, dark place but not the refrigerator, which will quickly affect the cocoa butter and make the chocolate "bloom" a white coating.

Sugar. In addition to granulated sugar, we often use light brown sugar in baking for its toasty caramel flavor. Dark brown sugar is not a direct substitute because of its strong molasses character, but you can make light brown sugar by combining equal parts of dark brown and granulated sugar. In addition, we love the crunchy texture of coarse sugar for sprinkling on cookies and tart crusts, and it provides just the right thickness for caramelizing. Coarse, turbinado, and raw or raw-style sugar are all good for this purpose.

Salads and Appetizers

Fresh Lemon-Basil Vinaigrette

Apple-Walnut Vinaigrette

Roasted Tomato–Garlic Vinaigrette

Balsamic-Orange Vinaigrette

Crunchy Green Salad with Goat Cheese and Warm Bacon Vinaigrette

Salade Niçoise with Roasted Tomato–Garlic Vinaigrette

Chilled Asparagus, Shaved Fennel, and Pecorino with Lemon-Basil Vinaigrette

Roquefort and Pear Salad with Grapes and Spiced Pecans

Riviera Caesar Salad

Dandelion Salad with Beaujolais-Poached Eggs and Roasted Shallots

Roasted Stuffed Artichokes with Toasted Nuts, Lemon, and Tomato

Caramelized Onion Tart

Truffled Chicken Liver Mousse

Crab Cakes and Baby Greens with Citrus Vinaigrette and Spicy Aioli

Steamed Mussels with Fennel, Cream, and Pernod

Escargots with Lots of Garlic

Grilled Shrimp with Aiolis

Panzanella
(Tuscan Sourdough Salad)

Bluepoint Oysters with Mignonette Salsa

Fresh Lemon-Basil Vinaigrette

MAKES ABOUT 1 CUP

$1/4$ cup freshly squeezed lemon juice
1 teaspoon finely chopped lemon zest
2 medium garlic cloves, finely chopped
12 leaves fresh basil, finely chopped
$1/4$ cup red wine vinegar
$1/2$ teaspoon sugar
1 cup extra-virgin olive oil
Kosher salt and freshly ground black
   pepper

In a mixing bowl, whisk together the lemon juice, lemon zest, garlic, basil, vinegar, and sugar. In a thin stream, add the oil, whisking constantly until well blended. Add salt and black pepper to taste. Use immediately or refrigerate in a tightly closed jar. Shake well before using.

Apple-Walnut Vinaigrette

MAKES ABOUT 1 CUP

$1/2$ Granny Smith or other tart apple,
   peeled, cored, and cut into chunks
1 shallot, peeled
$1/4$ cup cider vinegar
1 teaspoon sugar
$1/3$ cup walnut oil
$2/3$ cup canola or light olive oil
Kosher salt and freshly ground black
   pepper

In a blender or food processor, combine the apple chunks and shallot and process until smooth. Add the vinegar and sugar and blend. Add the oils and blend until creamy. Add salt and pepper to taste and pulse to combine. Use immediately or refrigerate in a tightly closed jar. Shake well before using.

Roasted Tomato–Garlic Vinaigrette

Preheat the oven to 375°F. On a baking sheet, toss the tomato halves with the garlic oil, pepper, and salt. Arrange them cut side down and bake 20 minutes, until the edges begin to turn golden brown. Transfer the tomatoes, with any juices that have accumulated in the pan, to a blender or food processor. Add the vinegar and herbs and blend until smooth. Still processing, pour in the oil in a thin stream. Add salt and pepper to taste and pulse to combine. Use immediately or refrigerate in a tightly closed jar. Shake well before using.

1 pound ripe plum tomatoes, halved, seeded, and rinsed

1/4 cup Garlic Oil and Puree (page 292), or 1/4 cup olive oil mixed with 1 minced large garlic clove

1/2 teaspoon freshly ground black pepper

1 teaspoon kosher salt

6 tablespoons red wine vinegar

2 tablespoons finely chopped fresh parsley or chives, or a combination

1/2 cup plus 2 tablespoons olive or canola oil

Balsamic-Orange Vinaigrette

MAKES ABOUT 1 CUP

In a mixing bowl, whisk together the vinegar, juice, and shallots. In a thin stream, add the oils, whisking until well blended. Add salt and pepper to taste. Use immediately or refrigerate in a tightly closed jar. Shake well before using.

1/4 cup good-quality balsamic vinegar

1/4 cup freshly squeezed orange juice

2 shallots, minced

1/3 cup extra-virgin olive oil

1/3 cup canola oil

Kosher salt and freshly ground black pepper

Crunchy Green Salad with Goat Cheese and Warm Bacon Vinaigrette

SERVES 6 TO 8 AS AN APPETIZER, 4 AS AN ENTREE

This appealing salad has a direct lineage to the French brasserie classic frisée aux lardons, *which combines fresh young chicory, chunks of crisp bacon, and an addictive dressing strong enough to make your mouth water. The warm, smoky vinaigrette contrasts beautifully with the cool greens. At Vaudeville, a lively late-night Paris brasserie across from the solemn Bourse (the stock exchange), this generous salad comes topped with Roquefort cheese and a perfectly poached egg—and that's just an appetizer!*

We've expanded on the theme by adding favorite American salad ingredients like cucumbers, tomatoes, and celery, and made it substantial with boiled new potatoes and crumbled goat cheese. Feel free to add and subtract from the ingredients below. When you use all the elements, this makes a satisfying one-dish meal. Add our creamy, spicy Curried Pumpkin Soup with Apple and Toasted Pumpkin Seeds (pages 40–41) and crusty bread, and you can serve salad for dinner even in the middle of winter. Dividing the salad in serving bowls as you make it ensures an even distribution of potatoes, vegetables, dressing, and cheese.

For the salad:

- **1 pound (about 12) small red-skinned boiling potatoes**
- **1/2 head frisée (curly endive), well washed and torn into pieces**
- **4 cups mixed salad greens (mesclun) or a mixture of at least 3 lettuces such as red leaf, romaine, endive, radicchio, arugula, frisée, watercress, and Boston**

1) Put the potatoes in a saucepan and cover with cold water. Cover the pan and bring to a boil over high heat. Uncover and boil until the potatoes are tender, about 12 to 15 minutes. Drain.

2) While the potatoes are cooking, make the dressing: in a skillet, sauté the bacon over medium-high heat until most of the fat has been rendered and the bacon is golden and beginning to crisp, about 5 minutes. Turn off the heat and pour off the fat into a glass

measuring cup. Remove the bacon from the pan and let drain on paper towels.

3) You now have an empty skillet with a thin coating of bacon fat. Add the garlic and shallots and cook over medium heat, stirring, until softened, about 5 minutes. Add the brown sugar and cook, stirring, until dissolved. Scrape the mixture into a blender or food processor and add all the remaining dressing ingredients except the salt and pepper. Add ¼ cup of the bacon fat and process, pulsing, just until smooth. Season to taste with salt and pepper.

4) Make the croutons: preheat the oven to 350°F. Arrange the baguette slices on a baking sheet; brush the tops with garlic oil and sprinkle with salt and pepper. Bake 10 to 12 minutes, until golden.

5) Slice the warm potatoes ¼ inch thick and combine with half of the warm vinaigrette (reheat the vinaigrette in a microwave if necessary) and half of the bacon pieces. Divide among roomy serving bowls.

6) In a large bowl, combine the frisée, salad greens, chives, tomatoes, cucumber, and celery. Toss with the remaining vinaigrette, season to taste with salt and pepper, and divide on top of the potatoes in the serving bowls.

7) Sprinkle the crumbled goat cheese and reserved bacon pieces over the salads, place 3 or 4 croutons on each, and serve.

4 teaspoons chopped fresh chives

2 plum tomatoes, seeded and diced

½ long English cucumber, peeled, halved lengthwise, and sliced into half moons

2 stalks celery, sliced ¼ inch thick

Kosher salt and freshly ground black pepper

6 ounces fresh mild goat cheese, crumbled

For the dressing:

3 cups (about 1 pound) diced slab bacon

2 tablespoons minced garlic

½ cup chopped shallots

6 tablespoons packed light brown sugar

6 tablespoons balsamic vinegar

½ cup extra-virgin olive oil

6 tablespoons freshly squeezed orange juice

Kosher salt and freshly ground black pepper

For the croutons:

16 to 20 baguette slices, about ¼ inch thick

3 tablespoons Garlic Oil and Puree (page 292), or 3 tablespoons olive oil mixed with 1 minced garlic clove

Kosher salt and freshly ground black pepper

PILSNER URQUELL, WITH ITS CRISP TASTE, FRESH BOUQUET, AND SALTY, COMPLEX FLAVORS, WOULD WORK WELL WITH THIS MULTIFLAVORED SALAD.

SANCERRE, POUILLY-FUMÉ, OR CALIFORNIA SAUVIGNON BLANC WILL MATCH PERFECTLY.

Salade Niçoise with
Roasted Tomato–Garlic Vinaigrette

SERVES 4 TO 6

The classic brasserie lunch of the French Riviera, Salade Niçoise is wonderful with a tall pilsner on a hot day. From Marseilles to Monaco, where we had an exemplary Niçoise at the legendary Hotel Negresco, the Mediterranean is lined with all kinds of restaurants, many of them right on the beach. The best way to enjoy a Niçoise is in bare feet and a wet bathing suit, on any beach you can find—or just in the sun, in your own backyard. To take it on a picnic, divide the salad on split baguettes and wrap tightly until serving. That's a pan bagnat, the classic Provençal sandwich.

It's the meaty tuna and potatoes that give the salad its substance, and the creamy egg yolks blend with the dressing to make a delicious emulsion that brings out the flavors of the different vegetables. We prefer the tomato vinaigrette here, but lemon would also be excellent—and quicker, in case you're working on the spur of the moment. The raw onions are marinated to soften their bite. You probably know how to make hard-boiled eggs, but to prevent the usual gray color from forming on the yolk, try this method. If you boil the eggs, potatoes, and beans after breakfast, by lunchtime everything will be perfectly chilled. The tuna here can be grilled or sautéed; or you can do as the Niçoises do and use canned tuna in olive oil, drained and broken up with a fork.

4 large eggs

6 small Yukon Gold potatoes, scrubbed

4 ounces small string beans or haricots verts, ends trimmed

12 ounces fresh tuna steak, cut 1 inch thick

Kosher salt and freshly ground black pepper

1) In a small saucepan, cover the eggs with cold water and set over high heat. When the water boils, set the timer for 4 minutes. After 4 minutes, turn off the heat but let the eggs sit in the hot water for 4 minutes more (this is to ensure a firm yellow yolk). Then take the saucepan off the stove, put it in the sink, and run cold water into it until the eggs feel cool to the touch.

2) Meanwhile, put the potatoes in a saucepan and cover with cold salted water. Bring to a boil and cook 12 to 15 minutes, until tender but not falling apart. Fill a large bowl with ice cubes and cover with cold water. With a slotted spoon, lift the potatoes out of the pot and plunge them into the ice water to cool. Add the string beans to the pot and boil 3 to 5 minutes, just until bright green and crisp-tender. With a slotted spoon, lift the beans out of the pot and plunge them into the ice water to cool. (The recipe can be prepared to this point up to 12 hours ahead and refrigerated.)

3) When the potatoes are cool enough to handle, cut them in quarters. Peel the eggs and cut them in quarters lengthwise.

4) When you are ready to serve, heat the grill or a broiler and season the tuna on both sides with salt and pepper.

5) Compose the salad: in a large salad bowl, toss the greens with 1/4 cup of the vinaigrette.

6) On top of the greens, arrange the vegetables: working clockwise, place the tomato halves at 12:00, then place the potatoes at 2:00, beans at 4:00, eggs at 6:00, drained onion rings at 8:00, and artichoke hearts at 10:00, leaving a space in the center for the tuna. Scatter the olives over the bowl.

7) Grill the tuna for 2 minutes, then turn and grill another minute. (Or sear on both sides in a very hot skillet in a teaspoon of vegetable oil.) It will be quite rare; cook it longer on the second side if you prefer to cook it through. Slice the tuna 1/2 inch thick and arrange it in the center of the bowl. Drizzle more vinaigrette over the tuna and vegetables. Sprinkle with chives and serve.

8 ounces mixed salad greens (mesclun) or a mixture of at least 3 lettuces such as red leaf, romaine, endive, radicchio, arugula, frisée, watercress, and Boston

1 recipe Roasted Tomato–Garlic Vinaigrette (page 3) or Fresh Lemon-Basil Vinaigrette (page 2)

12 cherry tomatoes, halved

1/2 small red onion, sliced into thin rings and marinated in 2 tablespoons cold water, orange juice, or wine vinegar

One 10-ounce can artichoke hearts, well drained and quartered

1/2 cup Niçoise, Gaeta, or oil-cured black olives

2 teaspoons chopped chives

ANY CLASSIC PILSNER, WELL CHILLED, WOULD BE A GREAT COMPLEMENT TO THIS SUMMERY SALAD; A GERMAN *HEFE-WEIZEN* WOULD ADD GOOD CITRIC NOTES.

A CHILLED DRY PROVENÇAL ROSÉ FROM THE BANDOL OR CASSIS IS THE NATURAL WINE CHOICE.

Chilled Asparagus, Shaved Fennel, and Pecorino with Lemon-Basil Vinaigrette

SERVES 6

This salad, inspired by the simplicity of Italian vegetable cookery, should be served very cold and very crisp. Keep the cooked and trimmed vegetables chilled until just before serving, then toss with the vinaigrette and dot with diced tomato and shavings of pecorino Romano. True pecorino Romano can only come from the Mediterranean island of Sardinia, where thousands of sheep, salt air, and a cheesemaking tradition evolved over centuries conspire to create a strong, wonderfully salty cheese that sharpens the flavors of any dish. It's well worth seeking out—and especially good with vegetables, whether cooked or in salads.

The crunch and contrast of this salad make it an ideal prelude to a hearty Osso Buco with Saffron Risotto and Orange Gremolata (pages 178–80), Rigatoni with Olive-Lamb Ragu (pages 104–5), or almost any entree with big flavors. If you always serve lettuce salads, try this easy one for a refreshing change.

2 pounds thin, tender asparagus stalks, woody bottoms trimmed off

1 large bulb fennel, stalks trimmed off

1 recipe Fresh Lemon-Basil Vinaigrette (page 2)

3 plum tomatoes, chopped

2 ounces pecorino Romano cheese, in one piece

Kosher salt and freshly ground black pepper

1) Bring a large pot of salted water to a boil. Add the asparagus, return to a boil, and blanch for 2 to 3 minutes. Fill a large pot or bowl with ice cubes, then add cold water to cover. When the asparagus are crisp-tender, lift them out of the pot and plunge into the ice water to stop the cooking and set the color. When chilled, remove and set aside to drain. Refrigerate until ready to use, up to 12 hours.

2) With a sharp knife, cut the fennel bulb in half lengthwise. Cut the tough core out of the fennel and slice crosswise into very thin half-moons. Drop into cold water to refresh and soften. Refrigerate in water until ready to use, up to 12 hours.

3) When ready to serve, toss the asparagus with about $\frac{1}{3}$ cup of the vinaigrette. Arrange on a platter with all the tips facing the same way.

4) In the same bowl, toss the drained fennel with a few tablespoons of dressing. Arrange on top of the asparagus. Sprinkle the chopped tomatoes over the fennel. With a vegetable peeler, shave curls of pecorino over the salad. Add salt and pepper to taste and serve.

FOR A CRISP EFFECT, CHOOSE A GOOD LAGER; FOR CONTRAST, TRY A FRUITY, SPICY TRAPPIST TRIPLE ALE.

CHILL A SAUVIGNON BLANC FROM NORTHERN ITALY OR CALIFORNIA.

Roquefort and Pear Salad
with Grapes and Spiced Pecans

SERVES 4 TO 6

All the Roquefort cheese in the world is aged in the limestone caves of Roquefort-sur-Soulzon, in a rocky region of south-central France that we visited in 1982. When the round cheeses arrive at the caves, they are creamy white and firm, giving no indication of the miraculous changes that are about to take place. The damp, fragrant air in these caves contains a particular blend of microorganisms that enter the cheese through precisely thirty-six carefully pierced holes, which results in the sharp, blue-green-veined cheese we love.

As we entered the caves for the first time, we were astonished by the sight of thousands of wheels of Roquefort stacked up to the necks of the workers who, dressed all in white, are responsible for piercing, brushing, salting, and turning the cheeses during the three-month ripening process. As the cheeses become strong and ripe, they are removed, and new ones come to take their place, in a carefully calibrated procedure that has constantly revived itself over centuries. The caves have never been empty since a long-ago shepherd discovered the miraculous effect the air had on a forgotten cheese sandwich—or so the legend goes.

We love the combination of earthy, salty Roquefort cheese and crisp, sweet pears so much that we built an entire salad around it, bringing in red grapes to back up the fruitiness of the pears and toasted pecans to enhance the nuttiness of the cheese. There's a distinct autumn spirit to this salad, so serve it with Toasted Barley and Mushroom Soup with Scamorza (pages 42–43) or a Cassoulet (pages 168–70) from the Roquefort region.

1) Make the spiced pecans: preheat the oven to 350°F. In a mixing bowl, combine the cayenne, cumin, and brown sugar. Add the oil and mix thoroughly. Add the pecans and toss until thoroughly coated. Spread the pecans out on a baking sheet and bake for 15 to 20 minutes, watching carefully to make sure the nuts do not burn. Stir the pecans halfway through the cooking. When toasty, remove from the oven and set aside to cool. (The pecans can be made up to 2 days ahead and kept in an airtight container.)

2) In a large salad bowl, combine the pecans, salad greens, beans, pears, grapes, and drained onion rings. Add about half of the vinaigrette and toss thoroughly. Sprinkle salt and pepper over the top of the salad.

3) Crumble the Roquefort over the salad with your fingers, or chop it with a knife and sprinkle it over. Sprinkle the chives over the top of the salad.

4) Toss at the table and serve, passing the remaining dressing separately.

For the spiced pecans:

1/4 teaspoon cayenne pepper
1/4 teaspoon ground cumin
1 tablespoon light brown sugar
2 teaspoons olive oil
1 cup pecan halves

For the salad:

8 ounces mixed salad greens (mesclun) or a mixture of at least 3 lettuces such as red leaf, romaine, endive, radicchio, arugula, frisée, watercress, and Boston

6 ounces haricots verts or string beans, blanched in boiling salted water until crisp-tender, then rinsed under cold water until cool

2 ripe but firm pears, cored and sliced lengthwise 1/4 inch thick

8 ounces seedless red grapes, stemmed

1/2 small red onion, sliced into thin rings and soaked in cold water or wine vinegar

1 recipe Apple-Walnut Vinaigrette (page 2)

Kosher salt and freshly ground black pepper

6 ounces Roquefort cheese, chilled

1 tablespoon chopped chives

A NUTTY BROWN OR DARK ALE WOULD WORK WELL WITH THIS COMBINATION OF SWEET AND SALTY INGREDIENTS.

SERVE A FRUITY VOUVRAY OR A WASHINGTON STATE RIESLING.

Riviera Caesar Salad

We always knew there had to be a way of combining everyone's favorite salads: the crisp Caesar and the summery Caprese, with its fresh-milk mozzarella, fragrant basil, and meaty tomatoes. The ingredient that pulls everything together here is the slow-roasted tomatoes, which we first tasted at Alain Ducasse's stunning restaurant in Monte Carlo. No one has taught us more than Ducasse about how to appreciate and experience great food, from perfecting an ingredient as basic as the tomato to creating brilliant twelve-course tasting menus. The tomatoes of the Riviera really do have a special flavor: the salt air and sunshine make the difference. However, this slow-roasting technique brings out the Mediterranean in every tomato.

Serve this on its own or before pastas and pizzas, especially a light Linguine with Manila Clams and Fresh Basil (pages 102–3).

For the tuiles and croutons:

1 cup freshly grated Parmesan or grana Padano cheese

3 to 4 small slices French, Italian, or sourdough baguette per serving, tops lightly brushed with olive oil or Garlic Oil and Puree (page 292)

For the dressing:

1 tablespoon Dijon mustard

1 tablespoon plus 1 teaspoon freshly squeezed lemon juice

1 tablespoon plus 1 teaspoon red wine vinegar

1) Make the tuiles and croutons: preheat the oven to 400°F. At one end of a nonstick baking sheet or a baking sheet lined with parchment paper, spread the cheese in an even layer about 1/4 inch thick. Don't spread the cheese over the whole pan; it will be too thin. On the remaining pan surface, arrange the baguette slices in a single layer. Bake until the cheese is crisp and light golden brown, 8 to 12 minutes. Remove from the oven and set the croutons aside. Let the cheese cool until hard. With your hands, carefully break into large pieces. (To store for later use, layer the pieces in an airtight container, placing a sheet of parchment or wax paper between the pieces to prevent sticking.)

2) Make the dressing: in a food processor or blender, combine the mustard, lemon juice, vinegar, anchovies, and pepper. Blend well, then add the egg yolk and blend until emulsified. Still blending, pour in the oil in a thin stream. Add the cheese just until combined. Set aside.

3) In a large bowl, combine the lettuce, mozzarella, and croutons and toss with the dressing.

4) Serve in wide bowls, with a cheese tuile stuck vertically into each bowl, tomato halves around the edge, basil sprinkled over, and a little black pepper ground over the top.

2 anchovy fillets

1/2 teaspoon freshly ground black pepper

1 large egg yolk

1/2 cup olive oil

1/2 cup freshly grated Parmesan or Romano cheese, or a combination

For the salad:

2 very fresh heads romaine lettuce, dark outer leaves discarded, leaves separated and well washed

3 ounces fresh lightly salted mozzarella, cut into 1/2-inch cubes

18 halves Slow-Roasted Tomatoes (page 303)

12 fresh basil leaves, julienned

Freshly ground black pepper

SLIGHTLY CHILLED BEAUJOLAIS OR A FRUITY ITALIAN ROSÉ WORKS BEAUTIFULLY HERE.

Dandelion Salad with Beaujolais-Poached Eggs and Roasted Shallots

SERVES 4

Brasserie Georges is one of the greatest brasseries in Lyons, a city of great restaurants. A central character in the life of the city, its soaring ceilings and murals of Alsatian life serenely overlook the crowds that surge in and out all day, every day. It's not uncommon to wait up to three hours for a table; to the faithful Lyonnais, this is considered time well spent, and we'd have to agree. Founded by master Alsatian brewer Georges Hofherr in 1836, la Georges, as it is known to its many regulars, serves both the traditional rich food of the Beaujolais region and Alsatian specialties. In fact, the largest choucroute garnie *ever assembled—involving over three thousand pounds of sauerkraut—was served there in 1986 to mark the 150th anniversary of the restaurant.*

This salad is our own creation, although it includes several building blocks of la cuisine lyonnaise: *onions (we like shallots for roasting), bacon, eggs, the spicy mustard of nearby Dijon, and the fruity red wine of the Beaujolais. The wine and vinegar will turn the poached egg whites a delicate pink. This is also a terrific brunch or light supper dish.*

8 shallots, peeled and left whole

1 teaspoon olive oil

4 ounces slab or thick-cut bacon, cut into ¹/₄-inch matchsticks

1 cup ¹/₂-inch cubes sourdough bread

1 tablespoon Dijon mustard

¹/₃ cup plus ¹/₄ cup red wine vinegar

²/₃ cup extra-virgin olive oil

Kosher salt and freshly ground black pepper

1) Preheat the oven to 400°F.

2) Rub the shallots with the teaspoon of oil, wrap tightly in foil, and bake 35 to 45 minutes, until tender and sweet. Set aside to cool.

3) Meanwhile, in a skillet, cook the bacon over medium-high heat until golden brown. Remove and drain on paper towels. Pour off all but 2 tablespoons of fat from the skillet, add the bread cubes, and stir well to coat evenly. Cook, stirring, until golden brown. Remove and drain on paper towels. Set aside.

4)   Whisk the mustard, the 1/3 cup vinegar, and the 2/3 cup extra-virgin olive oil together, then add salt and pepper to taste. In a large bowl, toss the frisée, dandelion greens, beans, and bacon with the vinaigrette. Divide among 4 serving plates. Add 2 shallots to each plate, then sprinkle the croutons around the perimeter.

5)   Combine the water, remaining 1/4 cup vinegar, and the wine in a saucepan and bring to a gentle boil. One at a time, break the eggs into a large spoon or small bowl and slip gently into the liquid. After about 3 minutes, the whites should be cooked through and the yolks still soft. Remove with a slotted spoon and place in the center of each salad. Serve immediately.

1 head frisée (curly endive), washed, cut into 2-inch pieces, and refrigerated

2 cups dandelion greens or additional frisée, washed, cut into 2-inch pieces, and refrigerated

1 cup haricots verts or small string beans (optional), blanched

8 cups water

1/4 cup light-bodied red wine, preferably Beaujolais

4 large eggs, at room temperature

SERVE A WELL-CHILLED ITALIAN OR PROVENÇAL ROSÉ OR A YOUNG BEAUJOLAIS.

Roasted Stuffed Artichokes with Toasted Nuts, Lemon, and Tomato

SERVES 6

Stuffed artichokes can be a glorious dish—if they are not packed with damp stuffing until the character of the artichoke is lost. In our version toasted nuts provide a light crunch, and the fresh acidity of tomato and lemon helps to coax out the delicate flavor of the artichokes. This is a fun, sociable, slow-eating dish to start off a dinner party for friends. Have plenty of warm bread standing by.

Warm-flavored nut oils are an easy way to revitalize your cooking: walnut, sesame, and hazelnut oils are easy to find and intensely flavorful. Always store them in the refrigerator. This dish makes a light vegetarian entree or a lunch as well.

For the artichokes:
6 large globe artichokes
2 lemons, halved

For the stuffing:
1 cup toasted, peeled hazelnuts
   (see the headnote on page 184)
   or pecan halves (see page xxxiii)
2 cups dry breadcrumbs
2 garlic cloves, minced
1 tablespoon freshly grated lemon zest
¹/4 cup freshly grated Parmesan
   cheese
1 tablespoon fresh thyme leaves

1) Make the artichokes: cut the stem of each artichoke to a length of about 1 inch. Swish the artichokes in a sinkful of water to remove any grit. With a sharp knife, cut off the top inch of each artichoke and snip any pointed ends off the leaves with scissors.

2) Squeeze the lemons into a large pot of salted water. Cover and bring to a boil, then add the artichokes. Put an upside-down dinner plate on top of them to keep them fully submerged in the water. Boil for about 40 minutes, until an artichoke leaf pulls out easily and is tender to the bite. Lift the artichokes out of the liquid and let cool upside down on a kitchen towel or baking pan. Do not discard the cooking liquid.

3) Meanwhile, make the stuffing: put the nuts, breadcrumbs, garlic, lemon zest, Parmesan, and thyme in a food processor. Process until the mixture is finely ground, then drizzle in the oil, pulsing just until combined. Season to taste with salt and pepper.

4) When the artichokes are cool enough to handle, preheat the oven to 450°F. Remove the tiny center leaves and the choke from each artichoke with a pointed teaspoon. Stuff the center of each artichoke and between the leaves with the breadcrumb mixture, packing tightly. Use half the butter to dot the tops of the artichokes.

5) Place the artichokes upright in a small roasting pan and moisten with about 2 cups of the cooking liquid, pouring around the artichokes. Bake 20 minutes, then remove the artichokes to shallow bowls or soup plates.

6) Meanwhile, make the sauce: in a skillet, heat the olive oil over medium-high heat. Add the garlic and onion and cook, stirring, until softened, about 3 minutes. Add the carrots and celery and cook, stirring occasionally, 5 minutes more. Add the wine and simmer until reduced by half. Add the stock and simmer until reduced and the vegetables are just tender, about 5 minutes more. Whisk in the butter and season to taste with salt and pepper. Whisk in the herbs and tomato. Spoon about 1/2 cup of the sauce around (not over) each artichoke, then add lemon wedges and sprinkle with Parmesan cheese. Serve immediately.

1/4 cup hazelnut or walnut oil
Kosher salt and freshly ground black pepper

For the sauce:
3 tablespoons extra-virgin olive oil
2 garlic cloves, minced
1 large onion, chopped
2 medium carrots, chopped
2 stalks celery, chopped
1 cup dry white wine
2 cups Chicken Stock (page 307) or low-sodium canned broth
4 tablespoons (1/2 stick) cold unsalted butter, cut into small pieces
Kosher salt and freshly ground black pepper
2 tablespoons chopped fresh parsley
1 tablespoon fresh thyme leaves
2 plum tomatoes, diced
Lemon wedges
Freshly grated Parmesan cheese

A NUTTY BROWN ALE WITH BUTTERY FLAVOR WILL HIGHLIGHT THE TOASTED NUTS AND EARTHY ARTICHOKE FLAVOR.

TRY A CRISP YOUNG PINOT GRIGIO FROM FRIULI OR A SPANISH ALBARINO.

Caramelized Onion Tart

Tarte à l'oignon *is one of the most versatile of Alsatian specialties: it's on every menu, from the simplest* bierstub *(the Alsatian word for brasserie) to the most elegant restaurants in the cosmopolitan capital of Strasbourg. The lightest, most finely flavored tart we ever tasted was served to us high in the Vosges Mountains at a tiny auberge called Les Alisiers in Lapoutroie. We let the perfect filling melt in our mouths as we watched the clouds and the cows slowly drift across the mountainsides below.*

Tarte à l'oignon *is equally at home as an appetizer for a robustly flavored dinner (such as our Chicago Choucroute, pages 148–49) or as a complete lunch with a green salad or vegetable soup. The olives and anchovies, if used, add a more Mediterranean flavor, bringing the tart into the family of the Provençal* pissaladière, *perfect for rounding out a meal of Salade Niçoise with Roasted Tomato–Garlic Vinaigrette (pages 6–7).*

1 tablespoon light olive oil

3 garlic cloves, minced

3 tablespoons unsalted butter

2 pounds yellow onions, thinly sliced

2 teaspoons all-purpose flour

3 large eggs

2/3 cup heavy cream

1/8 teaspoon freshly grated nutmeg

1 teaspoon finely chopped fresh basil

1 teaspoon finely chopped fresh parsley

1/2 cup freshly grated Gruyère cheese

1/2 cup oil-cured black olives, pitted
   and chopped (optional)

1) In a skillet, heat the olive oil over medium-high heat. Reduce the heat to medium, add the garlic, and cook, stirring, 2 to 3 minutes. Add the butter and swirl it around the pan until it melts, then add the onions. Reduce the heat to low and cook, uncovered, stirring occasionally, until the onions are soft, golden brown, and caramelized, about 25 minutes. Sprinkle the flour over the onions and cook, stirring, 3 minutes more. Set aside to cool at least 20 minutes. (The recipe can be prepared to this point up to 1 day ahead and refrigerated.)

2) Preheat the oven to 350°F.

3) In a mixing bowl, whisk together the eggs, cream, nutmeg, basil, and parsley. Stir in the cooled onions, cheese, and olives, if using. Add salt and pepper to taste. Pour into the pie crust and arrange the anchovies, if using, in a spoke pattern on top of the filling.

4) Bake 25 to 30 minutes, until the custard is set and the top is golden brown. Let cool 5 minutes. (The recipe can be prepared to this point up to 3 days ahead and refrigerated. Reheat in the oven before serving.) Slice and serve immediately.

Kosher salt and freshly ground black pepper
1 Myrna's Pie Crust (see The Best Banana Cream Pie, pages 240–42), made up to and including step 7
6 anchovy fillets (optional)

A TRAPPIST ALE WITH COMPLEX, REFRESHING CHARACTER AND WARM TOASTY NOTES WILL MATCH WELL WITH THE CREAMY CUSTARD AND SWEET ONIONS.

FOR A CLASSIC COMBINATION, SERVE A DRY ALSATIAN RIESLING OR PINOT GRIS.

Truffled Chicken Liver Mousse

SERVES 10

The great pride of an Alsatian restaurant kitchen is often its smooth, delicate foie gras maison, *homemade pâté crafted from fresh livers of duck or goose and infused with the region's marc, or grape brandy. The classic mousses, pâtés, and terrines of the French kitchen may seem like complicated chefly mysteries, but there's no reason this classic preparation can't be the pride of your kitchen as well. The black truffles add another dimension but are by no means necessary. Made with easily obtained fresh chicken livers and a little bit of care, this is an impressive hors d'oeuvre with remarkable flavor.*

1 pound fresh chicken livers, cleaned of all fat, veins, and sinews

1 cup tawny port

¹/₄ cup Cognac

8 large egg yolks

12 tablespoons (1¹/₂ sticks) unsalted butter, melted

5 ounces fresh pork fatback or larding fat, melted

1 teaspoon white truffle oil

¹/₈ teaspoon freshly ground white pepper

2 pinches freshly grated nutmeg

2 pinches cayenne pepper

1 teaspoon kosher or sea salt

2 cups cold heavy cream

¹/₄ cup finely chopped fresh or canned black truffles (optional)

1) Two or three days before you plan to serve the mousse, rinse the livers well under cold running water and dry them on paper towels. Put them in a mixing bowl and pour the port over. Cover and refrigerate overnight. Grease a terrine mold or a glass or ceramic loaf pan with butter, cover, and refrigerate overnight.

2) The next day, preheat the oven to 350°F.

3) Drain the livers well, discarding the port, and transfer to a food processor or blender. Add the Cognac, egg yolks, melted butter, fatback, truffle oil, white pepper, nutmeg, cayenne, and salt. Process until very smooth. Add the cream and pulse just until combined. Do not overprocess.

4) Pour and press the mixture through a chinois or fine sieve into another bowl. Whisk in the truffles, if using, and pour the mixture into the buttered terrine.

5) Cover with a double layer of foil, pressing firmly around the edges to make a tight seal. Place in a roasting pan and pour hot water into the pan until it comes halfway up the sides of the dish. Bake for about 90 minutes, until barely set. Give the dish a little shake to test for doneness; when the center is almost set but still soft, the mousse is done. It will firm up in the refrigerator.

6) Refrigerate, covered, overnight or up to 2 days. Serve chilled but not cold, with hot toast.

SERVE WITH A YEASTY, AROMATIC TRAPPIST ALE FROM BELGIUM OR THE NETHERLANDS.

A FRUITY, CRISP MÜLLER-THURGAU OR RIESLING FROM TRENTINO IN NORTHERN ITALY MARRIES BEAUTIFULLY TO THIS RICH DISH.

Crab Cakes and Baby Greens
with Citrus Vinaigrette and Spicy Aioli

SERVES 6 AS AN APPETIZER, 4 AS AN ENTREE

We never gave the proper deep thought to crab cakes until a memorable meal at Joe's Stone Crab House in Miami snapped us to attention. French restaurants treat quenelles of crab as a rare delicacy, so we knew that hearty, spicy American crab cakes had to be on our brasserie menu. Since our brasserie is in Chicago, miles from the nearest crab, we always use lump crabmeat for this dish, and you can too—as long as you buy it fresh from a busy fish store. To make this dish even more irresistible, top each crab cake with a swirl of spicy garlic mayonnaise.

This simply perfect dish with subtle Creole seasoning makes an elegant opening to almost any meal—or a terrific summer dinner with some grilled bread and a juicy tomato-basil salad alongside the greens. If you've never made your own breadcrumbs, here's your chance. Just collect all the bits and pieces of stale bread you have in the house, put them in the food processor, and pulse into fine crumbs. The results will be much tastier and less salty than store-bought. If you can find panko, Japanese bread-crumbs, the texture will be even better.

For the citrus vinaigrette:
- **¼ cup freshly squeezed lemon juice**
- **¼ cup freshly squeezed orange juice**
- **1 tablespoon freshly squeezed lime juice**
- **6 tablespoons extra-virgin olive oil**
- **½ teaspoon honey**
- **1 teaspoon kosher salt**
- **¼ teaspoon freshly ground black pepper**

1) Make the dressing: in a bowl, whisk all the dressing ingredients together and set aside.

2) Make the crab cakes: lightly squeeze any liquid out of the crabmeat and pick over to remove any bits of cartilage. Put the crabmeat in a bowl. Add the egg, egg white, parsley, cilantro, bell pepper, lemon juice, cayenne, and cumin and mix thoroughly.

Add the mayonnaise, breadcrumbs, and salt and pepper to taste and mix just until moistened and well combined.

3) Divide the mixture into 12 cakes about 1 inch thick and 2^1/$_2$ inches across. Spread out on a baking sheet and set aside until ready to use. (The recipe can be prepared to this point up to 8 hours ahead and refrigerated.)

4) When ready to serve, toss the greens and tomatoes with the citrus vinaigrette and divide among the serving plates.

5) Heat the oil in a skillet over medium-high heat. Working in batches to avoid crowding the pan, sauté the crab cakes just until golden brown, about 3 minutes on each side.

6) Serve warm on the plates with greens and tomatoes. Spoon a little aioli on each crab cake, or pass it separately at the table.

For the crab cakes:

1 pound lump crabmeat

1 large egg

1 large egg white

2 teaspoons finely chopped fresh parsley, or a combination of parsley and chives

2 teaspoons finely chopped fresh cilantro

1 small red bell pepper, seeded and finely diced

1 teaspoon freshly squeezed lemon juice

^{1}/$_4$ teaspoon cayenne pepper, or to taste

^{1}/$_2$ teaspoon ground cumin

^{1}/$_3$ cup Mayonnaise, homemade (page 299) or store-bought

^{2}/$_3$ cup plain breadcrumbs

Kosher salt and freshly ground black pepper

To finish the dish:

6 cups mixed salad greens (mesclun) or a mixture of at least 3 lettuces such as red leaf, romaine, endive, radicchio, arugula, frisée, watercress, and Boston

2 plum tomatoes, quartered lengthwise into wedges

1 tablespoon light olive oil

1 recipe Spicy Aioli (page 300)

AN AMBER ALE WITH FRUITY FLAVORS AND A LONG FINISH WILL BE ABLE TO HANDLE THE SPICE AND COMPLETE THE DISH.

BOTH LIGHT, FRESH GERMAN RIESLINGS FROM THE MOSEL AND FRENCH VOUVRAY MARRY WELL WITH THE CRAB.

Steamed Mussels with Fennel, Cream, and Pernod

The popular anise-flavored aperitifs Pernod and Ricard are the legitimate descendants of the now-illegal liqueur called absinthe, which swept Paris as the narcotic of choice in the late nineteenth century. Known to poets and painters as "the green muse," absinthe causes vivid hallucinations and, if taken too often, permanent brain damage. Absinthe was made palatable by pouring it through a sugar cube; modern versions are mixed with cold water to make the thirst-quenching Provençal aperitif known as pastis. Pastis will cause nothing more than a vivid sense of well-being or perhaps an observation of how well its fennel flavor blends with mussels and cream in this classic French dish. However, the dish is also delicious when made with all wine.

We call for Prince Edward Island mussels in this recipe, as the PEI producers use the "rope-raising" method that keeps the mussels clean, plump, and healthy. We first witnessed this phenomenon off the coast of New Zealand, where literally millions of mussels thickly cluster around ropes that dangle from the producers' floats. Out on the harvest boats, the winches haul as fast as the workers can scrape the mussels off the ropes and into the hold. Those "greenlip" mussels, which are available in some U.S. fish stores, are so fresh that we have eaten them raw—but most should be cooked quickly and simply, as in the Belgian brasserie classic of mussels cooked in gueuze ale. Serve this easy but very impressive dish with plenty of warm bread or toast.

1) Clean the mussels: put the mussels in the sink and cover them with cold water. Swish them around vigorously in the sink, rubbing them against each other to remove sand, slime, and grit, then drain the water and rinse out the sand that remains. Repeat until no sand remains in the sink. Rinse the mussels well, then discard any with cracked or open shells. Pull the beard from the side of each mussel with your fingers, or use your fingers and a paring knife for a better grip.

2) In a large, heavy pot with a lid, heat the olive oil over medium-high heat. Add the garlic, shallots, and fennel and cook, stirring, until softened, about 3 minutes.

3) Add the wine and Pernod and bring to a boil. Add the mussels, stir, and cover. Cook, shaking the pan occasionally, until most of the mussels are open, 4 to 5 minutes. Add the cream and salt and pepper to taste, mix gently, and continue cooking, covered, until all the mussels are open.

4) Transfer to a large serving bowl or serve from the pot into large bowls at the table. Ladle cooking liquid over each serving until about a third of the mussels are covered. Sprinkle parsley over each serving.

4 pounds black mussels in their shells, preferably Prince Edward Island

2 tablespoons olive oil

2 garlic cloves, minced

2 shallots, minced

1 small bulb fennel, stalks trimmed off, halved lengthwise and thinly sliced

1 cup dry white wine

1/4 cup Pernod, Ricard, or other pastis or anise-flavored liqueur

1 cup heavy cream

Chopped fresh parsley for garnish

A CLASSIC FRENCH *BIÈRE DE GARDE*, WITH ITS AMBER COLOR AND HINTS OF LICORICE, WOULD COMBINE BEAUTIFULLY WITH THE SUBTLE ANISE FLAVOR HERE.

CRISP, FRESH MUSCADET OR POUILLY-FUMÉ PAIRS PERFECTLY WITH THIS DISH.

Escargots with Lots of Garlic

The classic dish of snails baked in a flavor bath of butter, garlic, and parsley is known throughout France as a Burgundian creation—except in Alsace, where the dish is considered a local specialty and always called escargots à l'Alsacienne. *To us the most important thing is to include plenty of garlic and enough fragrant parsley to make the butter turn a vibrant green.*

Fresh snails are now rarely used for this dish, even in France. At Brasserie T we simmer imported canned snails in seasoned water to improve the flavor, then bake them in butter and herbs. They can be made in special snail dishes with an indentation for each snail, small ramekins, or one large dish. For an entree, just toss the whole dish with a pound and a half of freshly cooked linguine.

For the snail butter:

- **1 cup peeled garlic cloves**
- **2 cups chopped fresh parsley**
- **1 cup (2 sticks) unsalted butter, at room temperature**
- **1 tablespoon freshly squeezed lemon juice**
- **1 tablespoon plain breadcrumbs**
- **¹/₂ teaspoon kosher salt**
- **¹/₄ teaspoon freshly ground black pepper**

1) Make the snail butter: finely mince the garlic cloves. In the bowl of a mixer, combine the garlic and parsley. Add the butter and whip, using the whipping attachment, until well combined and fluffy. With the mixer running, add the lemon juice, breadcrumbs, salt, and pepper and mix until combined. With a rubber spatula, scrape the butter out onto a piece of plastic wrap and shape into a log. Roll tightly in plastic wrap and refrigerate until chilled and firm, at least 1 hour or up to 3 days.

2) Simmer the snails: rinse the snails in cold water. In a large, heavy pot, heat the oil over medium heat. Add the onion and garlic and cook, stirring, until softened, about 5 minutes. Do not let them brown. Add the snails, rosemary, thyme, and wine and bring

to a simmer. Cook until the liquid is reduced by a third. Add water to cover, bring to a boil, then reduce the heat and simmer for 10 minutes. Turn off the heat and let the snails cool in the liquid.

3) When ready to serve, preheat the oven to 425°F.

4) Cut the butter log in half. Use half of the butter to dot the bottom of 6 special snail dishes, 6 medium ramekins, or 1 medium baking dish. Arrange the snails in the dish or dishes, then top each snail with the remaining butter.

5) Bake 15 to 20 minutes, until bubbly and very hot. Serve immediately.

For the snails:

2 tablespoons light olive or canola oil
1 large onion, chopped
3 garlic cloves, crushed
36 fresh or canned extra-large snails
2 sprigs fresh rosemary
2 sprigs fresh thyme
$^1/_2$ cup dry white wine

TO CUT THE RICHNESS OF THE BUTTER, EAT THIS WITH A SPARKLY, TOASTY BELGIAN *GUEUZE* FROM A TRADITIONAL BREWER, OR A LAGER WITH A SIMILAR CHARACTER.

COMPLEMENT WITH A MÂCON BLANC OR A SIMPLE FRENCH CHABLIS WITH GOOD ACIDITY.

Grilled Shrimp with Aiolis

SERVES 4 OR 5

Our favorite, most colorful finger food. Swaths of light green, bright yellow, salmon pink, and cream look beautiful on plates, but we sometimes serve this dish on brightly colored tiles or glass bricks for even more visual punch. Lots of people who claim to dislike mayonnaise have never tried the homemade version, and only the strictest diehards can resist aioli—fresh mayonnaise with plenty of garlic beaten in. The Provençal tradition of the grand aioli—a day-long feast centered around aioli and all the things you can dip into it—is one we envy. If you'd like to add steamed vegetables such as cauliflower and broccoli florets or asparagus, that would be very much in the aioli tradition. In fact, you can leave the shrimp out altogether if you like.

See pages 300–301 for additional aiolis and make whichever ones you like—or all. Aim for a mix of colors and flavors. All aiolis can be made a day ahead and refrigerated.

For the aioli base:
2 cups cold Mayonnaise (page 299)
1 garlic clove, finely minced
1/2 lemon, seeds removed
**Kosher salt and freshly ground black
    pepper**

For the basil aioli:
**1 tablespoon Pesto (see Pesto Mashed
    Potatoes, pages 208–9) or any
    store-bought pesto**

For the red pepper aioli:
1 small red bell pepper

1) Make the aioli base: combine the mayonnaise and garlic in a mixing bowl. Squeeze the lemon over the mixture, stir, and add salt and pepper to taste.

2) Make the basil aioli: transfer 1/2 cup of aioli base to a bowl and whisk in the pesto until well blended. Chill.

3) Make the red pepper aioli: spear the pepper on the end of a long fork and roast on a hot griddle or over a medium flame on your gas stove, turning, until blackened and charred all over. Place in a thick plastic or brown paper bag, close the top, and set aside.

When cool enough to handle, slip off the skins with your fingers, split the pepper open, remove the seeds, and dice. Do not rinse; the flavor is in the oils. In a blender, combine the red pepper pieces with 1/2 cup aioli base. Blend well, transfer to a bowl, and chill.

4) Make the saffron aioli: in a small saucepan, simmer the saffron and water together until reduced to 1 teaspoon of liquid. Transfer 1/2 cup of aioli base to a bowl and whisk in the saffron essence. Chill.

5) Preheat a grill or broiler for at least 20 minutes, until very hot. Push a thin skewer through each shrimp from tail to head so that the shrimp is straightened and surrounds the skewer. Wrap each shrimp in a slice of pancetta and brush with garlic oil.

6) Grill the shrimp 2 to 3 minutes on each side, until the pancetta shrivels and browns but the shrimp are pink and juicy. Do not overcook.

7) To serve, place a large dab of each kind of aioli on each serving plate or spread the aiolis in swatches. Rest the shrimp on top of the aiolis (one per swatch), sprinkle with sesame seeds, and serve immediately.

For the saffron aioli:

1 pinch saffron threads
1/4 cup water

For the shrimp:

20 large raw shrimp, peeled and deveined
20 thin slices pancetta
2 tablespoons Garlic Oil and Puree (page 292), or 2 tablespoons olive oil mixed with 1 minced garlic clove
2 tablespoons black or white sesame seeds, or a combination, lightly toasted (see page xxxiii) (optional)

MATCH WITH A FRIULIAN PINOT GRIGIO OR TOCAI OR WITH ANOTHER LIGHT, FRESH ITALIAN WHITE.

Panzanella

Tuscan Sourdough Salad

SERVES 6

A traditional way of using up stale bread and summer's excess of tomatoes, panzanella is brightly citrusy and full of vegetables, like a salad form of gazpacho. Using slightly dry bread, which soaks up the delicious liquids better than fresh, means that the textures and flavors stay true. Panzanella can be as simple as bread, tomatoes, and seasoning, but cucumbers make the salad crunchy and colorful. A dusting of aged imported Asiago, a cow's milk cheese from the Dolomite mountains north of Venice, adds both sharpness and creaminess. The flavor of true Asiago is almost like a cross between Parmigiano and Romano, so if you are a fan of those popular cheeses, seek out a chunk of Asiago. Kalamata and Gaeta olives are large enough to pit with a cherry pitter.

2 large kirby cucumbers or 1 English cucumber, well washed (do not peel)

2 pounds plum tomatoes, diced

1 cup pitted Gaeta or Kalamata olives, halved lengthwise

1 small red onion, sliced into thin rings and soaked in cold water

3 tablespoons capers, drained and rinsed

1 small loaf crusty sourdough or olive bread (preferably at least 2 days old), cut into 1-inch cubes

1 cup red wine vinegar

1 ½ cups olive oil

¼ cup julienned fresh basil leaves

3 large garlic cloves, finely minced

1 tablespoon freshly squeezed lemon juice

1 teaspoon freshly grated orange or lemon zest

Kosher salt and freshly ground black pepper

Freshly grated or shaved aged Asiago cheese for garnish

1) Halve the cucumbers lengthwise, then use the tip of a teaspoon to scrape out the seeds. Slice into half-moons ⅛ inch thick and transfer to a large salad bowl.

2) Add all the remaining ingredients except the Asiago cheese, then toss well to blend.

3) Cover and refrigerate at least 30 minutes or up to 3 hours to let the flavors blend. Serve chilled or bring to room temperature before serving. Garnish each plate with plenty of Asiago, or shave curls of Asiago over each plate with a vegetable peeler at the table.

TRY A CRISP VERNACCIA DI SAN GIMIGNANO OR
A PINOT BIANCO FROM FRIULI.

Bluepoint Oysters with Mignonette Salsa

SERVES 4 OR 6

One reason for the cluster of fine brasseries in the Paris neighborhood of Montparnasse is the nearby Gare Montparnasse—the train station where trains from Brittany used to unload their sparkling-fresh Atlantic seafood every day. The oyster market has moved elsewhere, but nearby shellfish restaurants like Le Dôme still serve Belon oysters from Brittany, often with a mignonette sauce of shallots marinated in red wine vinegar. We don't know of a better way to start off a great meal. Here's our all-American rendition, made with meaty eastern Bluepoints and lots of fresh vegetables. As always, nestling the raw oysters in a bed of crushed ice is a good idea—gastronomically and aesthetically.

1) In a mixing bowl, combine the shallots, tomato, cucumber, pepper, dill, mint, and chives to make the salsa. Whisk together the vinegar, oil, and salt and pepper to taste and pour over the vegetables. Toss well, cover, and refrigerate 30 minutes.

2) Meanwhile, prepare a large serving platter by filling it with crushed ice. Keep in the freezer until ready to use.

3) Open the oysters: wrap your left hand (or right if you're a lefty) with a kitchen towel. With your wrapped hand, hold the oyster firmly on a flat surface (with the convex side down to catch the liquor) and use the other hand to push the tip of an oyster knife into the hinge of the oyster. Push and turn the knife until the hinge pops open. Run the blade of the knife along the inside of the shell to loosen. Lift off the top shell and discard. Run the blade under the oyster, severing it from the shell. Return the oyster to the bottom of the shell and place it on the ice bed, and repeat with remaining oysters.

4) Just before serving, top each oyster with a teaspoon of salsa. Scatter the lemon wedges on the platter and serve.

2 medium shallots, finely minced

1 large beefsteak tomato, seeded and diced

1 small cucumber (do not peel), seeded and diced

1 large yellow pepper, seeded and diced

1 teaspoon finely chopped fresh dill

1 teaspoon finely chopped fresh mint

1 teaspoon snipped chives

¼ cup red wine vinegar

⅓ cup extra-virgin olive oil

Kosher salt and freshly ground black pepper

24 very fresh Bluepoint or other meaty oysters, rinsed clean

2 lemons, cut into wedges

A FRESH, CRISP MUSCADET IS THE CLASSIC ACCOMPANIMENT TO OYSTERS.

Soups and Chowders

French Onion Soup with Gruyère and Country Mustard

Spring Vegetable Minestrone with White Beans and Pesto

Roasted Red Pepper Soup with Herbed Fresh Ricotta

Curried Pumpkin Soup with Apple and Toasted Pumpkin Seeds

Toasted Barley and Mushroom Soup with Scamorza

Fresh Tomato-Basil Soup with Focaccia Croutons

Roasted Garlic Soup with Polenta Croutons

Italian Lentil Soup with Smoked Bacon and Spinach

Clam, Corn, and Chimay Chowder

Four-Pepper Oyster Stew

Gazpacho with Crabmeat and Croutons

Leek and Potato Soup with Smoked Fish

French Onion Soup
with Gruyère and Country Mustard

SERVES 6

Who can resist homemade onion soup with croutons and a layer of bubbly melted cheese on top? No one, it seems. For many Americans onion soup gratinée is the first French food they encounter; in France the soup is practically an institution, especially at the brasserie Au Pied de Cochon in the old market district of Paris. The days when Les Halles was the wholesale meat market for all of Paris is reflected on the menu in offerings like liver, sweetbreads, calf's foot soup, and the following fond poem to the pig:

> *Je ne connais q'un animal*
> *qui chaque jour de sa substance*
> *comme toi fasse un don total*
> *c'est le bon citoyen de France!*
>
> I know of only one animal
> That every day gives, as you do,
> a total gift of itself;
> That's a good French citizen!

We use an herbal chicken stock that brings out the flavor of the onions, and punch up the soup with a flavor jolt of mustard. The result is a real dinner soup that needs only a big composed salad like our Crunchy Green Salad with Goat Cheese and Warm Bacon Vinaigrette (pages 4–5) and a dessert of Individual Caramelized Apple Tarts (pages 234–35) to make a hearty but not heavy meal. Caramelized onions are important here for sweetness, flavor, and color; don't rush the caramelizing process. Be careful when maneuvering the bowls of hot soup around; we find it's best to place them in a roasting pan for the final cooking.

1) In a large, heavy pot, heat the olive oil over medium-high heat. Add the onions, reduce the heat to low, and cook, stirring occasionally, until very soft and caramelized, 35 to 45 minutes.

2) Add the brandy and stir, scraping up the browned bits from the bottom of the pan with a wooden spoon. Cook briefly, just until syrupy, then add the chicken stock, bay leaf, thyme, and peppercorns. Bring to a boil, then reduce the heat and simmer until reduced by one-fourth. Stir in the mustard. Add salt and pepper to taste. (The recipe can be prepared to this point up to 3 days in advance. Reheat over low heat when ready to serve.)

3) When ready to serve, preheat the broiler or heat the oven to 500°F. Ladle the soup into 6 deep, flameproof bowls. Leave at least $1/2$ inch of space at the top of each bowl. Top each with 3 baguette toasts to cover the surface, then cover the toasts with 2 slices of Gruyère and 1 slice of mozzarella.

4) Arrange the bowls in a roasting or baking pan placed on the oven rack, then carefully slide the rack into the oven. Broil for 1 minute (or bake for 3 minutes), then sprinkle each bowl with Parmesan and parsley, rotate the pan, and return to the oven until the cheese is melted and golden brown. Serve immediately.

2 tablespoons olive oil

3 pounds yellow onions, peeled, halved, and thinly sliced

1 tablespoon brandy or Cognac

12 cups Chicken Stock (page 307) or low-sodium canned broth

1 bay leaf

$1/4$ teaspoon fresh thyme leaves

12 black peppercorns

1 tablespoon grainy "country-style" Dijon mustard

Kosher salt and freshly ground black pepper

18 small baguette slices, about $1/4$ inch thick, lightly toasted

12 thin slices Gruyère cheese

6 thin slices fresh mozzarella cheese

3 tablespoons freshly grated Parmesan cheese

2 tablespoons chopped fresh parsley, chives, or a combination

A DARKER LAGER WITH COFFEE AND CARAMEL CHARACTER WOULD SET OFF THE HEARTY FLAVORS OF THE SOUP NICELY.

PAIR WITH CLASSIC BISTRO WINES LIKE BEAUJOLAIS AND CÔTES-DU-RHÔNE, OR TRY A LIGHT CALIFORNIA SYRAH.

Spring Vegetable Minestrone with White Beans and Pesto

SERVES 8

This soup turns up all along the Riviera, whether as a classic Ligurian minestrone with the marvelous Genoese pesto, or a Provençal soupe au pistou. However, it also turns up far from the Mediterranean: in New York City's Grand Central station, where one of our favorite American brasseries, Cafe Centro, is located. Cafe Centro has entirely captured the authentic bustle and the graceful lines of classic Parisian brasseries.

We love the extra fragrance and flavor provided by the cubes of fresh fennel here. This soup is a great project for a late-spring afternoon, with lots of therapeutic slicing and dicing of the season's freshest new vegetables to be done. The vegetables are combined and lightly cooked just before serving, so that their flavors and textures stay true. Rick grew up on this soup: his grandmother Adeline was serving it drizzled it with extra-virgin olive oil long before he became a chef!

1 cup dried cannellini or great Northern beans

3 tablespoons extra-virgin olive oil

2 medium carrots, diced

3 stalks celery, diced

1 medium onion, diced

1 small bulb fennel, diced

2 large red bell peppers, diced

2 small zucchini, diced

2 small yellow (summer) squash, diced

8 ounces domestic mushrooms, quartered

1) Make the beans: cover the beans with plenty of water and soak overnight. The next day, discard the soaking liquid, cover the beans with fresh water, and simmer, covered, until cooked through but not soft, adding more boiling water as necessary.

2) In a large pot, heat the oil over medium-high heat. Add the carrots, celery, onion, fennel, red bell pepper, zucchini, yellow squash, and mushrooms and cook, stirring, until softened, about 8 minutes. Do not let the vegetables brown; reduce the heat if necessary.

3) Stir in the beans, tomatoes, and basil and mix to combine, breaking up the tomatoes with a wooden spoon.

4) Add the stock and bring to a boil, then reduce the heat to a simmer. Simmer 15 minutes, then stir in the pasta and cook 10 more minutes. Stir in the escarole and salt and pepper to taste.

5) Serve in heated bowls, with a spoonful of pesto dolloped on top and sprinkled with Parmesan cheese.

One 28-ounce can Italian plum tomatoes, with juice

10 cups Chicken Stock (page 307), or 5 cups low-sodium canned broth plus 5 cups water

1 cup ditalini pasta

1 medium head escarole (curly endive), tough outer leaves removed, remaining leaves separated, well washed, and cut into 2-inch lengths

Kosher salt and freshly ground black pepper

1 recipe Pesto (see Pesto Mashed Potatoes, pages 208–9), for garnish

Freshly shaved Parmesan cheese, for garnish

AN ITALIAN PILSNER WOULD HARMONIZE WITH THIS LIGHT, FRESH SOUP.

TRY SIMPLE, FRESH REDS AND FLORAL WHITES FROM NORTHERN ITALY.

Roasted Red Pepper Soup with Herbed Fresh Ricotta

SERVES 6 TO 8

What are roasted peppers not good for? We can't think of anything. In sandwiches, pasta, sauces, pizzas, salads, or just draped over chunks of crusty bread, roasted peppers offer silky texture and deep, smoky-sweet flavor that no other vegetable can provide. What makes this soup really special is the easy-to-make topping: the fresh-milk flavor of good ricotta, the brightness of orange zest, and the green notes of fresh herbs contrast beautifully with the velvety red soup.

For the soup:

3 tablespoons olive oil

2 large carrots, chopped

2 stalks celery, chopped

1 large onion, chopped

4 garlic cloves, minced

1/2 medium bulb fennel, diced

1 Bouquet Garni (page 297)

2 tablespoons tomato paste

8 Roasted Red Peppers (page 304), diced

12 cups Chicken Stock (page 307), Vegetable Stock (page 311), or low-sodium canned broth

Kosher salt and freshly ground black pepper

Chopped fresh parsley, for garnish

1) Heat the oil in a large pot over medium-high heat. Add the carrots, celery, onion, garlic, and fennel and cook, stirring, until softened, about 8 minutes. Do not let the vegetables brown; reduce the heat if necessary. Add the bouquet garni and tomato paste and cook, stirring, about 5 minutes more. Add the red peppers and cook, stirring, about 3 minutes more.

2) Add the stock and bring to a boil, then reduce the heat and simmer until reduced by one-third.

3) Remove the bouquet garni from the soup. With a hand blender, puree the soup in the pot, or let cool slightly, puree in batches in a blender, and return to the pot. (You can prepare the soup to this point up to 1 day in advance. Reheat over low heat when ready to serve.) Add salt and pepper to taste.

4)   Meanwhile, make the topping: In a mixer or food processor, whip all the ingredients together. Refrigerate until ready to serve.

5)   Serve the soup, topping each bowl with a dollop of the herbed ricotta and a generous sprinkling of parsley.

For the topping:

$^1/_2$ cup fresh ricotta cheese
$^1/_4$ teaspoon freshly grated orange zest
$^1/_2$ teaspoon minced fresh basil
1 teaspoon minced fresh tarragon

MATCH A BRIGHT, YOUNG CHIANTI CLASSICO OR FRUITY PINOT NOIR
TO THE SWEETNESS IN THIS SOUP.

Curried Pumpkin Soup with Apple and Toasted Pumpkin Seeds

SERVES 6 TO 8

The ultimate autumn soup, sweetened with apple juice, sparked with cider vinegar, and warmed with curry powder. Canned and frozen pumpkin purees are available at the supermarket; so are winter squash purees, which can be substituted for the pumpkin if necessary. But the best results come from starting with a whole fresh pumpkin, easily found from September through December. Small pumpkins are easy to work with and have the best flavor.

Here's how to treat your fresh pumpkin: Use your largest knife to cut the pumpkin into halves. Snap off and discard the stem, then use your hands to scrape out the seeds and pulp and transfer them to a colander. Pick out the stringy pulp and wash the seeds until clean. Place pumpkin in a roasting pan dotted with 4 tablespoons of butter and filled with 1/2 cup of water. Cover with foil and bake at 400°F until the pumpkin is soft, 20 to 30 minutes. Scoop pulp from the skins and puree in a food processor or with a hand blender and proceed with the soup. Save a cup of the puree to make luscious Pumpkin Polenta (page 203).

1 tablespoon light olive oil

2 medium carrots, chopped

2 stalks celery, chopped

1 medium onion, chopped

2 garlic cloves, minced

1 leek, including 3 inches of green, sliced into rings and well washed

1 teaspoon best-quality curry powder

1/4 teaspoon freshly grated nutmeg

1) Heat the olive oil in a large pot over medium-high heat. Add the carrots, celery, onion, garlic, leek, curry powder, nutmeg, cinnamon, star anise, and brown sugar and cook, stirring, until softened, about 8 minutes. Do not let the vegetables brown; reduce the heat if necessary.

2) Add the apple juice and vinegar and simmer, stirring, until the liquid is reduced to a thick syrup. Add the pumpkin puree and

cook, stirring, 4 minutes. Stir in the stock, bring to a boil, reduce the heat, and simmer 30 minutes.

3)   Remove the star anise. With a hand blender, puree the soup in the pot until very smooth, or let cool slightly, carefully puree in batches in a blender, and return to the pot. (You can prepare the soup to this point up to 1 day in advance. Reheat over low heat when ready to serve.)

4)   Add the hot cream to the hot soup and simmer until slightly thickened. Whisk in the butter and add salt and pepper to taste.

5)   Meanwhile, make the garnish: preheat the oven or a toaster oven to 375°F. Spread the pumpkin seeds on a baking sheet and toast, stirring occasionally, until golden brown, about 8 minutes. Check frequently to make sure they do not burn.

6)   Melt the butter in a saucepan and whisk in the cinnamon and brown sugar. Add the pumpkin seeds and stir to coat. Transfer to a serving bowl. (You can prepare the seeds up to 2 days in advance.)

7)   Put the diced apple in a serving bowl and bring the orange and a hand grater to the table.

8)   To serve, ladle the soup into bowls and top with apple pieces and pumpkin seeds. Grate a little orange zest over each bowl.

$1/4$ teaspoon ground cinnamon

2 pieces star anise

1 teaspoon dark brown sugar

1 cup apple juice or cider

$1/2$ cup cider vinegar

4 cups pumpkin puree, fresh or canned (not pumpkin pie mix)

10 cups Chicken Stock (page 307), Vegetable Stock (page 311), or water

1 to 2 cups heavy cream, heated

2 tablespoons cold unsalted butter, cut into pieces

Kosher salt and freshly ground black pepper

For the garnish:

$1/2$ cup fresh pumpkin seeds, hulled or store-bought

1 tablespoon unsalted butter

2 pinches ground cinnamon

2 pinches dark brown sugar

1 Granny Smith apple, peeled, cored, diced small, and tossed with 1 tablespoon freshly squeezed lemon juice

1 whole orange

PAIR WITH A RICH PINOT GRIS FROM ALSACE OR EXPERIMENT WITH AN EXOTIC MUSKETELLER FROM AUSTRIA'S STYRIAN REGION.

Toasted Barley and Mushroom Soup
with Scamorza

SERVES 6 TO 8

Domesticated mushroom-barley soup goes wild. Plentiful vegetables, fresh herbs, extra-virgin olive oil, and creamy scamorza cheese combine with deep-woods-flavored mushrooms to create a straightforward, satisfying soup with extraordinary taste. Scamorza is a member of the mozzarella cheese family, which are boiled in water and stretched rather than dried or pressed like most cheeses. At the Lago Monate cheesemakers outside Milan, we watched the workers pull huge armfuls of pure white, springy cheese from boiling vats, swiftly divide it into balls, and then, just as swiftly, sculpt each ball into the traditional piglet shape.

Scamorza can be bought fresh, when it is very springy; later, when it is slightly ripened and creamy; or smoked. We recommend the smoked version for this recipe; fresh smoked mozzarella would be fine too. In cooking the soup, make sure to use enough salt to bring out the distinct flavors of the vegetables. Salad, fruit, and Tangerine Angel Food Cake with Tangerine Glaze (pages 244–45) would round out a light but deeply satisfying meal.

For the soup:

2 tablespoons olive oil
2 medium carrots, chopped
3 stalks celery, chopped
1 medium onion, chopped
3 garlic cloves, minced
1 cup pearl barley
10 cups Chicken Stock (page 307)
or Vegetable Stock (page 311),
or 5 cups low-sodium canned broth
plus 5 cups water

1) Heat the oil in a large pot over medium-high heat. Add the carrots, celery, onion, and garlic and cook, stirring, until softened, about 8 minutes. Do not let the vegetables brown; reduce the heat if necessary.

2) Add the barley and cook, stirring, until the barley is well coated with oil and slightly toasted. Add the stock and bouquet garni and bring to a boil, then reduce the heat and simmer until the barley is cooked through but not mushy, about 20 minutes.

3) Meanwhile, cook the vegetables: heat 1 tablespoon of the oil in a large skillet, add the garlic, shallot, and fennel, and cook, stirring, until softened, about 5 minutes. Add the remaining 1 tablespoon oil and swirl it around in the pan to heat. Add the mushrooms, yellow squash, and zucchini and cook, stirring, until tender, 3 to 5 minutes more. Stir in the tomatoes, basil, and sage and cook 5 minutes more.

4) Stir the cooked vegetables into the soup and add salt and pepper to taste.

5) Top each serving with cheese and parsley and serve.

1 Bouquet Garni (page 297)

Kosher salt and freshly ground black pepper

Shredded smoked scamorza or mozzarella cheese, for garnish

Chopped fresh parsley, for garnish

For the vegetables:

2 tablespoons olive oil

2 garlic cloves, minced

1 shallot, minced

$1/2$ medium bulb fennel, diced

2 cups (4 ounces) sliced fresh mushrooms, such as porcini (cèpes), shiitakes (caps only), oysters (pulled apart), cremini, or a combination

1 small yellow (summer) squash, sliced $1/4$ inch thick

1 small zucchini, sliced $1/4$ inch thick

One 8-ounce can crushed tomatoes

4 fresh basil leaves, chopped

2 fresh sage leaves, minced

MATCH WITH FLORAL, EARTHY WHITES LIKE CALIFORNIA VIOGNIER OR FRENCH CÔTES DU RHÔNE BLANC.

Fresh Tomato-Basil Soup
with Focaccia Croutons

Tomatoes and basil are the definitive Mediterranean combination, but it takes olive oil to bring them into perfect unity. At the Ligurian olive oil mill run by the Crespi family, we tasted their new-pressed olive oil straight from underground storage cisterns. We had attended wine tastings before, but the experience of tasting olive oil through its various stages of development was new to us. Olive oil does not age like wine, but it does go through stages of filtration: the thick, creamy chartreuse of the initial mixture is gradually clarified into the translucent green-gold liquid we love.

This soup is best made with super-ripe tomatoes, especially the soft and squishy ones you might otherwise discard as overripe: they have the most natural sweetness. Less ripe tomatoes can be improved by the molasses flavor in dark brown sugar. Cold or hot, this makes a great summer lunch with fresh Parmesan–Black Pepper Biscuits (page 80), a green salad, and thinly sliced prosciutto di Parma.

For the croutons:

One 8-inch-square piece day-old Rosemary–Red Onion Focaccia (page 81) or store-bought focaccia, cut into 1/2-inch cubes

2 tablespoons Garlic Oil and Puree (page 292), or 2 tablespoons olive oil mixed with 1 minced garlic clove

2 tablespoons freshly grated Parmesan cheese

Kosher salt and freshly ground black pepper

1) Make the croutons: preheat the oven to 350°F. Toss the focaccia cubes with the oil and cheese. Season with salt and pepper and spread out on a baking sheet. Bake until golden, crisp, and just beginning to brown around the edges, about 12 minutes.

2) Make the soup: heat the oil in a large pot over medium-high heat. Add the onion and garlic and cook, stirring, until softened, 3 to 5 minutes.

3) Coarsely chop the tomatoes, adding them to the pot as you go. Stir well, add the tomato paste and brown sugar to taste, bring to a simmer, and cook 10 minutes.

4)   Add the stock and bring to a boil over high heat, then reduce the heat to a simmer and cook 20 minutes more.

5)   With a hand blender, puree the soup in the pot, or let cool slightly, carefully puree in batches in a blender, and return to the pot. Add the vinegar and salt and pepper to taste, then stir in the basil. Serve immediately, garnished with chives and a drizzle of oil. (Or let cool, cover, refrigerate overnight, and serve cold.)

For the soup:

2 tablespoons olive oil

1 large onion, chopped

4 garlic cloves, minced

5 pounds very ripe tomatoes, red, yellow, or a combination, cored (do not peel)

$^1/_2$ cup tomato paste

Up to 1 tablespoon dark brown sugar

10 cups Chicken Stock (page 307) or low-sodium canned broth

3 tablespoons balsamic vinegar, or to taste

Kosher salt and freshly ground black pepper

$^1/_4$ cup julienned fresh basil

1 teaspoon chopped fresh chives

Extra-virgin olive oil for drizzling

MATCH WITH A FLINTY SAUVIGNON BLANC, ESPECIALLY POUILLY-FUMÉ.

Roasted Garlic Soup
with Polenta Croutons

Though garlic soup might sound like a radical new idea from garlic-mad American chefs, in Provence soupe à l'ail or aïgo bouïdo is an ancient brew, and Spanish sopa de ajo is daily fare. Garlic, of course, provides an unparalleled depth of flavor; when it is boiled or roasted beforehand, its bite turns to sweetness. For substance we've added light croutons with the roasted corn flavor of polenta, and the last-minute leeks continue the flavor theme while varying the texture. However, the soup can certainly be served adorned with nothing more than a few snipped chives.

For the croutons:

3¹/₂ cups water

1 cup polenta

¹/₄ cup freshly grated Parmesan cheese

2 tablespoons unsalted butter

1 teaspoon kosher salt

Freshly ground black pepper to taste

1 tablespoon all-purpose flour

2 tablespoons olive oil

For the soup:

5 whole large garlic heads, with the skin

¹/₄ cup plus 2 teaspoons olive oil

2 large carrots, chopped

3 stalks celery, chopped

1 large onion, coarsely chopped

1 Bouquet Garni (page 297)

1 cup dry white wine

1) One day in advance, begin the croutons: generously oil a small baking pan or baking dish with olive oil. Bring the water to a boil in a heavy-bottomed saucepan. In a very thin stream, add the polenta while whisking constantly. Cook over medium-low heat, stirring constantly, until cooked through and no longer grainy, 30 to 40 minutes. Add more boiling water as needed to keep the mixture soft. When cooked, whisk in 2 tablespoons of the cheese, the butter, salt, and pepper and pour the mixture into the oiled pan. The polenta should be about ¹/₂ inch deep in the pan. Cover and refrigerate overnight.

2) The next day, make the soup: preheat the oven to 400°F.

3) With a sharp knife, cut the top ¹/₈ inch off the garlic heads. Rub the heads with 2 teaspoons of the oil and wrap tightly in foil. Bake about 45 minutes, until very soft and aromatic. Set aside to cool.

4) Heat the remaining ¹/₄ cup oil in a skillet over medium-high heat. Add the carrots, celery, and onion and cook, stirring, until

soft, about 8 minutes. Do not let the vegetables brown; reduce the heat if necessary. Add the bouquet garni.

5) Squeeze out the roasted garlic cloves by holding each garlic head upside down and pressing the center down with your thumbs, as though you were trying to turn the garlic head inside out. Remove any bits of peel and fiber and add the garlic cloves to the pan.

6) Add the wine and Cognac and stir. Cook until the liquid has almost evaporated.

7) Add the stock and bring to a boil, then reduce the heat and simmer until reduced by half.

8) Remove the bouquet garni from the soup. With a hand blender, puree the soup in the pot, or let cool slightly, carefully puree in batches in a blender, and return to the pot. (You can prepare the soup to this point up to 1 day in advance. Reheat over low heat when ready to serve.)

9) Meanwhile, finish the croutons: turn the firmed polenta out onto a clean surface and line the baking pan with parchment paper or aluminum foil. With the tip of a knife, cut the polenta into matchsticks 1/2-inch wide and 2 1/2 inches long. Sprinkle with flour on both sides. Working in batches if necessary to avoid crowding the pan, heat the olive oil in a skillet over medium-high heat and quickly brown the croutons on all sides. Remove to the baking pan and sprinkle with the remaining 2 tablespoons Parmesan cheese.

10) Stir the hot cream into the hot soup.

11) Whisk in the 3 tablespoons cold butter until it is melted and smooth.

12) Melt the butter in a skillet over medium-high heat. When it foams, add the leeks and sauté until soft, about 8 minutes. Season with sugar and salt and pepper to taste. Stir into the soup.

13) Serve the soup topped with polenta croutons and a sprinkling of chopped parsley.

1/4 cup Cognac or brandy

10 cups Chicken Stock (page 307) or low-sodium canned broth

2 to 3 cups heavy cream, heated

3 tablespoons cold unsalted butter

2 tablespoons unsalted butter

2 medium leeks, including 3 inches of green, halved lengthwise, well washed, and cut lengthwise into julienne

1/4 teaspoon sugar

Kosher salt and freshly ground black pepper

Chopped fresh parsley for garnish

CHIMAY WHITE, A TRAPPIST ALE WITH DISTINCTIVE SPICINESS, IS DELICIOUS WITH THIS SOUP.

TRY AROMATIC PINOT GRIGIO FROM ITALY'S ALTO ADIGE REGION, OR ITS COUSIN, ALSATIAN PINOT GRIS.

Italian Lentil Soup with Smoked Bacon and Spinach

We had wonderfully eye-opening soups in Italy's Umbria region and came to the conclusion that Italian lentil soups, in which the lentils always keep their pleasing shape and nutty flavor, are our favorites. Lentil soup in America has a pretty uninspiring reputation, probably because of the thick brown sludge often served under that name. Let this soup change your mind. The small tender lentils of Umbria, called Castellucio, are available in this country under that name or the French name of lentilles de Puy. When cooked together with diced fresh vegetables, smoky bacon or pancetta, and lemon-spiked spinach, the earthy lentils are at their best. The golden garlicky croutons can go on top of the soup or at the bottom of the bowl.

3 tablespoons olive oil

2 garlic cloves, crushed

1 1/2 cups 1/2-inch cubes sourdough bread

8 ounces slab bacon or smoked pancetta, cut into 1/2-inch cubes

2 garlic cloves, minced

1 medium onion, chopped

3 stalks celery, chopped

2 medium carrots, chopped

1 large leek, including 3 inches of green, sliced into thin rings and well washed

1 teaspoon caraway seeds

1 Bouquet Garni (page 297)

2 cups green or brown lentils, rinsed

1/2 cup dry sherry

1) In a large, heavy pot, heat 2 tablespoons of the oil and the garlic cloves over medium-high heat. Add the bread cubes and cook, stirring, until golden. Remove the croutons and garlic cloves and drain on paper towels. Discard the garlic cloves.

2) Add the remaining 1 tablespoon oil to the pot and heat over high heat. Add the bacon and cook, stirring, just until golden brown. Remove and drain on paper towels.

3) Add the minced garlic and onion to the pot and cook, stirring, until translucent. Add the celery, carrots, and leek and cook, stirring, until softened, about 8 minutes.

4) Lower the heat to medium, add the caraway seeds, bouquet garni, lentils, and stir.

5) Add the sherry and stir, scraping up the browned bits from the bottom of the pot with a wooden spoon. Cook until the liquid has almost disappeared. Add the wine and cook until the liquid has almost evaporated.

6) Add the stock and tomato paste and bring to a boil, then reduce the heat and simmer, uncovered, until the lentils are tender, 30 to 40 minutes. Remove the bouquet garni.

7) Add the spinach and lemon juice and stir to combine. Return the bacon to the soup and simmer just to heat through. Add salt and pepper to taste and serve garnished with the croutons.

1 cup Alsatian Riesling or other full-bodied dry white wine

10 cups Chicken Stock (page 307), Vegetable Stock (page 311), or low-sodium canned broth

2 tablespoons tomato paste

8 ounces fresh spinach, thick stems removed, well washed and coarsely chopped

Juice of $1/2$ lemon

Kosher salt and freshly ground black pepper

A LIGHT GEWURZTRAMINER FROM ALTO ADIGE, A PINOT GRIGIO, OR ANOTHER FLORAL WHITE WILL WORK WELL HERE.

Clam, Corn, and Chimay Chowder

SERVES 6 TO 8

When fresh corn is at its peak and clams are plentiful, make a dinner out of this fragrant soup, or stir it up in the middle of winter to remind you of warm days past and future. Although we think of clambakes as an oceanside phenomenon, the annual Tramonto family clambake used to take place on the shores of Lake Ontario, near Rochester, New York. In those days the chowder was made with clams flown in from Boston and the favorite local beer, Genesee cream ale. Chimay ales are by far the best known of the traditional Trappist beers, made at monasteries in and around Belgium. Trappist monks are commanded to live off their own land, labor, and resources, a restriction that has helped them maintain a brewing tradition that has been lost to more worldly orders. Chimay's Red Cap, or Capsule Rouge, beer is typical of the Trappist style: strong, yeasty, almost sweet, and very full-bodied.

A tomato salad with shredded basil, extra-virgin olive oil, and plenty of freshly ground pepper makes the meal almost complete. Summer Berry Pudding (pages 252–53) is the ultimate ending.

For the soup:

2 teaspoons light olive oil

6 ounces salt pork, diced

2 stalks celery, chopped

1 medium bulb fennel, chopped

1 medium onion, chopped

3 garlic cloves, minced

2 large bell peppers, red, green, or a combination, seeded and diced

¹/₄ cup all-purpose flour

1) Heat the olive oil in a large pot over medium-high heat, add the salt pork, and cook, stirring, until the edges begin to brown. Add the celery, fennel, onion, and garlic and cook, stirring, until softened, about 5 minutes. Do not let the vegetables brown; reduce the heat if necessary. Add the bell peppers and cook, stirring, 5 minutes more.

2) Add the flour and cook, stirring, 3 minutes. Stir in the beer and simmer to reduce by half. Add the stock, clam juice, canned clams with their liquid, bouquet garni, potatoes, and corn and simmer about 20 minutes. Remove the bouquet garni. (You can prepare the soup to this point up to 1 day in advance. Reheat over low heat when ready to serve.)

3) Add the hot cream and simmer 10 minutes more, until slightly thickened and the potatoes are cooked through.

4) When the soup is nearly cooked, make the garnish: combine the beer, garlic, and shallot in a skillet with a lid and bring to a simmer. Add the clams, stir, cover, and cook, shaking the pan occasionally, until the clams open, about 3 minutes.

5) Finish the soup: whisk in the butter and add the Tabasco, Worcestershire sauce, and salt and pepper to taste.

6) To serve, ladle the chowder into bowls and top each serving with two steamed clams in the shell.

1$\frac{1}{4}$ cups Chimay Red beer or another strong, sweetish, yeasty ale

4 cups Fish Stock (page 310), Chicken Stock (page 307), or water

4 cups clam juice

One 16-ounce can best-quality chopped clams, with their liquid

1 Bouquet Garni (page 297)

3 boiling potatoes, peeled (if you like) and cut into $\frac{1}{2}$-inch cubes

2 cups corn kernels, fresh or frozen

2 cups heavy cream, heated

4 tablespoons ($\frac{1}{2}$ stick) cold unsalted butter, cut into pieces

$\frac{1}{2}$ teaspoon Tabasco sauce, or to taste

$\frac{3}{4}$ teaspoon Worcestershire sauce

Kosher salt and freshly ground black pepper

For the garnish:

$\frac{3}{4}$ cup Chimay Red beer, or whatever beer you used for the soup

1 shallot, minced

2 garlic cloves, minced

12 to 16 littleneck clams in their shells

ENJOY WITH CHIMAY RED TO ECHO THE BEER IN THE DISH AND TO TASTE THE COOKED AND CHILLED VERSIONS SIDE BY SIDE.

MATCH WITH A RIPE CALIFORNIA OR AUSTRALIAN CHARDONNAY.

Four-Pepper Oyster Stew

SERVES 6 TO 8

The Belon oysters of Brittany are the favorites of the patriotic French, and at the best brasseries, Parisians down them by the dozen, piled on platters with cracked ice, lemon wedges, and drifts of seaweed. Belons are very briny and surprisingly metallic compared to our creamy Malpeques and Bluepoints. American oysters are a better choice for this thick soup, traditionally known as a stew or a pan-roast.

By any name, shellfish and cream are an elemental pairing. No other liquid is able to coax so much subtle flavor from the delicate morsels. We've sparked the flavor of the soup with a pack of peppers—white, red, black, and Tabasco. You can buy shucked oysters at any good fish store, but make sure that they are very, very fresh.

1 cup peeled, diced Idaho potatoes

About 30 freshly shucked oysters, with their liquor (4 oysters per person)

1 tablespoon light olive oil

1 cup diced carrots

1 cup diced celery

1 cup diced onions

6 garlic cloves, finely minced

1 bay leaf

4 sprigs fresh thyme

1 cup dry white wine

8 cups Fish Stock (page 310) or water

3 tablespoons minced fresh parsley

1 large red bell pepper, seeded and diced

1 ¹/₂ teaspoons kosher salt

¹/₄ teaspoon ground white pepper

1) Put the potatoes in a saucepan and cover with cold salted water. Cover and bring to a boil, then cook for 10 to 12 minutes, until the potatoes are tender all the way through but still firm (they will cook more later in the recipe).

2) Strain the oysters and reserve the liquor. Pick the oysters over for shells and debris.

3) In a large skillet, heat the oil over high heat. Add the carrots, celery, onions, and garlic and cook, stirring, until the onions are translucent, about 8 minutes. Add the bay leaf, thyme, and wine and cook 1 minute. Add the oyster liquor and cook 30 seconds more. Add the stock and reduce the liquid by one-fourth.

4)   Add the parsley, bell pepper, salt, white pepper, and black pepper and bring to a simmer. Stir in the Tabasco and Worcestershire sauce and simmer 1 minute. Add the hot cream and cook, stirring, 3 minutes.

5)   With the mixture at a gentle simmer, add the scallions and oysters and cook just until the edges of the oysters turn opaque and start to curl up, about 2 minutes. Do not let them overcook; they will continue cooking as long as the soup is simmering. Remove the bay leaf and thyme and discard.

6)   Serve immediately in shallow soup plates, topped with a sprinkling of fresh basil and a few grinds of the black pepper mill.

1 teaspoon freshly ground black pepper
$1/4$ to $1/2$ teaspoon Tabasco sauce
$1/2$ teaspoon Worcestershire sauce
2 cups heavy cream, heated
2 scallions, finely chopped
1 tablespoon chopped fresh basil

DRY STOUT IS A TRADITIONAL BEER CHOICE FOR OYSTERS, SAID TO AWAKEN THEIR SALTY-SWEET FLAVORS.

TRY A BORDEAUX BLANC WITH A SAUVIGNON/SÉMILLON BLEND OR AN AUSTRALIAN SÉMILLON.

Gazpacho with Crabmeat and Croutons

SERVES 8

Gazpacho has come a long way from its ancient roots as a paste of olive oil, bread, vinegar, and almonds, but the principle remains the same: the soup is blended rather than cooked, highly seasoned, and eaten cold. Although tomatoes seem integral to the soup, they are a relatively recent introduction. When tomato plants were first brought back to Spain from Peru, in the sixteenth century, they were used strictly for decorative purposes, as houseplants. It was not until the eighteenth century that the Spanish discovered that tomatoes—members of the dangerous nightshade family that also includes potatoes and eggplant—were not poisonous.

The gazpacho we serve in the hot Chicago summers at Brasserie T is a sort of liquid salad, with cucumbers and fresh citrus juices providing cool flavor notes on top of ripe tomatoes and piquant Spanish sherry vinegar. Crabmeat adds luxury and texture but is by no means necessary for a successful gazpacho; if good lump crabmeat is beyond your reach, feel free to leave it out and use more of the other garnishes instead. When preparing the soup, the vegetables can be cut quite large because they will be blended together; the garnishes will be most pleasant to eat if diced small. Use red onions rather than yellow here; the bite is much less intense.

For the croutons:
3 tablespoons olive oil
2 garlic cloves, crushed
2 cups ¹/₂-inch cubes sourdough bread
Kosher salt

1) Make the croutons: heat the olive oil and garlic cloves in a skillet over medium-high heat. Add the bread cubes and cook, stirring, until golden brown. Drain on paper towels, sprinkle lightly with salt, and set aside to cool. Discard the garlic cloves.

2) Make the soup: in a food processor or blender, combine all the ingredients except the salt and pepper. Process until smooth, then add salt and pepper to taste. Transfer to a large serving bowl, cover, and refrigerate at least 1 hour or up to 24 hours. (Refrigerate the serving bowls you plan to use as well.)

3) When ready to serve, prepare the garnishes: pick over the crabmeat and discard any bits of shell and cartilage. Put the other garnishes in small bowls for passing at the table.

4) To serve, ladle the soup into the chilled serving bowls, top with crabmeat, and pass the other garnishes at the table.

PAIR THIS FRESH SOUP WITH A WHEAT BEER THAT HAS LIGHT SPICINESS AND HINTS OF CITRUS.

A YOUNG, UNOAKED WHITE RIOJA OR A LIGHT, CRISP RIESLING FROM THE MOSEL COMPLEMENTS THE VEGETABLE FLAVORS BEAUTIFULLY.

For the soup:

4 large ripe beefsteak tomatoes, cut into chunks, or one 32-ounce box Pomi crushed tomatoes (not strained)

1 large cucumber, peeled, seeded, and cut into chunks

2 stalks celery, chopped

1 red bell pepper, seeded and cut into chunks

1 green bell pepper, seeded and cut into chunks

1/2 small red onion, chopped

2 garlic cloves, finely minced

3 cups tomato juice

4 teaspoons best-quality sherry vinegar or red wine vinegar

2 tablespoons freshly squeezed lime juice

2 tablespoons freshly squeezed lemon juice

1/4 cup light olive oil

3 dashes Tabasco sauce, or to taste

Kosher salt and freshly ground black pepper

For the garnishes:

8 ounces lump fresh crabmeat

1/4 cup slivered almonds, toasted

2 tablespoons chopped fresh chives

2 tablespoons chopped fresh cilantro

1 small red onion, finely diced

1 stalk celery, finely diced

2 plum tomatoes, seeded and finely diced

1 avocado, peeled and diced

Freshly ground black pepper

Leek and Potato Soup with Smoked Fish

SERVES 8

This classic soup of many names (potage Parisien, crème de poireaux, potage Parmentier) is one of the elemental dishes of French home cooking; the basic recipe of potatoes, leeks, stock, and salt is transformed into any number of wonderfully light concoctions with watercress, spinach, scallions, and other flavorful greens. (All those soups have their own names too; it's no wonder French menus can be so challenging.) Some hearty versions include bacon; in our variation on that theme, flaky smoked fish accents the silky soup. The soup can be served hot or cold (vichyssoise, anyone?)

This is a substantial first course, best served before a light entree such as Crab Cakes and Baby Greens with Citrus Vinaigrette and Spicy Aioli (pages 22–23) or Linguine with Manila Clams and Fresh Basil (pages 102–3). Or serve large bowls of soup and add nothing more than a green salad with endive for crispness, warm bread, and a deep-flavored dessert like Roasted Fruits with Cinnamon–Red Wine Glaze and Toasted Almonds (pages 232–33).

2 tablespoons olive oil

4 large Idaho potatoes, peeled and cut into 1/2-inch cubes

2 medium carrots, chopped

3 stalks celery, chopped

1 large onion, chopped

4 garlic cloves, minced

1 large leek, including 3 inches of green, sliced into rings and well washed

1) Heat the oil in a large pot over medium-high heat. Add the potatoes, carrots, celery, onion, garlic, and leek and cook, stirring, until softened, about 8 minutes. Do not let the vegetables brown; reduce the heat if necessary.

2) Stir in the bouquet garni, thyme, and bay leaf and pour in the wine. Cook, stirring, until the liquid has almost evaporated. Add the stock and bring to a boil, then reduce the heat and simmer until reduced by half.

3) Remove the bouquet garni, thyme, and bay leaf. With a hand blender, puree the soup in the pot, or let cool slightly, carefully puree in batches in a blender, and return to the pot. (You can prepare the soup to this point up to 1 day in advance. Reheat over low heat when ready to serve.)

4) Add the hot cream to the hot soup. Add salt and pepper to taste.

5) To serve, put about ¼ cup of fish in the bottom of each bowl, then ladle the hot soup over it. Sprinkle tomato and chives on top of each bowl.

1 Bouquet Garni (page 297)

2 sprigs fresh thyme

1 bay leaf

¹/₂ cup light-bodied dry white wine

12 cups Chicken Stock (page 307) or Vegetable Stock (page 311), or 6 cups low-sodium canned broth plus 6 cups water

1 to 2 cups heavy cream, heated

Kosher salt and freshly ground black pepper

2 cups flaked smoked white-fleshed fish, such as haddock, trout, or whitefish

2 cups diced plum tomatoes, for garnish (optional)

Chopped fresh chives, for garnish

A MÂCON BLANC WILL WORK WELL, OR TRY A CONDRIEU FOR AN INTERESTING COMBINATION OF TEXTURES.

Pizzas

Semolina Pizza Crust

Pizza Sauce

Caramelized Onion Pizza

Four-Cheese Pizza

Asparagus and Goat Cheese Pizza

Tuscan Arugula Pizza

Prosciutto and Artichoke Pizza

Italian Sausage, Wild Mushroom and Roasted Pepper Pizza

Barbecued Pepperoni, Mushroom, and Red Onion Pizza

Pizza Bianco with Porcini

Calzones Stuffed with Chicken, Spinach, and Ricotta

AT BRASSERIE T THE BLUE-TILED WOOD-BURNING PIZZA OVEN is the warm heart of the restaurant, bringing a piece of the kitchen out into the dining room and irresistibly drawing everyone in the room toward its warmth and light. To us, pizza is almost a magical food. Being able to quickly transform dough, sauce, vegetables, and cheese into a complete meal in the oven is the easiest cooking method we know of. And the results—melting, crisp, hearty, and healthy—are both impressive and universally popular. Everyone likes pizza, and there are so many interesting things to do with it. The semolina flour in our dough gives the pizzas a notably crisp crust. Our Tuscan Arugula Pizza is a refreshing salad pizza with lemony notes; our special barbecued pepperoni adds heft and spice to red onion and mushroom pizza; and fontina cheese and porcini mushrooms take our Pizza Bianco upscale as an elegant appetizer or hors d'oeuvre. A fluffy stuffed calzone is a great dinner that kids love to make and eat.

Like pizza itself, our pizza oven was imported from Italy. The first known pizzeria, established in Naples in 1830 (though the dish is much older), was lined with volcanic rock from nearby Mount Vesuvius for maximum heat retention. Our professional oven is also specially constructed (and burns wood), but you actually don't need any special equipment for making pizza at home. You will get better results from using round pizza pans rather than rectangular baking sheets, but unless you are an aficionado, a pizza stone is not necessary. Just follow these general guidelines:

- A HOT oven is very important. Preheat it for a long time, at least half an hour.

- If you're cooking more than one pizza at a time, whichever pizza is closer to the bottom of the oven will cook faster and be crisper. Switch the pans in the middle of the baking so that each gets a chance near the bottom of the oven.

- The dough should be stretchy and elastic; use plenty of olive oil in the dough and try to work in a warm kitchen. Don't worry if your crust doesn't turn out perfectly even and smooth. Holes can be patched.

- The dough should be rolled out to 1/4-inch thickness at the most, or it will not crisp.

- Your pizzas do not have to be round. We like ovals for some of our pizzas, and freeform is always fine. If you don't want to roll the dough out, you can always press it into a baking pan instead.

- All pizzas can be made "bianco," without tomato sauce.

- Keep your toppings light—not too heavy in character (such as thick eggplant slices) and not too plentiful (such as a thick blanket of mozzarella)—or the other elements will be lost.

Semolina Pizza Crust

MAKES 2 MEDIUM PIZZAS OR 4 INDIVIDUAL ONES

1 package (¹/₄ ounce) active dry yeast
¹/₂ cup warm water, preferably filtered
    or spring water
1 tablespoon honey
1 tablespoon extra-virgin olive oil
1 cup semolina flour
1³/₄ cups all-purpose flour
1 teaspoon kosher salt

1) In the bowl of a mixer fitted with a dough hook or a food processor fitted with a plastic blade, combine the yeast, warm water, honey, and olive oil. Mix (at low speed if possible) for 1 minute, or until well combined.

2) Let stand for 1 minute, then turn the mixer back on (at low speed, if possible). Gradually add all the semolina flour and ¹/₂ cup of the all-purpose flour. Continue mixing for another 3 minutes. If the mixture still seems stiff or dry, add more warm water and keep mixing until it is smooth and soft. If it seems sticky, add more flour 2 tablespoons at a time.

3) Cover the bowl tightly with plastic wrap and let stand at room temperature about 30 minutes, until the mixture begins to bubble.

4) Remove the plastic wrap and turn the mixer back on at low speed. Gradually add the salt and remaining flour, then mix just until the dough forms a ball and pulls away from the sides of the bowl, 2 to 3 minutes. Do not overmix the dough; it should be a bit sticky and elastic.

5) Lightly oil a bowl or large container, turn the dough into it, and cover with a dry kitchen towel. Let stand in a warm place (inside the oven is OK) until the dough doubles in volume, about 45 minutes.

6) Punch down the dough and turn it onto a lightly floured surface. Divide it in half or in quarters and use your hands to firmly shape the dough into balls. Rest at least 10 minutes at room temperature, or up to 2 days tightly covered and refrigerated. Bring to room temperature before using.

7) Proceed as directed in the recipe.

Pizza Sauce

1) In a large nonreactive skillet, heat the oil over medium-high heat. Add the onion, stir, and reduce the heat to medium. Cook, stirring, until soft and translucent, 3 to 5 minutes. Do not let the onion brown.

2) Add the pepper flakes and stir, then add the tomatoes with their juices. Simmer, uncovered, for 10 minutes, then add the basil and oregano. Simmer another 15 to 20 minutes, until thickened and reduced to about 2 cups. Season to taste with salt and pepper. Use immediately or let cool and refrigerate for up to 4 days.

2 tablespoons Garlic Oil and Puree (page 292), or 2 tablespoons olive oil mixed with 1 minced garlic clove

$^1/_2$ medium onion, diced

$^1/_2$ to 1 teaspoon red pepper flakes

One 28-ounce can crushed Italian plum tomatoes, or 2 pounds ripe fresh plum tomatoes, peeled, seeded, and diced

2 tablespoons finely chopped or julienned fresh basil

2 teaspoons dried oregano

Kosher salt and freshly ground black pepper

Caramelized Onion Pizza

2 tablespoons olive or canola oil

2 large yellow onions, halved and thinly sliced

Kosher salt and freshly ground black pepper

1 recipe Semolina Pizza Crust (page 60)

2 tablespoons Garlic Oil and Puree (page 292), or 2 tablespoons olive oil mixed with 1 minced garlic clove

3/4 cup shredded fontina cheese

3/4 cup shredded fresh mozzarella cheese

1/4 cup pitted oil-cured black olives, quartered

Roasted Eggplant (page 302) or 2 cups Slow-Roasted Tomatoes (page 303), or a combination

Freshly grated Parmesan or Romano cheese, or a combination, for garnish

Chopped fresh parsley, chives, basil, or a combination, for garnish

1) Preheat the oven to 450°F.

2) Heat a large skillet over medium heat. Add the olive oil and onions, stir well, and reduce the heat to low. Cook, stirring only every 5 to 10 minutes, until the onions are very soft and golden brown—about 30 minutes. Season with salt and pepper to taste.

3) Meanwhile, on a lightly floured surface, pat or roll out the pizza dough into rounds about 1/4 inch thick. Transfer onto pizza pans or baking sheets and let rest 10 minutes.

4) Brush the entire surface with the garlic oil and sprinkle with the fontina and mozzarella. In the center of each pizza, arrange the caramelized onions and sprinkle with the olives. Around the onions, arrange the eggplant and/or tomatoes, leaving a 3/4-inch border all the way around each pizza.

5) Bake about 15 minutes, until the crust is browned and crisp underneath.

6) Sprinkle with Parmesan cheese and fresh herbs and serve immediately.

Grilled Portobello Mushrooms with
Polenta Cakes, Mesclun, and Balsamic Sauce

*Roquefort and Pear Salad
with Grapes and Spiced Pecans*

Provençal Lamb Shanks with
Roasted Vegetables, Roasted Garlic, and Tapenade

Portofino Bouillabaisse

*Pan-Roasted Salmon with
Coriander Seed and Wilted Spinach*

Creamy Three-Grain Risotto with
Artichokes and Mushrooms

Rigatoni with Olive-Lamb Ragù

*Osso Buco with Saffron Risotto
and Orange Gremolata*

Four-Cheese Pizza

1) On a lightly floured surface, pat or roll out the pizza dough into rounds about ¼ inch thick. Transfer onto pizza pans or baking sheets and let rest 10 minutes.

2) Brush the entire surface with the garlic oil, then spoon the pizza sauce into the center of each round. Spread the sauce out toward the edges, leaving a ¾-inch border all the way around each pizza. Sprinkle the mozzarella, fontina, and provolone over the pizzas.

3) Bake 15 minutes, until the crust is browned and crisp underneath.

4) Sprinkle with Parmesan cheese and herbs and serve immediately.

1 recipe Semolina Pizza Crust (page 60)

2 tablespoons Garlic Oil and Puree (page 292), or 2 tablespoons olive oil mixed with 1 minced garlic clove

1 recipe Pizza Sauce (page 61)

¾ cup shredded fresh mozzarella cheese

¾ cup shredded fontina cheese

¾ cup shredded provolone cheese

¼ cup freshly grated Parmesan or Romano cheese, or a combination

Chopped fresh parsley, basil, chives, or a combination, for garnish

Asparagus and Goat Cheese Pizza

1 whole head garlic, with the skin

1 teaspoon olive oil

16 stalks asparagus, woody bottoms trimmed off

1 recipe Semolina Pizza Crust (page 60)

2 tablespoons Garlic Oil and Puree (page 292), or 2 tablespoons olive oil mixed with 1 minced garlic clove

1 recipe Pizza Sauce (page 61) (optional)

$^3/_4$ cup shredded fresh mozzarella cheese

$^3/_4$ cup crumbled soft, fresh goat cheese

Freshly grated Parmesan or Romano cheese, or a combination, for garnish

Chopped fresh parsley, chives, basil, or a combination, for garnish

1) Preheat the oven to 400°F. On a piece of aluminum foil, rub the garlic head with the olive oil. Wrap the foil tightly around the garlic and bake 30 to 40 minutes, until very soft and aromatic. Remove from the oven and set aside to cool.

2) Raise the oven temperature to 450°F.

3) Meanwhile, bring a shallow pan of salted water to a boil. Add the asparagus and blanch until tender but still crisp, about 4 minutes. Drain, then plunge into ice water to stop the cooking and set the color.

4) On a lightly floured surface, pat or roll out the pizza dough into rounds about $^1/_4$ inch thick. Transfer onto pizza pans or baking sheets and let rest 10 minutes.

5) Brush the entire surface with the garlic oil, then spoon the pizza sauce into the center of each round. Spread the sauce out toward the edges, leaving a $^3/_4$-inch border all the way around each pizza. Sprinkle the mozzarella, then the goat cheese, over the pizzas. Squeeze the cooled garlic cloves out of their peels and arrange them on the pizzas. Arrange the asparagus on top, pointing out like the spokes of a wheel.

6) Bake about 15 minutes, until the crust is browned and crisp underneath.

7) Sprinkle with Parmesan cheese and fresh herbs and serve immediately.

Tuscan Arugula Pizza

1) Preheat the oven to 400°F. On a piece of aluminum foil, combine the garlic cloves and 2 tablespoons of the olive oil. Using your hands, mix together until the garlic is well coated with oil. Wrap the foil tightly around the garlic and bake 30 to 40 minutes, until very soft and aromatic. Remove from the oven and set aside to cool, reserving the oils that have accumulated.

2) Raise the oven temperature to 450°F.

3) On a lightly floured surface, pat or roll out the pizza dough into ovals about 1/4 inch thick. Transfer to pizza pans or baking sheets and let rest 10 minutes.

4) When the garlic is cool enough to handle, squeeze the soft flesh out of the peels and mash it with a fork or finely chop with a knife. Mix well or puree with the reserved oil. Brush the entire surface with the garlic-oil mixture, leaving a 3/4-inch border around the edge of each pizza, and sprinkle the mozzarella over.

5) Bake about 15 minutes, until the crust is browned and crisp underneath.

6) Meanwhile, combine the lemon juice, lemon zest, sugar if using, and vinegar in a large mixing bowl. Whisk in the remaining olive oil (about 1/4 cup), then season to taste with salt and pepper. Add the arugula, tomatoes, and olives and toss to coat.

7) When the pizzas are ready, remove from the oven and slice into wedges with a pizza cutter. Spread the arugula mixture evenly over the pizzas, then place a lemon wedge in the center of each one. Sprinkle with Parmesan and serve immediately.

8 to 10 large garlic cloves, unpeeled

1/4 cup plus 2 tablespoons extra-virgin olive oil

1 recipe Semolina Pizza Crust (page 60)

1 1/2 cups shredded fresh mozzarella cheese

1 tablespoon freshly squeezed lemon juice

1/2 teaspoon finely chopped lemon zest

1/2 teaspoon sugar (optional)

1 teaspoon red wine vinegar

Kosher salt and freshly ground black pepper

4 cups loosely packed arugula, thick stems removed, well washed and dried

4 plum tomatoes, seeded and diced

1/2 cup pitted oil-cured black olives, quartered

Lemon wedges for garnish

Freshly grated Parmesan or Romano cheese, or a combination, for garnish

Prosciutto and Artichoke Pizza

1 recipe Semolina Pizza Crust
(page 60)

2 tablespoons Garlic Oil and Puree
(page 292), or 2 tablespoons olive
oil mixed with 1 minced garlic clove

1 recipe Pizza Sauce (page 61)
(optional)

$^3/_4$ cup shredded provolone cheese

$^3/_4$ cup shredded fresh mozzarella
cheese

One 10-ounce can artichoke hearts,
well drained and quartered, or one
10-ounce package frozen artichoke
hearts, thawed and quartered

2 ounces very thinly sliced prosciutto

Freshly grated Parmesan or Romano
cheese, or a combination, for
garnish

Chopped fresh parsley, chives, basil, or
a combination, for garnish

1) Preheat the oven to 450°F.

2) On a lightly floured surface, pat or roll out the pizza dough into rounds about $^1/_4$ inch thick. Transfer onto pizza pans or baking sheets and let rest 10 minutes.

3) Brush the entire surface with the garlic oil, then spoon the pizza sauce into the center of each round. Spread the sauce out toward the edges, leaving a $^3/_4$-inch border all the way around each pizza. Sprinkle the provolone and mozzarella over the pizzas, then arrange the artichoke pieces on top.

4) Bake about 15 minutes, until the crust is browned and crisp underneath.

5) As soon as the pizzas come out of the oven, lay the slices of prosciutto across the top. Sprinkle with Parmesan cheese and fresh herbs and serve immediately.

Italian Sausage, Wild Mushroom, and Roasted Pepper Pizza

MAKES 2 MEDIUM PIZZAS OR 4 INDIVIDUAL ONES

1) Preheat the oven to 450°F.

2) Make the mushroom topping: heat a heavy skillet over medium-high heat. Add the garlic oil and swirl it around the pan, then add the mushrooms in the order listed, stirring well after each addition. When all the mushrooms are in the pan, add salt and pepper to taste; cook, stirring, just until the mushrooms are browned but still firm. Remove to a plate and spread out to cool; the mushrooms will continue to cook as they cool.

3) Crumble the sausage meat into the skillet and heat over medium-high heat. Cook until the meat is browned and cooked through, stirring occasionally. Remove from the pan with a slotted spoon and drain on paper towels.

4) On a lightly floured surface, pat or roll out the pizza dough into rounds about 1/4 inch thick. Transfer onto pizza pans or baking sheets and let rest 10 minutes.

5) Brush the entire surface with the garlic oil, then spoon the pizza sauce into the center of each round. Spread the sauce out toward the edges, leaving a 3/4-inch border all the way around each pizza. Sprinkle the provolone over the pizzas, then sprinkle on the sausage, peppers, and mushrooms.

6) Bake 15 minutes, until the crust is browned and crisp underneath.

7) Sprinkle with Parmesan cheese and herbs and serve immediately.

For the mushroom topping:

1 tablespoon Garlic Oil and Puree (page 292), or 1 tablespoon olive oil mixed with 1 minced small garlic clove

2 ounces button mushrooms, sliced about 1/4 inch thick

2 ounces sliced cremini mushrooms, sliced about 1/4 inch thick

2 ounces shiitake mushrooms, stems removed, caps sliced about 1/4 inch thick

Kosher salt and freshly ground black pepper

For the pizza:

8 ounces hot or sweet Italian sausage, bulk or in casings

1 recipe Semolina Pizza Crust (page 60)

2 tablespoons Garlic Oil and Puree (page 292), or 2 tablespoons olive oil mixed with 1 minced garlic clove

1 recipe Pizza Sauce (page 61) (optional)

1 1/2 cups shredded provolone cheese

1 cup coarsely chopped Roasted Red Peppers (page 304), or store-bought

Freshly grated Parmesan or Romano cheese, or a combination, for garnish

Chopped fresh parsley, chives, basil, or a combination, for garnish

Barbecued Pepperoni, Mushroom, and Red Onion Pizza

MAKES 2 MEDIUM PIZZAS OR 4 INDIVIDUAL ONES

1 recipe Semolina Pizza Crust (page 60)

2 tablespoons Garlic Oil and Puree (page 292), or 2 tablespoons olive oil mixed with 1 minced garlic clove

1 cup Barbecue Sauce (pages 312–13), or 2 cups Pizza Sauce (page 61)

1^1/2 cups shredded mozzarella cheese

2 cups Mushroom Mix (pages 294–95) or 2 ounces cremini mushrooms, sliced about ^{1}/4 inch thick

2 ounces aged pepperoni, preferably Italian, thinly sliced

1 cup very thinly sliced red onions

Freshly grated Parmesan or Romano cheese, or a combination, for garnish

Chopped fresh parsley, chives, basil, or a combination, for garnish

1) Preheat the oven to 450°F.

2) On a lightly floured surface, pat or roll out the pizza dough into rounds about ^{1}/4 inch thick. Transfer onto pizza pans or baking sheets and let rest 10 minutes.

3) Brush the entire surface with the garlic oil. Spoon barbecue sauce into the center of each round. Spread the sauce out toward the edges, leaving a ^{3}/4-inch border all the way around each pizza. Sprinkle the mozzarella over the pizza, then the mushrooms. Place the pepperoni slices on top, then sprinkle on the red onions.

4) Bake 15 minutes, until the crust is browned and crisp underneath.

5) Sprinkle with Parmesan cheese and herbs and serve immediately.

Pizza Bianco with Porcini

MAKES 2 MEDIUM PIZZAS OR 4 INDIVIDUAL ONES

1) In a skillet, heat the olive oil over high heat. Add the mushrooms and cook, stirring, until the liquid has cooked off and the mushrooms are beginning to brown around the edges. Do not overcook; the mushrooms will continue to cook as they cool. Remove from the heat and set aside.

2) Preheat the oven to 450°F.

3) On a lightly floured surface, pat or roll out the pizza dough into rounds about 1/4 inch thick. Transfer onto pizza pans or baking sheets and let rest 10 minutes.

4) Brush the crusts with truffle oil, then with garlic oil, brushing all the way out to the edges. Sprinkle with a little salt and plenty of pepper. Sprinkle the fontina cheese over the pizzas, leaving a 3/4-inch border all the way around each pizza. Repeat with the Parmesan cheese, then the mushrooms. Add the anchovy fillets if using, arranging them on top in a spoke pattern.

5) Bake 15 minutes, until the crust is browned and crisp underneath.

6) Sprinkle with extra Parmesan and parsley and serve immediately.

1 tablespoon olive oil

1 garlic clove, finely minced

4 ounces fresh porcini or other deep-flavored mushrooms, such as portobello or shiitake caps, sliced 1/8 inch thick

1 recipe Semolina Pizza Crust (page 60)

1 tablespoon plus 1 teaspoon white truffle oil

2 teaspoons Garlic Oil and Puree (page 292) or extra-virgin olive oil

Kosher salt and freshly ground black pepper

1 cup grated fontina cheese

1/2 cup freshly grated Parmesan or Romano cheese, or a combination, plus extra for garnish

Anchovy fillets to taste (optional)

2 tablespoons chopped fresh parsley

Calzones Stuffed with Chicken, Spinach, and Ricotta

MAKES 2 LARGE CALZONES (4 SERVINGS)

For the filling:

5 to 6 ounces boneless, skinless chicken breast (about 1 breast half)

1 tablespoon Garlic Oil and Puree (page 292), or 1 tablespoon olive oil mixed with 1 minced small garlic clove

Kosher salt and freshly ground black pepper

1¹/₂ cups Mushroom Mix (pages 294–95)

8 ounces fresh ricotta cheese

1¹/₂ cups shredded fresh provolone cheese

2 tablespoons freshly grated Parmesan cheese

2 tablespoons chopped fresh parsley or chives, or a combination

¹/₂ teaspoon kosher salt

¹/₄ teaspoon freshly ground black pepper

For the calzone:

1 recipe Semolina Pizza Crust (page 60)

2 large eggs, beaten

1 recipe Pizza Sauce (page 61) (optional)

Freshly grated Parmesan or Romano cheese, or a combination, for garnish

Chopped fresh parsley, chives, basil, or a combination, for garnish

1) Preheat the oven to 450°F.

2) Make the filling: brush the chicken breast with a little garlic oil, then season with salt and pepper. Heat a skillet over medium-high heat, add the remaining oil and the chicken, and cook until the underside is golden brown, about 3 minutes. Turn and continue cooking just until cooked through. Remove from the pan and dice into ¹/₂-inch pieces. (Or brush the chicken breast with the garlic oil and grill or broil on both sides just until cooked through.)

3) In a mixing bowl, combine the remaining ingredients for the filling and mix well. Add the chicken and mix to combine. Set aside.

4) On a lightly floured surface, roll out the pizza dough into large rounds about ¹/₄ inch thick. Transfer onto pizza pans or baking sheets and let rest 10 minutes.

5) Keeping in mind that you are going to fold the calzone in half, place half the filling on the right half moon of one dough round. Smooth it gently toward the edges of the half moon, leaving plenty of room around the edges. Brush the edges of the dough with egg, then carefully fold the dough over the filling. With your fingers, press the edges together. Starting at the one end of the sealed edge, make a series of overlapping folds, folding 2-inch sections of crust at a time toward the filling to make a thick, decorative crust.

6) Brush the entire surface with egg. Transfer to pizza pans or baking sheets. Bake 12 to 15 minutes, until golden brown.

7) Spread serving plates with pizza sauce if using, and place the calzones on top. Cut in half to serve four.

8) Sprinkle with Parmesan cheese and herbs and serve immediately.

Breads and Sandwiches

Zigzag Breadsticks

Seeded Multigrain Rolls with Golden Raisins

Roasted Corn Bread

Ricotta-Stuffed Flatbread

Parmesan–Black Pepper Biscuits

Rosemary–Red Onion Focaccia

Brioche

Rosemary Roasted Lamb Sandwiches with Zucchini and Red Onions

Vegetable–Goat Cheese Sandwich

Smoked Salmon BLTs

Croque Monsieur

Skirt Steak Sandwiches with Roasted Shallots and Horseradish Mayonnaise

WITH THE OPENING OF OUR VANILLA BEAN BAKERY, WE SEIZED the opportunity to really think about bread. We wanted to be able to make our own bread for the breadbaskets at Brasserie T and not have to rely on outside suppliers for this most fundamental part of any meal. We rarely eat without a chunk of bread close at hand, and to make bread for people has always seemed like the most basic and rewarding form of nourishment. In working with bread, we have been constantly reminded that yeast is a living thing, to be treated with care and respect. We've found that being aware of this simple fact has carried over to the rest of our ingredients and equipment: our appreciation and understanding of cooking in general have increased tremendously. And we are far from alone: bakers all over the country are experimenting with new ideas and reviving old styles, much as microbrewers are doing with the world's other yeast staple: beer.

At our bakery and in our home, bread doesn't only mean bread: it includes focaccia, brioche, muffins, scones, biscuits, rolls, cookies, baguettes, flatbread, corn bread, and a host of other baked goods we are still inventing and evolving every day. We couldn't have known that we would become fascinated with yeasts, glutens, sourdoughs, and all the reactions that make baking as much a science as an art. The breads we present here are just a small sampling of the rich possibilities. You'll find new takes on old-world classics (for example, Gale's experiments with traditional French brioche techniques resulted in her easy three-step method; the texture of a focaccia benefits from sweet red onions added to the dough; *grissini* get a new zigzag shape) as well as new ideas (Roasted Corn Bread has fresh corn and garlic in the mix; a savory Ricotta-Stuffed Flatbread encloses melted cheese between two crisp cracker layers). And, of course, we pass on a couple of old favorites: perfect Parmesan–Black Pepper Biscuits and nutty multigrain rolls can make a special meal out of salad, cheese, and fruit. Check out the Cheese Plates chapter for some thought-provoking combinations.

It's just a short hop from rediscovering bread to rediscovering sandwiches. Although sandwiches aren't traditionally a restaurant food, they are very much a brasserie food: a quick, flexible meal that can be dressed up or down and eaten any time of day—and always tastes great. Since we both grew up on sandwiches like bologna, salami and brick cheese, and peanut butter on white bread, the toppling mounds of overstuffed, colorful sandwiches and *panini* we first encountered at sandwich shops in Europe made a tremendous impression on us. At our first stop, England, we discovered wonderful sandwiches like cheddar cheese and ham with chutney, cream cheese and cucumber, and watercress with sweet butter, which are equally at home as a pub lunch with an amber ale as they are at a tea shop in the afternoon. (We also discovered a new junk-food sandwich: the "chip butty," a soft roll spread with butter and stuffed with hot French fries.)

Farther south, we were dazzled by the many colors, layers, breads, and stuffings at the sandwich shops of France and the *paninotecas* of Italy. We learned that Paris is the home of the grilled ham and cheese *croque monsieur* (and the meatless *croque madame*), and we worked our way south eating slim baguettes with butter and *jambon de Paris*; dripping *pan bagnat*, the Provençal sandwich that is just like a *salade niçoise* on a roll; and rolled Venetian sandwiches stuffed with prosciutto, roasted peppers, and eggplant. In fact, our entire memory of the city of Venice is dominated by the sandwiches, but Florence also offers its famous *frittata panini*, for which an omelet is stuffed into bread, and Milan makes thin, elegant salami sandwiches.

All that we learned, we've put into practice here. A contrast in textures and flavors is important, as in the salty, spicy, and sweet elements of our Steak Sandwich with Horseradish Mayonnaise and Roasted Shallots. We like to put cool and hot together, as in the crisp lettuce and hot bacon on our silky Smoked Salmon BLT. Sandwiches stuffed into whole loaves, like our Vegetable–Goat Cheese Sandwich, are the most substantial. If possible, buy your bread from a bakery rather than a supermarket bread section. There really is a difference.

Zigzag Breadsticks

2 cups all-purpose flour

2 cups bread flour

2 teaspoons kosher salt

$^1/_4$ cup freshly grated Parmesan
cheese

2 teaspoons active dry yeast

1$^1/_4$ cups warm water

1 pinch freshly ground black pepper

2 tablespoons Garlic Oil and Puree
(page 292), or 2 tablespoons olive
oil mixed with 1 minced garlic clove

Cornmeal

1) In the bowl of a mixer fitted with a dough hook, blend the flours, salt, and cheese together. Dissolve the yeast in the water and add to the dry ingredients, then add the pepper and garlic oil.

2) Mix at low speed for 3 minutes, then at high speed for 1 minute. Cover the bowl with a damp towel and let the dough rise in a warm place until doubled in bulk, about 1 hour.

3) Lightly grease 2 large baking sheets and sprinkle lightly with cornmeal.

4) Punch down the dough and form the breadsticks: pull off a small handful of dough and roll it out into a thin snake as long as your baking sheet. Transfer to the baking sheet, then run your finger down its length, pushing the breadstick into a zigzag pattern as you go. Repeat with the remaining dough.

5) Cover the pans and let the dough rise in a warm place until doubled in bulk.

6) Preheat the oven to 400°F.

7) Uncover the pans and bake the breadsticks until golden brown, about 20 minutes. Rotate the pans halfway through the baking.

Seeded Multigrain Rolls with Golden Raisins

MAKES ABOUT 16 ROLLS

1) In a bowl, combine the honey, water, and yeast.

2) In the bowl of a mixer fitted with a dough hook, combine all the dry ingredients and the raisins.

3) Check the yeast mixture for activity. When it is slightly bubbly and creamy-looking, add it to the dry ingredients. Add the oil and mix at low speed for 6 minutes.

4) Lightly grease a mixing bowl and turn the dough into it. Cover with a damp cloth and let the dough rise in a warm place until doubled in bulk, about 1 hour.

5) Lightly grease a baking sheet and sprinkle it with cornmeal.

6) Punch the dough down and knead it briefly, sprinkling with flour if it seems sticky. Using your hands or a dough divider, divide the dough into about 16 pieces and form into rounded rolls with your hands. Transfer to the baking sheet.

7) Cover with a damp towel and let the dough rise in a warm place until doubled in bulk, about 1 hour.

8) Preheat the oven to 400°F.

9) Using a mister, spritz the rolls with water, then dust lightly with flour.

10) Bake until golden brown, 15 to 20 minutes, rotating the pan halfway through the baking.

^{1}/$_4$ cup honey
1^1/$_4$ cups warm water
2 teaspoons active dry yeast
2^1/$_2$ cups bread flour
1^1/$_2$ cups whole wheat flour
2^1/$_4$ teaspoons kosher salt
^{1}/$_8$ cup cracked wheat
^{1}/$_8$ cup millet or additional cracked wheat
^{1}/$_8$ cup rolled oats
^{1}/$_4$ cup hulled sunflower seeds
^{1}/$_4$ cup hulled pumpkin seeds
^{1}/$_4$ cup chopped walnuts
^{2}/$_3$ cup golden raisins
5 tablespoons plus 1 teaspoon olive oil
Cornmeal

Roasted Corn Bread

SERVES 6 TO 8

We like to experiment with putting vegetables, cheese, and herbs in our breads, and this is one of our successes. In corn season, use an ear of fresh corn instead of the frozen kernels. Remove the husk and grill it for a smoky flavor, cut the kernels from the cob, and add to the batter along with the roasted garlic puree in step 8 (do not sauté them together). Great with mild fresh goat cheese and Roasted Vegetable–White Bean Chili (pages 120–21).

10 whole garlic cloves, unpeeled

2 tablespoons plus 1 teaspoon olive oil

One 10-ounce package frozen corn kernels

³/₄ cup all-purpose flour

2 teaspoons baking powder

3 tablespoons light brown sugar

1 teaspoon salt

1¹/₄ cups yellow cornmeal

14 tablespoons (1³/₄ sticks) unsalted butter

1 cup whole milk

1 large egg

1 tablespoon chopped fresh chives

1) Preheat the oven to 400°F.

2) Rub the garlic with 1 teaspoon of the olive oil, wrap in aluminum foil, and bake 30 to 40 minutes, until very soft. When cool enough to handle, pierce the cloves with a knife and squeeze out the roasted flesh. Mash to a smooth paste with a knife or mortar and pestle.

3) Heat the remaining 2 tablespoons olive oil in a skillet over medium-high heat. Add the roasted garlic and the corn and cook, stirring, until the garlic and corn are well combined and the corn kernels are lightly browned, about 8 minutes.

4) Generously butter the sides of a 9-inch round cake pan. Line the bottom with wax paper.

5) Preheat the oven to 400°F.

6) In a large mixing bowl, combine the flour, baking powder, brown sugar, salt, and cornmeal with a fork.

7) In a small saucepan, warm the butter and milk over low heat just until the butter is melted.

8) In a separate bowl, whisk the egg lightly, then whisk it into the warm milk mixture.

9) Make a well in the center of the dry ingredients and pour in the milk mixture. Add the corn-garlic mixture and chives and mix just to combine.

10) Pour the batter into the cake pan and bake 20 to 25 minutes, until a skewer inserted into the center comes out clean. Let cool in the pan, then slice into wedges.

Ricotta-Stuffed Flatbread

MAKES FOUR 8-INCH LOAVES

For the dough:

1 package (¹/₄ ounce) active dry yeast
1 cup warm water
1 tablespoon honey
1 tablespoon olive oil
¹/₃ cup semolina flour
2¹/₃ cups all-purpose flour
1 teaspoon kosher salt

For the filling:

1 large whole head garlic, with the skin
1 teaspoon olive oil
¹/₄ cup Garlic Oil and Puree (page 292), or ¹/₄ cup olive oil mixed with 3 minced garlic cloves
4 ounces ricotta salata cheese, grated
Freshly ground black pepper

1) Make the dough: in the bowl of a mixer fitted with a dough hook or a food processor fitted with a plastic blade, combine the yeast and warm water and let stand 1 minute. Add the honey, oil, semolina flour, and ²/₃ cup of the all-purpose flour and mix at a medium speed 3 minutes. (If using a food processor, pulse until the mixture forms a ball, then process for 1 minute.) Cover the bowl with plastic wrap and let stand in a warm place until the mixture bubbles, about 30 minutes.

2) Add the remaining flour and the salt and mix until the dough begins to pull away from the sides of the bowl and form a ball. If the mixture still seems stiff or dry, add more warm water and keep mixing until it is smooth and soft. If it seems sticky, add more flour 2 tablespoons at a time.

3) Brush the top of the dough with olive oil, cover the bowl with plastic wrap, and let the dough rise in a warm place until doubled in bulk. Punch the dough down and use your hands to divide it into 8 pieces. Roll into balls and arrange on a baking sheet. Cover lightly and let rest 20 minutes.

4) Meanwhile, begin the filling: preheat the oven or a toaster oven to 400°F.

5) With a very sharp knife, cut the top ¹/₈ inch off the garlic head. Rub with the olive oil, wrap tightly in foil, and bake 40 minutes, until very soft. Set aside to cool. When cool enough to handle, squeeze out the roasted garlic cloves by holding each garlic head upside down and pressing the center down with your thumbs, as though you were trying to turn the garlic head inside out. Remove any bits of peel and fiber and set the roasted cloves aside.

6)   Lightly flour a rolling pin. On a lightly floured surface, roll out 4 of the dough balls until very thin and about 8 inches in diameter. Transfer to a large baking sheet.

7)   Preheat the oven to 425°F.

8)   Brush the edges of the dough rounds with water and brush the centers with the garlic oil. Sprinkle the centers with cheese, then the roasted garlic cloves. Grind black pepper over the filling.

9)   Roll out the remaining dough balls to the same size, and place on top of the covered rounds. With your fingers, press the edges together to seal. With a lightly floured rolling pin, gently roll over each loaf to flatten slightly.

10) Brush the top of each loaf with garlic oil. Bake until the bottom crusts are golden brown, 12 to 15 minutes. Cut into wedges and serve immediately.

Parmesan–Black Pepper Biscuits

$1^1/_2$ cups heavy cream

2 cups all-purpose flour

2 tablespoons baking powder

2 teaspoons kosher salt

$^2/_3$ cup freshly grated Parmesan
cheese

$^1/_8$ teaspoon cayenne pepper

$^3/_4$ teaspoon dry mustard

$^3/_4$ teaspoon freshly ground black
pepper

1) Preheat the oven to 400°F.

2) In a mixing bowl, whip the cream until stiff peaks form.

3) In the bowl of a mixer, blend together all the remaining ingredients. Add the whipped cream and mix at low speed just until combined.

4) On a lightly floured surface, roll or pat out the dough to a 1-inch thickness. With a biscuit or cookie cutter or a clean empty can, cut out rounds about 2 inches in diameter. Transfer to an ungreased baking sheet. Knead the scraps together just until combined, then roll out again and continue cutting out circles until all the dough is used.

5) Bake until golden brown, about 20 minutes. Serve immediately.

Rosemary–Red Onion Focaccia

1) Put the potatoes in a saucepan, cover with cold water, and bring to a boil over high heat. Cook until very tender, 15 to 20 minutes. Drain.

2) Meanwhile, combine the garlic with ¹/₄ cup of the oil and set aside. Combine the remaining ¹/₄ cup oil with the rosemary leaves and set aside.

3) When the potatoes are well drained, return to the saucepan and add the milk. Warm slightly over low heat.

4) Meanwhile, in the bowl of a mixer fitted with a dough hook, blend the flours and 1 tablespoon of the salt. Add the garlic-oil mixture, onion, yeast, and the warm potato-milk mixture. Blend at low speed for 6 minutes.

5) Brush a little plain olive oil on the surface of the dough (leaving it in the bowl), cover with plastic wrap, and let the dough rise in a warm place until doubled in bulk, about 1¹/₂ hours.

6) Lightly oil a baking sheet about 11 × 16 inches and 1 inch deep.

7) Place the dough on the baking sheet and press it flat with a rolling pin or your hands, pushing it into the corners of the pan until it is a uniform thickness.

8) Brush the dough with the rosemary-oil mixture, then prick it all over with a fork. Cover with plastic wrap and let rise in a warm place (the oven is good) until it reaches the top of the pan, about 45 minutes.

9) Preheat the oven to 400°F.

10) Remove the plastic wrap and sprinkle the focaccia with the remaining ¹/₂ tablespoon salt. Bake until golden brown, 20 to 30 minutes. Let cool in the pan, then cut into large squares or wedges for serving.

12 ounces Idaho potatoes, peeled and quartered
1 large garlic clove, finely minced
¹/₂ cup extra-virgin olive oil
1 teaspoon chopped fresh rosemary
³/₄ cup whole milk
2 cups all-purpose flour
2 cups bread flour
1¹/₂ tablespoons kosher salt
1 small red onion, coarsely chopped
1 heaping tablespoon active dry yeast
Olive oil

Brioche

Here's delicious proof that homemade bread is as easy as—actually, much easier than—pie. It's a three-step overnight process, but each step takes only about 10 minutes. In between, let the yeasts and sugars do their magic, and Voilà! c'est la brioche, a slightly sweet, light, eggy bread that makes a perfect breakfast, wonderful bread pudding, and truly fabulous French toast. Or just toast it and spread with preserves.

The traditional brioche method requires lots of slamming and slapping of the dough, but ours is a less demanding process. To make sugar brioche, which is so popular with our staff and customers, we roll out this dough into a 2-inch-thick log and let it rise on a baking sheet lined with parchment paper. Sprinkle heavily with sugar, bake, and slice into strips, and you'll have the best breakfast treat or after-school snack ever.

3 cups all-purpose flour
2³/4 cups bread flour
1 tablespoon kosher salt
¹/4 cup sugar
1 ounce fresh yeast
¹/4 cup warm water
8 large eggs
1 pound (4 sticks) cold unsalted butter, cut into ¹/2-inch pieces

1) In the bowl of a mixer fitted with a dough hook, blend the flours, salt, and sugar.

2) Dissolve the yeast in the water and add to the flour mixture. Add the eggs and mix until well blended.

3) Add the butter and mix at medium speed until all the pieces disappear, about 10 minutes. This will ensure that the dough is properly kneaded.

4) Place the dough in a bowl and cover tightly with plastic wrap. Refrigerate overnight.

5)   Turn the dough out onto a floured surface and cut into 2 equal parts. Shape into loaves by rolling with your hands.

6)   Lightly grease 2 loaf pans and place the loaves in them. Cover with plastic wrap.

7)   Place in a warm spot and let rise until the dough touches the plastic wrap, about $1^1/2$ to 2 hours.

8)   Preheat the oven to 350°F.

9)   Remove the plastic wrap and bake the loaves until golden brown, about 45 minutes. Rotate the pans after 20 minutes.

10) Remove the loaves from the pans immediately and let cool on a wire rack.

Rosemary Roasted Lamb Sandwiches
with Zucchini and Red Onions

MAKES 4 DINNER-SIZE SANDWICHES

You can roast a smallish leg of lamb especially for sandwiches or, even better, make a larger roast as part of a simple dinner with Panzanella (page 30) or Roasted Stuffed Artichokes with Toasted Nuts, Lemon, and Tomato (pages 16–17) and/or Rosemary Roasted Potatoes (page 214). The next day, use the delicious leftovers in these sandwiches; the meat firms up overnight, making it more sandwich-friendly. This amount of vegetables makes 4 large sandwiches, but you can increase or decrease according to the number you want to feed.

For the lamb:

1 boneless leg of lamb (3 to 4 pounds), rolled and tied

$^1/_4$ cup Garlic Oil and Puree (page 292), or $^1/_4$ cup olive oil mixed with 3 minced garlic cloves

2 garlic cloves, minced

1 tablespoon chopped fresh rosemary

Kosher salt and freshly ground black pepper

For the sandwich:

2 medium zucchini, halved crosswise, then thinly sliced lengthwise into flat strips about $^1/_8$ inch thick

1 large red onion, sliced into rounds $^3/_8$ inch thick

2 tablespoons Garlic Oil and Puree (page 292), or 2 tablespoons olive oil mixed with 1 minced garlic clove

1) The day before serving, make the lamb: preheat the oven to 500°F.

2) Rub the lamb with the garlic oil, garlic, and rosemary and season generously with salt and pepper. Place on a rack in a roasting pan and roast 10 to 15 minutes, until well browned. Reduce the heat to 400°F and continue roasting until cooked to the desired degree of doneness, 30 minutes to 1 hour longer (an internal temperature of 140°F is medium-rare).

3) Let rest, covered with foil, for 20 minutes, then refrigerate whole. (If you are serving some lamb immediately, slice it off the leg but leave the remainder whole until ready to slice for sandwiches. Refrigerate, tightly wrapped.)

4) The next day, make the vegetables: preheat the oven to 425°F.

5)   Gently toss the zucchini strips and onion slices with the garlic oil and spread out on a baking sheet. Roast 10 to 15 minutes, until tender but firm and slightly browned.

6)   Combine the mayonnaise and olives in a blender and pulse just until blended.

7)   Slice the lamb about $1/8$ inch thick.

8)   Cut the bread into 4 large rectangles and split each rectangle for sandwiches. Spread both sides of the bread with the olive mayonnaise. Layer one-fourth of the lamb, zucchini, onions, tomatoes, and basil on each bottom half, then add the top halves and press down firmly. If possible, wait 20 minutes before serving to let the flavors blend.

$1/2$ cup cold Mayonnaise, homemade (page 299) or store-bought

6 pitted Kalamata olives

1 recipe Rosemary–Red Onion Focaccia (page 81), an equivalent amount of store-bought focaccia, or 4 large rolls

2 ripe medium tomatoes, sliced

12 whole basil leaves

Vegetable–Goat Cheese Sandwiches

3 tablespoons Garlic Oil and Puree (page 292), or 3 tablespoons olive oil mixed with 2 minced garlic cloves

1 medium zucchini, halved crosswise, then thinly sliced lengthwise into flat strips about $1/8$ inch thick

1 medium yellow (summer) squash, halved crosswise, then thinly sliced lengthwise into flat strips about $1/8$ inch thick

1 medium red onion, sliced into rounds $3/8$ inch thick

Kosher salt and freshly ground black pepper

4 ounces spinach, well washed

$1/2$ cup Mayonnaise, homemade (page 299) or store-bought

2 tablespoons Pesto (see Pesto Mashed Potatoes, page 208) or chopped fresh basil

1 large round loaf bread, preferably peasant, whole wheat, or multigrain

One 8-ounce jar roasted red peppers, drained

4 ounces soft fresh goat cheese, crumbled

1) Preheat the oven to 400°F.

2) In a mixing bowl, gently toss 2 tablespoons of the garlic oil with the zucchini, yellow squash, and onion. Season generously with salt and pepper. Spread out on a baking sheet. Roast 15 to 20 minutes, until tender but firm and slightly browned.

3) Meanwhile, heat the remaining tablespoon of oil in a skillet over high heat. Add the spinach and cook, stirring, just until wilted, 1 to 2 minutes. Add salt and pepper to taste, stir, and remove from the skillet, shaking off any liquid. When cool enough to handle, chop and squeeze lightly with your hands to get rid of excess moisture.

4) Whisk together the mayonnaise and pesto.

5) Cut the bread in half lengthwise and remove some of the crumb from the top half, making a cavity. Spread both cut surfaces of the bread with the pesto mayonnaise.

6) Fill the top cavity with the spinach and sprinkle with the goat cheese. Layer the roasted vegetables and roasted red peppers on top. Place the bottom half of the bread on top and flip the loaf over. Press down firmly. If possible, wait 20 minutes before serving to let the flavors blend. With a very sharp serrated knife, cut into wedges for serving.

Smoked Salmon BLTs

1) In a microwave or skillet, cook the bacon until browned and crisp. Drain on paper towels.

2) In a bowl, whisk together the mayonnaise and mustard.

3) Toast the bread and let cool slightly. Spread 4 slices with the mayonnaise-mustard mixture. Lay the smoked salmon on top, then top with lettuce, tomato, and bacon. Spread the 4 remaining toast slices with the mayonnaise-mustard mixture and place on top.

4) With a sharp knife, cut the sandwiches diagonally in half. Serve immediately.

8 thick-cut bacon strips

4 tablespoons Mayonnaise, homemade (page 299) or store-bought

1 tablespoon whole-grain mustard

8 slices Brioche (pages 82–83) or challah

8 ounces sliced smoked salmon

4 crisp large romaine leaves, halved crosswise

2 ripe large tomatoes, sliced

Croque Monsieur

MAKES 4 LUNCH-SIZE SANDWICHES

8 slices Brioche (pages 82–83),
  challah, or bakery white bread,
  cut $^3/_4$ inch thick

4 slices mozzarella cheese

8 thin slices ham, about the size of the
  bread slices

4 slices fontina cheese

$^1/_2$ cup freshly grated Gruyère cheese

2 tablespoons unsalted butter

Chopped fresh chives, for garnish

Dijon mustard

1) Preheat the oven to 400°F.

2) On a clean surface, lay 4 slices of the bread. Layer the mozzarella, then the ham, then the fontina and finally the Gruyère on top of the bread. Top with remaining bread slices.

3) In an ovenproof skillet, melt the butter over medium heat until very hot. Add the sandwiches—they should start to sizzle immediately—and fry gently until the bread is just golden brown on the bottom. Turn and cook on the other side.

4) Transfer the skillet to the oven and bake 5 minutes, until the filling is piping hot. Cut the sandwiches diagonally in half. Sprinkle with chives and serve immediately with mustard.

Skirt Steak Sandwiches with Roasted Shallots and Horseradish Mayonnaise

1) Pound the skirt steaks with a tenderizing mallet or another heavy implement until slightly flattened and tenderized.

2) In a shallow dish, combine the garlic, onion, rosemary, tarragon, and 1 cup of the olive oil. Add the steaks and turn to coat. Cover and marinate, refrigerated, 4 to 6 hours or overnight. Turn the steaks over occasionally.

3) Preheat the oven to 400°F.

4) Put the shallots on a sheet of aluminum foil, drizzle the teaspoon of olive oil over, wrap tightly, and bake 30 to 35 minutes, until soft and sweet. Set aside to cool, then slice 1/8 inch thick.

5) Combine the mayonnaise, drained horseradish to taste, and lemon juice in a bowl. Mix well and chill until ready to use.

6) Preheat a grill, broiler, or cast-iron pan until very hot. Remove the steaks from the marinade and drain on a rack. Season with salt and pepper to taste. Sear the meat on one side, then turn and cook on the other side until medium-rare. Remove from the heat and set aside.

7) Spread 4 slices of the bread with the horseradish mayonnaise. Lay the steaks on top. Top with the cheese and shallot slices, then the arugula. Season with more salt and pepper. Spread the remaining bread with horseradish mayonnaise, place on top, and press down firmly. If possible, wait 20 minutes before serving to let the flavors blend.

Four 6-ounce skirt steaks

2 garlic cloves, minced

1 medium red onion, chopped

2 sprigs fresh rosemary, leaves only

2 sprigs fresh tarragon or thyme, leaves only

1 cup plus 1 teaspoon olive oil

8 whole shallots, peeled

1/2 cup cold Mayonnaise, homemade (page 299) or store-bought

1 to 2 tablespoons grated horseradish, drained

1 teaspoon freshly squeezed lemon juice

Kosher salt and freshly ground black pepper

8 large slices rye bread, with or without seeds

4 ounces white cheddar cheese, thinly sliced

20 leaves arugula, well washed

Pastas, Risotti, and Grains

Farfalle with Many Mushrooms, Tomatoes, and Fresh Herbs

Spaghettini with Quick Tomato-Basil Sauce

Fusilli with Chicken and Asparagus in Thyme-Tomato-Cream Sauce

Orecchiette with Zucchini, Chickpeas, and Red Chile

Calamari alla Marinara with Angel Hair Pasta

Linguine with Manila Clams and Fresh Basil

Rigatoni with Olive-Lamb Ragu

Spinach and Ricotta-Stuffed Crespelle

Orange-Ricotta Gnocchi with Broccoli Rabe

Creamy Three-Grain Risotto with Artichokes and Mushrooms

Roasted Eggplant–Wild Rice Risotto

Butternut Squash Risotto with Crisped Pancetta

Grilled Portobello Mushrooms with Polenta Cakes, Mesclun, and Balsamic Sauce

Tramonto's Escarole, Sausage, and White Bean Stew

Roasted Vegetable–White Bean Chili

Farfalle with Many Mushrooms, Tomatoes, and Fresh Herbs

SERVES 4 TO 6

Pasta in a light sauce of stock, herbs, and aromatics is one of our favorite foods, and it's a theme that can easily be varied with different fresh herbs, vegetables, cheeses, spices, even seafood and sausages. Instead of cooking a separate sauce, you simply heat a well-seasoned broth and toss it with the cooked pasta, vegetables, and seasonings. The result is a pasta dish that never gets sticky, stays hot longer, and has plenty of delicious juice at the bottom of the bowl without a gloppy, oversauced effect. Serve this pasta with plenty of grilled or toasted bread to soak it all up.

We use quantities of aromatic fresh mushrooms every day at Brasserie T—stirred into pastas, spooned onto bowls of sunny polenta, or adding a deep, mysterious element to stews and soups. Mushrooms should never be washed under running water; their open pores absorb so much water that if you sauté them later, you'll find yourself steaming them in their juices instead. Simply wipe them clean with a damp paper towel. If they seem especially dirty, brush them gently first with a vegetable brush.

1 tablespoon kosher salt

1 teaspoon pure olive oil

4 tablespoons (1/2 stick) unsalted butter

3 large garlic cloves, finely minced

2 shallots, chopped

1 cup sliced button mushrooms, about 1/4 inch thick

1 cup sliced cremini mushrooms, about 1/4 inch thick

1) Bring a gallon of water with the salt and pure olive oil to a boil in a large covered pot.

2) Meanwhile, cook the mushrooms: in a pot large enough to hold the pasta and sauce later on, melt the butter over medium heat. Add the garlic and shallots and sauté until softened, about 3 minutes.

3) Add the mushrooms in the order listed, stirring between additions. Sauté for 1 minute and remove from the heat; the mushrooms will continue to cook as they cool. Remove the mushrooms to a bowl and put the pot back on the stove.

4) Add the pasta to the pot of boiling water. Stir, cover, and return to a boil. Cook, uncovered, until still quite firm, or al dente. (The pasta will cook a little more later in the recipe.)

5) Meanwhile, make the pasta sauce: in the pot you used to cook the mushrooms, heat the oil over medium heat. Add the garlic and pepper flakes and sauté for 1 minute.

6) Add the stock, thyme, and rosemary and bring to a simmer.

7) When the pasta is cooked, drain it and add it to the simmering stock.

8) Quickly add the mushrooms, cheese, parsley, tomatoes, butter, and salt and pepper to taste. Stir to combine, cover, and cook over high heat for about 2 minutes, until tomatoes are softened. Toss well before serving.

9) Serve in heated bowls, with extra sauce ladled over the top and sprinkled with extra parsley and cheese.

1 cup sliced shiitake mushroom caps, about $1/4$ inch thick (discard stems)

1 cup oyster mushrooms, pulled apart into bite-size pieces

1 pound dried farfalle (bowtie) pasta

1 tablespoon olive oil

1 large garlic clove, chopped

$1/4$ teaspoon red pepper flakes, or to taste

2 cups Chicken Stock (page 307) or low-sodium canned chicken broth

1 teaspoon fresh thyme leaves, or $1/2$ teaspoon dried

1 teaspoon chopped fresh rosemary, or $1/2$ teaspoon dried

$1/2$ cup freshly grated Parmesan cheese, or a mixture of Parmesan and Romano, plus extra for garnish

1 tablespoon chopped fresh parsley, or a combination of parsley and chives, plus extra for garnish

4 ripe plum tomatoes, seeded and diced

2 tablespoons unsalted butter

Kosher salt and freshly ground black pepper

LOOK FOR A BEER WITH CARAMEL OVERTONES TO COMPLEMENT THE MUSHROOMS IN THIS FULL-FLAVORED PASTA.

FRUITY DOLCETTO AND LIGHT SOUTHERN ITALIAN REDS WORK WELL HERE. IN SUMMER, CHILL THE REDS SLIGHTLY, OR TRY A WELL-CHILLED PROVENÇAL ROSÉ.

Spaghettini with Quick Tomato-Basil Sauce

SERVES 4 TO 6

Everyone should have a speedy pasta-and-tomato-sauce dinner in their repertoire. This one is so easy that you'll have it memorized after the first time you make it. We especially like the texture of spaghettini—easier to eat than spaghetti but not as fine as angel hair. The key to the success of this simple dish is using absolutely the best canned Italian plum tomatoes you can find. If necessary, you can use all canned tomatoes.

Rick grew up on this sauce, and we're already looking forward to making it for our son, Gio (although as we write this, he's still on the banana-and-squash diet). Spaghetti with tomato sauce is dependable kid food, but a well-made sauce turns it into a family dinner or very Italian appetizer course. If you've gotten in the habit of opening a jar from the store, try making this instead; it really is almost as easy. Freeze any leftover sauce for next time, or save it for Spinach and Ricotta-Stuffed Crespelle (pages 106–7), Roasted Eggplant–Wild Rice Risotto (pages 112–13), or Individual Veal Meat Loaves with Tomato-Basil Sauce (pages 146–47).

1 tablespoon plus 2 teaspoons kosher salt

1 teaspoon pure olive oil

$1/3$ cup plus 2 tablespoons extra-virgin olive oil

1 large onion, chopped

6 large garlic cloves, minced

$1/4$ teaspoon red pepper flakes

One 28-ounce can best-quality Italian plum tomatoes, or one 32-ounce box crushed Pomi tomatoes

1 pound ripe plum tomatoes, seeded and coarsely chopped

1) Bring a gallon of water with 1 tablespoon of the salt and pure olive oil to a boil in a large covered pot.

2) Meanwhile, make the sauce: heat 2 tablespoons of the extra-virgin olive oil in a large saucepan over medium-high heat. Add the onion, garlic and red pepper flakes and sauté until softened, 3 to 5 minutes.

3) Add the canned and fresh tomatoes with their liquid, and crush the canned ones with a wooden spoon.

4)   Add half of the basil, the remaining olive oil and salt, and pepper and mix thoroughly.

5)   Bring to a boil and cook, stirring frequently, until the sauce begins to reduce and thicken, about 15 minutes. (The sauce can be prepared through this step up to 2 days in advance.)

6)   When the sauce begins to thicken, add the pasta to the pot of boiling water. Stir, cover, and return to a boil. Cook, uncovered, 10 to 13 minutes, until done to your liking. Drain the pasta briefly and return it to the pot.

7)   Add the sauce and half of the cheese to the pasta and toss to combine. Add salt and pepper to taste. Cover, remove from the heat, and let rest 2 minutes.

8)   Serve in heated bowls, sprinkled with the remaining cheese and basil. Top each bowl with a drizzle of extra-virgin olive oil at the last minute.

$1/4$ cup finely shredded fresh basil, plus extra for garnish

$1/2$ teaspoon freshly ground black pepper

1 pound dried spaghettini

$1/2$ cup freshly grated Parmesan or Romano cheese, or a combination of the two

Kosher salt and freshly ground black pepper

Extra-virgin olive oil for drizzling

A YOUNG CHIANTI CLASSICO IS THE NATURAL CHOICE. ON A HOT DAY, TRY A CRISP ITALIAN WHITE INSTEAD.

Fusilli with Chicken and Asparagus in Thyme-Tomato-Cream Sauce

This kind of chunky one-dish pasta meal is a favorite at our house and probably at your house too. The most important element here is the sauce, which brings all the ingredients together and enhances their different flavors. That's why good tomatoes, fresh thyme, and even high-quality heavy cream are worth seeking out (some ultra-pasteurized brands have a strong cooked-milk taste that overwhelms even the freshest cream). The unique flavor of grilled asparagus is worth the effort, but sautéing them over high heat in a skillet will also yield good results. The chicken and asparagus can be cooked ahead of time through step 6 and reheated in the sauce, or you can use leftover chicken. This recipe can be halved, but do make a whole batch of sauce and freeze whatever you don't use.

For the sauce:

2 tablespoons olive oil

1 garlic clove, minced

¹/₂ medium red onion, thinly sliced

1 teaspoon fresh thyme leaves

2 tablespoons white wine

One 28-ounce can best-quality Italian plum tomatoes

³/₄ cup heavy cream

Kosher salt and freshly ground black pepper to taste

For the pasta:

6 tablespoons olive oil

2 garlic cloves, minced

1¹/₂ pounds boneless, skinless chicken breast

1) Make the sauce: in a large saucepan, heat the oil over medium heat. Add the garlic and cook until softened, then add the onion and thyme and cook for 5 minutes. Add the wine, raise the heat, and simmer until the liquid is reduced by half.

2) Add the tomatoes with their liquid and crush them with a wooden spoon. Add the cream, mix well, and bring to a boil. Reduce the heat and simmer gently, uncovered, for 30 to 40 minutes, until thickened. Season to taste with salt and pepper.

3) Meanwhile, cook the chicken and asparagus: preheat a grill or broiler.

4) In a bowl, combine 2 tablespoons of the olive oil with the garlic, then add the chicken and salt and pepper to taste and mix to coat. In another bowl, gently combine the asparagus, 2 tablespoons of the olive oil, and salt and pepper to taste.

5) When the grill is very hot, arrange the chicken on it and grill on both sides just until cooked through, 4 to 5 minutes on each side. Set aside to cool.

6) Carefully arrange the asparagus on the grill in a single layer, with the stalks pointing across the grill to prevent them from falling through. Grill until browned, 2 to 3 minutes. To turn them, place the back of a spatula across the stalks, press down gently, and roll them over. Repeat until all are turned, then continue cooking just until browned. Remove the asparagus from the grill as they are cooked. (Or brown the asparagus and then the chicken in a small amount of vegetable oil in a skillet over very high heat.)

7) Cut the chicken crosswise into $1/2$-inch-wide strips. Cut the asparagus into $3/4$-inch lengths.

8) Bring 6 quarts of water with the 2 tablespoons of salt and pure olive oil to a boil in a large covered pot.

9) Meanwhile, in a pot large enough to hold the pasta and sauce later on, heat the remaining 2 tablespoons of olive oil over medium-high heat. Add the onions, thyme, sliced chicken, and sliced asparagus and cook, stirring, until heated through. Add the wine and simmer until reduced by half. Add the tomato-cream sauce, mix well, and bring to a simmer. Season to taste with salt and pepper.

10) Add the fusilli to the pot of boiling water. Stir, cover, and return to a boil. Cook, uncovered, 10 to 13 minutes, until done to your liking. Drain the pasta briefly and add it to the finished sauce. Toss well to coat.

11) Transfer to a large serving bowl. Grind plenty of black pepper over the top, sprinkle with the shredded basil, and pass the Parmesan cheese at the table.

Kosher salt and freshly ground black pepper

1 pound asparagus, woody bottoms trimmed off

2 tablespoons kosher salt

1 teaspoon pure olive oil

$1^1/2$ medium red onions, thinly sliced

1 teaspoon fresh thyme leaves

$3/4$ cup light-bodied dry white wine, such as Pinot Grigio

$1^1/2$ pounds dried fusilli or other short curly pasta

$1/2$ cup finely shredded basil

$1/2$ cup freshly grated Parmesan or Romano cheese, or a combination

MATCH WITH VERDICCHIO DI MATELICA AND CRISP PINOT GRIGIO OR TRY A LOIRE SAVENNIÈRES.

Orecchiette with Zucchini, Chickpeas, and Red Chile

Our honeymoon was the perfect excuse for making a three-month trip we'd dreamed of: driving from Paris to Rome, stopping to eat and see absolutely everything in between. When we finally arrived in Rome, our clothes were wrinkled, our car dusty, our palates jaded by too many two- and three-star multicourse dinners. But our very first, very simple dinner that night in Rome turned out to be one of the most memorable of our lives. An uncomplicated toss of pasta, red pepper flakes, green olives, and green-gold zucchini, it lives on in our minds as the easy and confident essence of Italian cooking.

Nothing beats pasta for quick one-dish dinners. Crisp-fried zucchini coins and nutty chickpeas are substantial enough to stand up to hearty orecchiette, "little ear" pasta rounds. With basil, hot chile, and tomatoes, the taste of Italy is complete.

1 tablespoon kosher salt

1 teaspoon pure olive oil

3 tablespoons olive oil

1 medium onion, chopped

4 garlic cloves, minced

1/2 to 1 teaspoon red pepper flakes

1 pound dried orecchiette or other short, thick pasta

3 small or 2 medium zucchini, sliced 1/4 inch thick

One 16-ounce can chickpeas, drained and rinsed

Juice of 1/2 lemon

4 plum tomatoes, diced

1) Bring a gallon of water with the salt and pure olive oil to a boil in a large covered pot.

2) Meanwhile, in a pot large enough to hold the pasta and sauce later on, heat the oil over medium-high heat. Reduce the heat to medium, add the onion, garlic, and pepper flakes and cook, stirring, until the onion is translucent, about 5 minutes.

3) Add the orecchiette to the pot of boiling water. Stir, cover, and return to a boil. Cook, uncovered, until tender, about 12 minutes.

4) Meanwhile, finish the sauce: to the onion mixture, add the zucchini, chickpeas, lemon juice, tomatoes, olives, and stock. Simmer until well combined and heated through, 6 to 8 minutes.

5) When the pasta is cooked, drain it briefly and add it to the sauce, tossing well to mix. Cover and cook over medium heat for 2 minutes, then turn off the heat and stir in the butter, cheese, basil, and salt and pepper to taste.

6) Serve immediately in heated bowls.

$1/2$ cup coarsely chopped pitted green olives, such as Atalanti, Cerignola, or another fleshy dark green olive

2 cups Chicken Stock (page 307) or low-sodium canned broth

3 tablespoons cold unsalted butter, cut into pieces

$1/2$ cup freshly grated Parmesan cheese

6 leaves fresh basil, chopped

Kosher salt and freshly ground black pepper

LOOK FOR A FLAVORFUL SICILIAN WHITE FROM MOUNT ETNA.

Calamari alla Marinara with Angel Hair Pasta

SERVES 6 TO 8

For seafood in general, and especially for calamari, Venice may be the most exciting city in the world. The morning's fish market is perfumed with the musky scent of squid ink, and the pavement grows black and slippery as the morning wears on. Later in the day, the squid turn up all over the city in pastas, seafood salads, casseroles, and stuffed with all kinds of aromatics.

Chicago is not exactly calamari country, so we have adapted our favorite dish to frozen calamari for Brasserie T. We use small ones from Point Judith in Rhode Island, where the producers freeze the squid when it is still very fresh. Also, Point Judith producers do not use the bleaching and tenderizing enzymes that are common among producers in Asia and which give a chemical taste to the squid. If you are buying fresh squid, remember that a purple tinge to the flesh means that the squid has been out of the water too long. All squid must be cooked either very briefly (as we do here) or very slowly; anything in between results in chewy squid.

2 tablespoons kosher salt

1 teaspoon pure olive oil

1/4 cup olive oil

1 medium onion, chopped

4 garlic cloves, minced

1/4 to 1/2 teaspoon red pepper flakes

1/2 cup light-bodied dry white wine, such as Pinot Grigio

2 cups Fish Stock (page 310) or clam juice

One 16-ounce can crushed tomatoes

1 pound frozen cleaned baby calamari (squid), tentacles left whole, caps sliced into 1/4-inch rings (no need to thaw first)

1) Bring 6 quarts of water with the salt and pure olive oil to a boil in a large covered pot.

2) Meanwhile, make the sauce: in a large pot, heat 2 tablespoons of the olive oil over medium-high heat. Reduce the heat to medium, add the onion, garlic, and pepper flakes and cook, stirring, until the onion is translucent, about 8 minutes. Add the wine and simmer until the liquid is reduced to a thick syrup.

3) Add the fish stock, bring to a boil, and reduce the liquid by one-fourth. Add the tomatoes and calamari and simmer until the calamari are tender. Frozen calamari will cook in about 5 minutes; thawed, in about 3 minutes. Do not overcook; the calamari will quickly become rubbery. Stir in the butter and add salt and pepper to taste.

4) Add the pasta to the pot of boiling water. Stir, cover, and return to a boil. Cook, uncovered, 10 to 13 minutes, until done to your liking. Drain briefly and toss with the remaining 2 tablespoons olive oil.

5) Mound the pasta in a serving bowl and top with the sauce. Serve immediately, sprinkled with fresh basil.

1 tablespoon unsalted butter

Kosher salt and freshly ground black pepper

1½ pounds dried angel hair pasta

2 tablespoons julienned fresh basil

DRINK CRISP WHITES FROM COASTAL WINE REGIONS: LIGURIAN VERMENTINO AND SPANISH ALBARINO ARE GOOD CHOICES.

Linguine with Manila Clams and Fresh Basil

SERVES 4 TO 6

What we simply call clams, the Italians know by many names: vongole, poveracce, arselle, capperozzoli, calcinelli, *and others, depending on the region, the variety, and the size of the clam. Sweet morsels of clam, fruity olive oil, and long strands of pasta are a truly great combination, one of the simplest and best in Italian cooking, especially with fresh basil to provide a green flavor note. Italians use clams from the Adriatic or the Mediterranean in this dish, but those are rarely imported to the United States; we find the best match comes from Pacific Manila clams, but any fresh cherrystones will do. Tiny littleneck clams may get lost in this dish; use the meatier cherrystone size.*

1 tablespoon kosher salt

1 teaspoon pure olive oil

2 pounds Manila clams or other cherrystones in their shells

2 cups clam juice

1 teaspoon extra-virgin olive oil

1 small garlic clove, finely minced

1/2 teaspoon fresh thyme leaves

1/4 teaspoon red pepper flakes

Kosher salt and freshly ground black
   pepper

1 cup best-quality canned clams, with
   their liquid

1/4 cup finely shredded basil, plus
   extra for garnish

2 tablespoons cold unsalted butter, cut
   into pieces

2 plum tomatoes, diced

1 pound dried linguine

1) Bring a gallon of water with the salt and pure olive oil to a boil in a large covered pot.

2) Meanwhile, clean the Manila clams: put them in the sink and cover with cold water. Let them stand for 5 minutes, then drain and rinse out the sand that remains. Cover with fresh water and swish the clams around vigorously in the water, rubbing them against each other to loosen sand and grit. Drain and repeat if necessary until no sand remains.

3) In a pot large enough to hold the pasta and clams later on, combine the clam juice, oil, garlic, thyme, pepper flakes, and salt and pepper to taste. Mix thoroughly.

4) Add both kinds of clams to the pot, cover, and bring the mixture to a simmer over medium-high heat. Simmer until the clams open, about 5 minutes.

5) Meanwhile, add the linguine to the pot of boiling water. Stir, cover, and return to a boil. Cook, uncovered, 10 to 13 minutes, until done to your liking.

6) Add the basil and butter to the clam mixture and simmer until the butter melts. Add the tomatoes and mix well.

7) Drain the pasta briefly and add it to the finished clam sauce. Toss well to coat, cover, remove from the heat, and let rest 2 minutes.

8) Lift the pasta out of the pot and into a large serving bowl or individual pasta bowls. Try to leave the whole clams in the pot as you remove the linguine. Arrange the clams on top of the bowl or bowls, and ladle over any broth that remains in the pot. Sprinkle with extra basil and serve.

MATCH WITH FRESH, CRISP NORTHERN ITALIAN WHITES LIKE
BIANCO DI CUSTOZA, SOAVE, OR PIGATO.

Rigatoni with Olive-Lamb Ragu

This thick ragu recalls the game sauces of Tuscany, which slowly cook hare, wild boar, or duck meat with wine and spices until all that's left is a rich concentrate with incredibly deep flavors. For us (and anyone else who grew up with spaghetti and meat sauce), these sauces are a revelation. We first encountered them on a 1994 trip to Tuscany, at La Tenda Rossa, a friendly family-run restaurant outside Florence that cooks both traditional and progressive food with equal skill. Expecting the light veal-and-vegetable sauce that goes under the name of ragu near Bologna, we were fascinated by the dark richness of the Tuscan ragus, which merge their flavors without ever acquiring the cooked taste of sauce that's been simmering too long.

Here is our easy interpretation of those gamy sauces. A dark, wine-infused meat sauce makes pasta into a dish as hearty and robust as beef stew, with much less meat and fat. Garnishing with sharp pecorino Romano rather than nutty Parmigiano completes the flavor balance.

1 tablespoon kosher salt
1 teaspoon pure olive oil
2 tablespoons olive oil
8 ounces pancetta, diced
2 medium carrots, diced
2 stalks celery, diced
1/2 bulb fennel, diced
1 medium onion, diced
4 garlic cloves, minced
1 teaspoon fennel seeds

1) Bring a gallon of water with the salt and pure olive oil to a boil in a large covered pot.

2) Meanwhile, in a large skillet, heat the oil over medium heat. Add the pancetta and cook, stirring, until golden and the fat is rendered, about 8 minutes. Add the carrots, celery, fennel, onion, garlic, fennel seeds, and pepper flakes and cook, stirring, until the onion is translucent, about 8 minutes. Stir in the thyme, bay leaf, and parsley.

3) Stir in the lamb, breaking it up with a spoon, and sauté, stirring, until the lamb is browned and cooked through, about 10 minutes. Raise the heat to medium-high if necessary to brown the meat.

4) Pour in the red wine and cook, stirring to scrape up the browned bits from the bottom of the pan with a wooden spoon, until the liquid is reduced to a thick syrup.

5) Add the tomatoes and tomato paste and simmer until slightly thickened, 10 to 15 minutes. Stir in the olives, Parmesan, and salt and pepper to taste.

6) When the sauce is almost done, add the rigatoni to the pot of boiling water. Stir, cover, and return to a boil. Cook, uncovered, 10 to 13 minutes, until done to your liking. Drain briefly, return to the pot, and toss with the lamb sauce.

7) Serve in heated bowls, topped with a sprinkling of fresh basil. Sprinkle with grated Romano cheese or use a vegetable peeler to shave curls of Romano over each bowl.

$1/2$ teaspoon red pepper flakes
$1/2$ teaspoon fresh thyme leaves
1 bay leaf
1 tablespoon chopped fresh parsley
1 pound lean ground lamb
$1/2$ cup dry red wine, such as a Cabernet or Chianti
One 16-ounce can crushed tomatoes
2 tablespoons tomato paste
$1/2$ cup chopped pitted oil-cured black olives
2 tablespoons freshly grated Parmesan cheese
Kosher salt and freshly ground black pepper
1 pound dried rigatoni or other tubular pasta
2 tablespoons julienned fresh basil
Romano cheese, grated or chunk

FOR CONTRAST, LOOK FOR A CLASSIC PILSNER WITH DRY, HOPPY FLAVOR.

THE DEEP FLAVOR OF THE RAGU CALLS FOR A CHIANTI CLASSICO, ROSSO DI MONTALCINO, OR STRUCTURED CALIFORNIA MERLOT.

Spinach and Ricotta-Stuffed Crespelle

These were first made for us by the passionate chef at a restaurant called Ambasciatta, in the town of Quistello in Emilia-Romagna. We were good friends of Chef Romano and called ahead to request a menu that would allow us to taste as many of his dishes as possible. The management was delighted to promise us a twelve-course menu—but didn't give us accurate directions to the restaurant. When we drove up one hour and forty-five minutes late, the great chef himself was walking off his emotions in the driveway, clearly fearing that all his work had been wasted. When he spotted us, he shook his fists, rushed back to the kitchen, and began sending out the most extraordinary pasta dishes we'd ever tasted.

Crespelle are really more like crêpes than pasta but take the same place in an Italian meal as pasta would: you can serve them as a first course or as a complete light din-ner or lunch dish with salad. If you've never made crêpes, do try these. They are easy, quick, and good. Any extra crêpes and filling can be layered, rolled, and sliced into spi-rals for a great hors d'oeuvre.

For the filling:

4 cups ricotta cheese, drained for 2 hours in cheesecloth or a coffee filter

2 large eggs

2 tablespoons olive oil

1 small onion, minced

2 garlic cloves, minced

8 ounces spinach, thick stems removed, well washed

4 leaves fresh basil, chopped

1) Make the filling: in a mixing bowl, mix together the drained ricotta and eggs. In a skillet, heat the olive oil over medium-high heat. Reduce the heat to medium, add the onion and garlic, and cook, stirring, until softened and translucent, about 8 minutes. Do not let them brown; reduce the heat if necessary.

2) Raise the heat to medium-high, add the spinach, and cook, stirring, just until wilted, 1 to 2 minutes. Turn off the heat, drain off any liquid in the pan, and mix in the basil, cheese, and lemon zest. Set aside to cool, then chop and mix with the ricotta mixture.

3) Make the crêpes: in a mixing bowl, whisk together the milk and eggs. Slowly whisk in the flour, salt, and pepper. Set aside to rest for 30 minutes. In an 8- or 9-inch nonstick skillet, melt about 1/4 teaspoon of the butter over medium heat, swirling to evenly coat the bottom of the pan. Ladle in about 3 tablespoons of the batter and quickly lift the pan off the heat, swirling to evenly coat the bottom of the pan. Cook until the crêpe is light golden brown on the bottom, then turn with a spatula and cook the other side. Remove to a piece of wax paper and repeat with the remaining batter, stacking the finished crêpes between sheets of wax paper.

4) Preheat the oven to 350°F. Lightly oil a large baking dish.

5) Assemble the crespelle: lay a crêpe on a clean work surface. Place about 3 tablespoons filling in a line down the center and fold over the 2 sides to cover the filling. Transfer, seam side down, to the oiled baking dish. Repeat with the remaining crêpes and filling.

6) Spoon the tomato-basil sauce over the crespelle and cover the dish with foil. Bake 10 to 15 minutes, then uncover and bake 10 minutes more, until the filling is piping hot. Sprinkle with the mozzarella and Parmesan, cover again with foil, and let stand 5 minutes. Uncover and serve immediately.

1/2 cup freshly grated Parmesan cheese
Grated zest of 1/2 lemon

For the crêpes:
1 1/2 cups whole milk
3 large eggs
1 1/2 cups all-purpose flour
1/2 teaspoon kosher salt
Pinch of freshly ground black pepper
About 2 tablespoons unsalted butter

To finish the dish:
2 cups (about 1/2 recipe) Quick Tomato-Basil Sauce (see Spaghettini with Quick Tomato-Basil Sauce, pages 94–95)
1 1/2 cups shredded fresh mozzarella cheese
1/4 cup freshly grated Parmesan cheese

TRY A SIMPLE SALICE SALENTINO OR A SICILIAN RED FROM MOUNT ETNA.

Orange-Ricotta Gnocchi with Broccoli Rabe

For a textbook definition of "family-style," the place to go is a popular restaurant outside Verona called Al Ponte. This friendly restaurant has served the same four pastas—meat-stuffed tortellini, spinach-stuffed ravioli, tagliatelle alla bolognese, and light gnocchi—for as long as anyone can remember. All of them are perfectly made. The pasta course at Al Ponte consists of just as much as you want of each kind of pasta (no need to make the agonizing choice); your hostess comes around with a smile and a heaping platter to ask if anyone wants more. "Yes, please. . ."

Gnocchi not only have a name that's hard to pronounce, but they have the reputation of being difficult to make. Well, here's how to pronounce the word: "nyaw-kee," spoken quickly and with the accent on the first syllable. And here's how to make the dish: with potatoes for moisture, ricotta cheese for light texture, and orange zest for flavor. It's hard to go wrong—if you can make mashed potatoes, you can make gnocchi.

For the gnocchi:

8 ounces Yukon Gold or other boiling potatoes (not Idahos or new potatoes), peeled and cut into 1-inch chunks

3¹/₄ cups all-purpose flour

2 large eggs, lightly beaten

¹/₂ cup ricotta cheese

¹/₂ cup freshly grated Parmesan cheese

Grated zest of 1 orange

Pinch of freshly grated nutmeg

1 tablespoon plus ¹/₄ teaspoon kosher salt

1) Put the potatoes in a saucepan, cover with cold salted water, and bring to a boil. Cook until very tender, about 20 minutes. Drain, return the potatoes to the pot, and shake them over medium heat for 30 seconds to dry them out. Mash smooth in the pot or transfer to the bowl of a mixer with a paddle attachment and mash until very smooth. Set aside to cool.

2) Meanwhile, begin the sauce: in a pot of boiling salted water, blanch the broccoli rabe for 2 minutes to remove the bitterness (it will finish cooking later in the recipe). Fill a bowl with ice cubes and cover with cold water. Lift the broccoli rabe out of the boiling water and plunge it into the ice water to stop the cooking. Drain, chop into 1-inch lengths, and set aside.

3) Make the gnocchi: line a large baking sheet with wax paper.

4) Mound the flour on a clean work surface. Make a large well in the center and pour the eggs into it. Working with your hands, gradually and gently work the potatoes and then the ricotta into the eggs. Sprinkle this mixture with the Parmesan, orange zest, nutmeg, 1/4 teaspoon salt, and pepper.

5) Working in circles, gradually expand the well by incorporating the flour into the potato-ricotta mixture. By the time you get to the outermost rim of flour, you should have a workable dough. Knead the whole thing together until smooth and soft, almost sticky.

6) Pull off a handful of dough and roll it between your hands to form a snake about 1/2 inch thick. Cut the snake with a sharp knife into 3/4-inch lengths and transfer to the lined baking sheet. If you like, use your fingers to gently roll each gnocchi against the back of a fork, creating the typical ridged pattern. (This helps them cook evenly and hold the sauce.) Repeat with the remaining dough.

7) Heat a gallon of water to boiling with the remaining salt and olive oil in a large covered pot.

8) Make the sauce: heat the oil in a skillet over medium-high heat. Reduce the heat to medium, add the onion and garlic, and cook 2 minutes, until softened. Add the broccoli rabe and cook, stirring, 5 minutes. Stir in the orange juice and stock and simmer until reduced by half, 8 to 10 minutes.

9) Meanwhile, cook the gnocchi: in batches of 2 dozen or so, drop the gnocchi into the boiling water and let them cook just until they float to the surface. Remove them with a slotted spoon and transfer them to the simmering stock.

10) Add the tomatoes, Parmesan, basil, and butter. Stir and simmer 3 minutes.

11) Stir in the orange segments.

12) Serve sprinkled with toasted almonds, if desired, and parsley.

2 pinches freshly ground black pepper
1 tablespoon olive oil

For the sauce:

8 ounces broccoli rabe
2 tablespoons olive oil
1 medium onion, chopped
4 garlic cloves, minced
Juice of 1 orange
4 cups Chicken Stock (page 307)
2 plum tomatoes, diced
1/4 cup freshly grated Parmesan cheese
6 leaves basil, finely chopped
2 tablespoons unsalted butter
1 orange, peeled and cut into segments

To finish the dish:

2 tablespoons slivered almonds, toasted (see page xxxiii) (optional)
1 tablespoon finely chopped fresh parsley

A TART TOCAI FROM ITALY'S FRIULI REGION— NO RELATION TO SWEET HUNGARIAN TOKAJI— IS PERFECT HERE.

Creamy Three-Grain Risotto
with Artichokes and Mushrooms

SERVES 4 TO 6

This risotto blends earthy mushrooms and nutty grains with the delicate flavors of arti-choke hearts and fresh Parmesan. It was inspired by an happy event: When we were cooking at Stapleford Park in Leicestershire in 1991, the notoriously picky inspectors for the Michelin guide awarded our year-old restaurant a "red M," the first step toward the coveted Michelin stars. We chose to celebrate with dinner at Chewton Glen, a lux-urious hotel nearby where our friend Pierre Chevillard ran the award-winning kitchen. And that's how two American chefs ate an Italian dish in an English kitchen, cooked by a French chef using a quintessentially American ingredient—wild rice. Until then, we would never have thought of using anything but traditional Italian arborio rice in risotto. The end result of Pierre's experiment is this three-grain concoction.

It's a winning combination—perfect as a winter first course with fish to follow (like our Pan-Roasted Salmon with Coriander Seed and Wilted Spinach, pages 128–29), or paired with a great salad for a complete vegetarian feast. Our final touch—the last-minute addition of whipped cream and herbs—lightens and smooths the mixture.

2 teaspoons olive oil

$^{1}/_{2}$ cup rinsed pearl barley

$^{1}/_{2}$ cup rinsed wild rice

4$^{1}/_{2}$ tablespoons unsalted butter

2 cups sliced shiitake, cremini, or oyster mushrooms, or a combination (discard shiitake stems)

Kosher salt and freshly ground black pepper

3 tablespoons cold heavy cream

1) In separate pots of boiling salted water, each with one teaspoon olive oil, cook the barley and wild rice, uncovered, until tender, about 45 minutes. Drain well and set aside.

2) In a small skillet, melt 1 tablespoon of the butter over medium-high heat. Add the mushrooms and sauté until softened and fragrant, about 3 minutes. Add salt and pepper to taste and set aside.

3) With a whisk, whip the cream until stiff peaks form. Cover and refrigerate until ready to use.

4) In a saucepan, bring the stock to a simmer.

5) In a deep heavy saucepan over medium heat, melt 1 tablespoon of the butter. Add the shallots and garlic, and sauté until transparent and soft, about 3 minutes.

6) Add the rice and stir until completely coated with butter.

7) Add a ladleful of stock and cook, stirring, until all the stock is absorbed by the rice. Add another ladleful of stock and continue cooking in the same manner, adding stock only as needed and stirring very frequently, until the rice is tender, about 25 minutes.

8) Stir in the barley, wild rice, artichokes, mushrooms, cheese, and remaining butter and mix to combine.

9) Fold in the whipped cream, parsley, chives, tarragon, and tomatoes.

10) Taste for salt and pepper and serve immediately.

3 cups Chicken Stock (page 307) or low-sodium canned chicken or vegetable broth

2 shallots, minced

2 large garlic cloves, minced

$^1/_2$ cup arborio rice

$1^1/_2$ cups quartered fresh baby artichokes (about 4 artichokes), cooked as described on pages xxxii–xxxiii, or frozen artichoke hearts (thawed), or canned brine-packed artichoke hearts (drained)

$^1/_2$ cup freshly grated Parmesan cheese

1 tablespoon finely chopped fresh parsley

1 tablespoon finely chopped fresh chives

1 tablespoon finely chopped fresh tarragon

1 large or 2 plum tomatoes, seeded and diced

ARTICHOKES CAN BE DIFFICULT FOR WINE, BUT HERE A CRISP PINOT GRIGIO
OR AUSTERE CALIFORNIA VIOGNIER WILL WORK WELL.

Roasted Eggplant–Wild Rice Risotto

SERVES 4 TO 6

October is white truffle season in Italy's northern realm of Piedmont, a cool, misty time of year when the tradition of hunting for truffles with trained dogs and pigs is in full swing. At season's end, a wonderfully lighthearted truffle festival is held in the capital, Alba, which includes an awards ceremony and celebration banquet for the most accomplished pigs and dogs. Most of the year, truffles are a very serious matter in Alba. White truffles are the most expensive in the world, and as with all truffles, no way of cultivating them has ever been discovered. No one knows just why truffles grow where and when they do.

We learned to appreciate their intensely sensual flavor in a dish much like this one. We had driven miles in the autumn's pitch dark, through forests and the hilly vineyards of Barbaresco, and were beginning to get that lost feeling. Finally we emerged into a village—really a clearing—consisting of an ancient church and a decrepit mansion, the first floor of which held a tiny restaurant. A fire was burning in the hearth, and we warmed up quickly and began to look forward to our meal. Cesare, the chef, was reputed to be both steeped in the traditions of the Piedmont and highly individualistic in his cooking. When the time came for the eggplant risotto, a huge pewter scale was placed in the center of our table, quickly followed by the largest truffle any of us had ever seen and a truffle shaver. At Cesare, each diner has the pleasure of shaving slices of truffle over his own plate, inhaling the incomparable scent. The scale is for weighing the truffle before and after, and the table is charged accordingly.

If you are going to invest in a white truffle, be sure to store it buried in rice, which will absorb excess moisture and preserve the flavor of the truffle; then the rice makes extraordinary risotto. Do use truffles quickly, as the true flavor is intense but fleeting. Shave it over pasta, roast chicken, or scrambled eggs. We've even made ice cream with the last few crumbs!

1) Toss the eggplant with the salt and let drain for 30 minutes in a sieve lined with paper towels.

2) Preheat the oven to 375°F.

3) Put the eggplant pieces in a roasting pan and drizzle with 1 tablespoon of the oil. Toss to coat and roast 10 minutes, then add the fennel, toss well, and roast until both vegetables are tender but not mushy, about 20 minutes more.

4) Meanwhile, cook the wild rice in plenty of boiling salted water until tender, about 40 minutes. Drain and set aside.

5) In a large heavy-bottomed saucepan, heat the remaining 1 tablespoon oil over medium-high heat. Reduce the heat to medium and add the onion, garlic, and pepper flakes. Cook, stirring, until the onion is translucent, 8 to 10 minutes.

6) In a saucepan, bring the stock to a simmer.

7) Add the rice to the onion-garlic mixture and stir until completely coated with oil. Add a ladleful of stock and cook, stirring, until all the stock is absorbed by the rice. Add another ladleful of stock and continue cooking in the same manner, adding stock only as needed and stirring very frequently, until the rice is tender, about 25 minutes.

8) Stir in the cooked wild rice and roasted eggplant and fennel. Stir in the tomato sauce, cheese, cream, and butter and heat through. Add salt and pepper to taste.

9) Serve in heated bowls, sprinkled with fresh basil and truffle shavings or drizzled with truffle oil.

1 medium eggplant, peeled and cut into $1/2$-inch cubes

1 teaspoon kosher salt

2 tablespoons olive oil

1 small bulb fennel, cut into $1/2$-inch cubes

$1/3$ cup wild rice

1 medium onion, chopped

2 garlic cloves, minced

$1/2$ teaspoon red pepper flakes

$3/4$ cup arborio rice

4 cups Chicken Stock (page 307), Vegetable Stock (page 311), or low-sodium canned broth

$1/2$ cup Quick Tomato-Basil Sauce (see Spaghettini with Quick Tomato-Basil Sauce, pages 94–95) or canned tomato puree (not paste)

2 tablespoons freshly grated Parmesan cheese

2 tablespoons heavy cream

2 tablespoons cold unsalted butter, cut into pieces

Kosher salt and freshly ground black pepper

Chopped fresh basil

Shaved black or white truffles or white truffle oil (optional)

A MELLOW DARK LAGER WITH MALT FLAVOR, AMBER COLOR, AND A HOPPY BOUQUET WOULD SET OFF THIS COMPLEX DISH.

LOOK FOR A STRUCTURED PIEDMONTESE OR CALIFORNIA CHARDONNAY TO STAND UP TO THE DEEP FLAVORS HERE.

Butternut Squash Risotto with Crisped Pancetta

The first time we drove over the Alps and through the valley of the Po River, we were appalled to see that much of the valley, obviously farmland, was covered with water. This seemed like an agricultural catastrophe of enormous proportions, and we couldn't wait to ask our hosts what had happened. Of course, all that had happened was that we had missed the opportunity to appreciate the enormous watery rice paddies of Lombardy, where short-grain arborio rice is grown. In nearby Milan, where risotto-making is a local obsession, the classic dish of risotto with winter squash is known by the delightful name of ris e zucca barucca.

The silky textures of butternut squash and arborio rice go naturally together, especially when spices, stock, and a bit of cream are included to make sure everything blends smoothly. Crisp salty pancetta, crunchy pistachio nuts, and fresh herbs balance out the dish, giving each mouthful a refreshing combination of tastes and textures. Try putting your dinner guests to work stirring the risotto: you've probably noticed that they always end up in the kitchen anyway! They'll enjoy feeling that they had a hand in the cooking.

1 medium butternut squash, peeled, halved, seeded, and cut into $^1/_2$-inch cubes (about 2 cups)

2 tablespoons cold heavy cream

2 teaspoons olive oil

4 ounces pancetta, diced

1 medium onion, chopped

2 garlic cloves, minced

$^3/_4$ cup arborio rice

4 cups Chicken Stock (page 307), Vegetable Stock (page 311), or low-sodium canned broth

1) In a large pot of boiling salted water, cook the squash until fork-tender, 12 to 15 minutes. Drain and set aside. (The squash can be made up to 1 day in advance.)

2) With a whisk, whip the cream until stiff peaks form. Cover and refrigerate until ready to use.

3) Heat the oil in a heavy-bottomed saucepan over medium-high heat. Add the pancetta and cook, stirring, until golden and crispy, about 5 minutes. Remove the pancetta and let drain on paper towels. Drain off all but 2 tablespoons of fat from the pan.

4) Add the onion and garlic and cook over medium heat, stirring, until the onion is translucent, about 8 minutes. Add the rice and stir until completely coated with oil.

5) Meanwhile, in a saucepan, bring the stock to a simmer.

6) Add a ladleful of stock to the rice and cook, stirring, until all the stock is absorbed by the rice. Add another ladleful of stock and continue cooking in the same manner, adding stock only as needed and stirring very frequently, until the rice is tender, about 25 minutes.

7) Stir in the turmeric, cinnamon, and brown sugar. Stir in the cooked squash and tomatoes, then gently stir in the cheese, butter, whipped cream, and basil and heat through. Add salt and pepper to taste.

8) Serve in heated bowls, sprinkled with pancetta, pistachios, and chives.

Pinch of ground turmeric
1/2 teaspoon ground cinnamon
1/2 to 1 teaspoon light brown sugar
2 plum tomatoes, diced
2 tablespoons freshly grated Parmesan cheese
2 tablespoons cold unsalted butter, cut into pieces
1 tablespoon chopped fresh basil
Kosher salt and freshly ground black pepper
1 tablespoon chopped pistachio nuts
1 tablespoon chopped fresh chives

ENJOY WITH A FULL-BODIED, REFRESHINGLY CRISP SOUTH GERMAN WHEAT BEER, DRUNK WITH THE TRADITIONAL SLICE OF FRESH LEMON.

BOTH RED AND WHITE WINES WORK WELL HERE. CHOOSE A BRIGHT DOLCETTO OR PINOT NOIR, OR A PINOT BIANCO OR A NON-OAKY CHARDONNAY.

Grilled Portobello Mushrooms with Polenta Cakes, Mesclun, and Balsamic Sauce

Balsamic vinegar appears not once but twice in this impressive dish, which is one of our favorite light entrees. In Modena, where all balsamic vinegar is made, we tasted vinegars from twelve to one hundred years old. In the traditional tasting method, drops of vinegar are deposited onto the fleshy part of the hand, where the thumb turns into the index finger, to warm before tasting. The sweet, woody character of balsamic vinegar comes not just from age but from the process of rotating the vinegar through thirteen different barrels as it ages and concentrates. During the process the vinegar— which begins as grape juice, not wine, which accounts for the sweetness—picks up the rich flavors of oak, juniper, cherry, and other woods. Balsamic vinegar has been prized for centuries: a complete set of aging barrels, called a batteria, *has been made part of the dowry for many a Modenese bride over the years, and vials of balsamic vinegar were among the luxury items confiscated from French aristocrats during the revolution. Some balsamic vinegars have been successfully aged as long as 360 years, much longer than any wine.*

Portobello caps are large and meaty, perfect for grilling because of their natural succulence. The portobellos you see in the market are actually very closely related to white button mushrooms but are much larger. They are flavorful because they are allowed to grow to the point when the caps are large, open, and mature.

1) The day before serving, make the sauce: in a skillet, heat the garlic oil over medium-high heat. Add the carrots, celery, and onion and cook, stirring, until softened, about 5 minutes. Add the thyme, vinegar, and wine and simmer until reduced by half. Add the stock and simmer until thickened and reduced to about 2 cups. Strain the sauce into another saucepan, whisk in the butter, and season with salt and pepper to taste. Cover and refrigerate until ready to use. (The sauce can be made up to 2 days in advance.)

2) Make the polenta: butter a 9- or 10-inch tart pan.

3) If using fresh corn, preheat a charcoal grill or broiler and brush the corn with garlic oil. Grill the corn (not too close to the heat) until smoky and lightly browned on all sides. Let cool and cut off the kernels with a sharp knife. If using frozen corn, thaw and toss with the garlic oil. Heat a skillet over high heat, add the corn, and sauté until aromatic and lightly browned. Set aside to cool.

4) In a saucepan, combine the milk, water, half of the butter, and salt and pepper to taste and bring to a boil. Gradually whisk in the polenta, then reduce the heat to low. Bring a pot or kettle of water to a boil.

5) Cook the polenta until tender, about 25 minutes, whisking constantly to prevent sticking and clumping. As needed, add boiling water, 1/2 cup at a time, to keep the polenta moist. When the mixture is smooth and cooked through (not grainy), stir in the cheese and cooked corn. Taste for salt and pepper. Scrape into the tart pan with a rubber spatula, smooth the top, and cover tightly with plastic wrap. Refrigerate at least 2 hours to set or as long as overnight.

6) Cook the mushrooms: in a large heavy pot, heat the oil. Add the carrots, celery, onion, garlic, and thyme and cook, stirring, until softened—about 5 minutes. Add about 2 quarts water to the pot, cover, and bring to a boil.

For the balsamic sauce:

2 tablespoons Garlic Oil and Puree (page 292), or 2 tablespoons olive oil mixed with 1 minced garlic clove

2 carrots, chopped

2 stalks celery, chopped

1 small onion, chopped

2 teaspoons fresh thyme leaves

1/3 cup balsamic vinegar

1/3 cup red wine

4 cups Veal Stock (pages 308–9), Chicken Stock (page 307), Vegetable Stock (page 311), or low-sodium canned broth

2 tablespoons cold unsalted butter, cut into pieces

Kosher salt and freshly ground black pepper

For the polenta:

2 ears fresh corn, husked, or one 10-ounce package frozen corn kernels

2 tablespoons Garlic Oil and Puree (page 292), or 2 tablespoons olive oil mixed with 1 minced garlic clove

1 1/2 cups whole milk

1 1/2 cups water

8 tablespoons (1 stick) unsalted butter

Kosher salt and freshly ground white pepper

1 cup imported polenta (not instant polenta or American cornmeal)

1 cup freshly grated Parmesan cheese

For the mushrooms:

2 tablespoons canola oil

2 carrots, quartered

2 stalks celery, quartered

1 onion, quartered

4 garlic cloves, crushed

1 teaspoon dried thyme, or 1 tablespoon fresh

6 large portobello mushrooms

To finish the dish:

About ¹/₂ cup Garlic Oil and Puree
(page 292), or ¹/₂ cup olive oil
mixed with 3 minced garlic cloves

Kosher salt and freshly ground black
pepper

12 ounces mixed salad greens
(mesclun) or a mixture of at least 3
lettuces such as red leaf, romaine,
endive, radicchio, arugula, frisée,
watercress, and Boston

¹/₄ cup Balsamic-Orange Vinaigrette
(page 3), or ¹/₄ cup extra-virgin
olive oil whisked with a few drops of
lemon juice, salt, and pepper

4 plum tomatoes, seeded and diced

1 cup freshly grated or shaved
Parmesan cheese

2 tablespoons chopped fresh chives,
plus 12 whole chives, for garnish

7) Meanwhile, remove the stems from the mushrooms and discard. Wipe the caps clean with a damp towel, then add to the pot of boiling vegetables. Put a plate on top of the mushrooms to make sure they are submerged. Cook about 8 minutes, until tender. Drain on a clean towel and discard the broth and vegetables (or strain the broth and save for making soup or cooking grains).

8) When ready to serve, bring the balsamic sauce to a simmer over low heat. Preheat a charcoal grill or broiler.

9) Brush the portobellos with some of the garlic oil and season with salt and pepper. Grill (not too close to the heat) until browned and smoky on both sides. Do not overcook.

10) Spoon about ¹/₄ cup of balsamic sauce onto each serving plate and keep the plates warm in a low oven. Cut the polenta into 6 triangular wedges, as you would cut a pizza.

11) In a skillet, heat 2 tablespoons of the garlic oil over medium heat. Working in batches if necessary, sauté the polenta wedges, turning once with a large spatula, until golden brown and crisp. If needed, add more oil to the pan between batches.

12) Remove the plates from the oven and place the polenta wedges off-center in the sauce. Lean a portobello mushroom against each wedge.

13) Toss the salad greens with the vinaigrette, season with salt and pepper to taste, and divide on top of the mushroom caps.

14) Sprinkle chopped tomato, Parmesan cheese, and chives over the top. Rest 2 whole chives, crossed, on top and serve immediately.

CHIANTI CLASSICO IS THE NATURAL CHOICE, BUT TRY ALSO NORTHERN RHÔNE REDS
OR A CALIFORNIA ZINFANDEL.

Tramonto's Escarole, Sausage, and White Bean Stew

Juicy sausages and bitter greens are a natural combination—and with creamy white beans added, they're one of our favorite one-pot dinners. This wonderful family-style stew can be made well in advance; it reheats beautifully over a low flame. It also freezes well, but as always, taste for salt and pepper before serving. Be sure to serve some crusty bread alongside to mop up the savory liquid at the bottom of the bowl. Thanks, Mom.

1) In a large deep skillet, heat the olive oil and cook the sausage pieces over medium-high heat until they begin to brown, about 10 minutes.

2) Add the garlic and pepper flakes to the skillet and sauté over medium-high heat just until the garlic softens, about 2 minutes. Add the escarole and cook, stirring, until wilted, about 2 minutes.

3) Add the beans and cook, stirring, 1 minute. Add the stock and bring to a gentle boil.

4) Add the butter, cheese, tomatoes, and half of the parsley. Mix to combine and cook until the mixture is heated through and the butter is melted. Add salt and pepper to taste.

5) Serve in heated bowls, sprinkled with the remaining herbs and drizzled with a bit of olive oil. Use a vegetable peeler to shave curls of Parmesan over each bowl or sprinkle each bowl with grated cheese.

1 teaspoon olive oil

8 ounces bulk Italian sausage, sweet and/or hot, broken into 1-inch chunks

5 large garlic cloves, minced

$1/2$ teaspoon red pepper flakes, or to taste

1 head escarole, leaves washed, dried, and chopped into 2-inch pieces

3 cups cooked or canned white beans (see page xxxii)

3 cups Chicken Stock (page 307) or low-sodium canned chicken broth

4 tablespoons ($1/2$ stick) unsalted butter

$1/2$ cup freshly grated Parmesan cheese or a combination of Parmesan and Romano

2 plum tomatoes, diced

2 tablespoons chopped fresh parsley

Kosher salt and freshly ground black pepper

Extra-virgin olive oil

Parmesan cheese, shaved or grated

TRY A BRIGHT, YOUNG DOLCETTO OR A RUSTIC RED FROM SOUTHERN ITALY.

Roasted Vegetable–White Bean Chili

SERVES 6

This chunky Mediterranean-influenced stew—in fact, it's somewhere between a Provençal vegetable ragoût and Texas chili—has plenty of deep, earthy flavors on its own, but it becomes positively luxurious with a top layer of melted cheddar and a cool dollop of sour cream. Or just top it with sliced avocado. It's the spices that earn the dish its chili status and make it a classic American accompaniment to beer. Try it with a wedge of Roasted Corn Bread (pages 76–77) or over Soft Polenta (page 202) for great alternatives to the traditional accompaniment of corn bread.

^{1}/$_4$ **cup Garlic Oil and Puree (page 292), or ^{1}/$_4$ cup olive oil mixed with 3 minced garlic cloves**

1 medium onion, diced

3 stalks celery, sliced ^{1}/$_2$ inch thick

2 medium carrots, sliced ^{1}/$_2$ inch thick

2 yellow bell peppers, seeded and diced

2 red bell peppers, seeded and diced

2 medium zucchini, diced

2 yellow (summer) squash, diced

^{1}/$_4$ cup chopped fresh cilantro, plus extra for garnish

1 bay leaf

1 teaspoon chili powder

One 28-ounce can crushed tomatoes

^{1}/$_2$ teaspoon cayenne pepper, or to taste

1 teaspoon ground cumin, or to taste

2 cups cooked white beans (see page xxxii), or one 19-ounce can white beans, drained and rinsed

1) Preheat the oven to 425°F.

2) In an ovenproof large heavy pot, heat the garlic oil over medium-high heat. Add the onion, celery, carrots, peppers, zucchini, yellow squash, cilantro, bay leaf, and chili powder and cook, stirring, just until softened, about 3 minutes. Transfer to the oven and roast about 25 minutes, stirring after 15 minutes, until the vegetables are tender but not mushy. They should still hold their shape.

3) Remove the pot from the oven, place over low heat, and add the crushed tomatoes, cayenne, cumin, white beans, and salt and pepper to taste. Simmer until thickened, 20 to 30 minutes, then stir in the butter. (The chili can be prepared to this point up to 3 days in advance.)

4) When ready to serve, preheat the broiler.

5) Ladle the chili into flameproof bowls and sprinkle the cheeses over them. Arrange the bowls in a roasting pan or on a baking sheet. Broil until the cheese is melted and brown, about 3 minutes. Garnish with a dollop of sour cream and a generous sprinkle of cilantro and serve immediately.

Kosher salt and freshly ground black pepper

2 tablespoons cold unsalted butter, cut into pieces

1 cup freshly grated cheddar cheese

1/2 cup freshly grated Parmesan cheese

1/2 cup sour cream or yogurt

A DRY, MEDIUM-BODIED PALE ALE THAT COMBINES FRUIT AND HOPS CHARACTERS IS A NATURAL WITH THIS LIGHTLY SPICY VEGETABLE DISH.

TRY A BRIGHT CALIFORNIA ZINFANDEL WITH SOFT TANNINS.

Main Courses

Stilton and Corn Soufflé

Spinach and Jack Cheese Omelet

Pan-Roasted Salmon with Coriander Seed and Wilted Spinach

Salmon Paillards with Mustard-Dill Sauce and Creamy Cucumber Salad

Sicilian Tuna with Braised Fennel, Tomato, and Capers

Sautéed Red Snapper with Tarragon Sauce

Brown-Butter Scallops with Braised Leeks

Chicken Pot Pie

Coq au Vin Rouge

Coq au Riesling

Sautéed Calf's Liver with Caramelized Onions and Balsamic Sauce

Individual Veal Meat Loaves with Tomato-Basil Sauce

Chicago Choucroute

Saucisson with Green Lentils and Potato-Onion Ragoût

Mediterranean Navarin of Lamb

Marinated Rib-Eye Steaks with Tobacco Onions

Stilton and Corn Soufflé

SERVES 4 TO 6

When we agreed to go to England to revitalize the flagging cuisine at Stapleford Park, a hotel owned by our friend Bob Payton, we had no idea what to expect. But having heard all the jokes about English cooking, we did wonder if they would like our food. As soon as we arrived in Melton Mowbray, a town dedicated to making strong, creamy Stilton cheese, we knew everything would be fine. The entire town of Melton Mowbray smells of Stilton, especially the fine cheeses of the firm of Tuxford & Tebbutt; that may be what inspired us to cook with it so often, creating new lunch and supper dishes like this one.

The richness of the local agricultural traditions quickly impressed us: the milk, butter, eggs, lamb, and vegetables were just as perfect and flavorful as the Stilton cheese. According to legend, Stilton was invented by a Mrs. Paulet in the 1700s. The cheese must be cylindrical, must ripen without ever being pressed, and must form its own coat, or crust. Red Leicester, a vibrant orange, crumbly, aged cheddar-style cheese, furthered our education in the best products of English kitchens.

More words and warnings have been devoted to the making of soufflés than for any other cooking subject, but this one doesn't rise perilously high. An airy egg batter, fresh milk and butter, savory cheese, and in this case, sweet corn kernels and a dash of mustard produce irresistible results. If you want to make your soufflés even more luxurious, follow the reheating instructions by pouring a dollop of heavy cream inside each one for the last 10 minutes of cooking.

Serve with Endive-Walnut Salad (page 194).

1)   Preheat the oven to 400°F. Butter and flour 1 large soufflé dish or 4 to 6 individual ones.

2)   Heat the milk in a saucepan over low heat.

3)   Melt the butter in a separate saucepan over medium heat, then add the flour, stirring with a whisk until smooth and creamy. The mixture should be about as thick as glue; add a little more flour if necessary. Cook about 3 minutes, until the mixture turns golden. Whisking, pour in the hot milk all at once and whisk constantly over medium heat until the mixture thickens.

4)   Remove from the heat and stir in the cheeses, egg yolks, corn, mustard, and salt and pepper to taste. Set aside to cool 5 minutes.

5)   Whip the egg whites until soft peaks form, then add to the cheese-corn mixture in thirds, folding with a rubber spatula after each addition.

6)   Pour the mixture into the soufflé dish or dishes, then place in a roasting pan. Pour hot tap water into the pan until it comes halfway up the sides of the dish. Bake 25 to 35 minutes for individual soufflés, 35 to 45 minutes for large ones, until risen and slightly firmed. (The dish can be prepared to this point up to 12 hours in advance. Let the soufflés cool in the dish, then turn out, cover, and refrigerate. To reheat, arrange on a baking sheet, drizzle a little heavy cream over the top of each soufflé, and bake at 400°F until hot and bubbly.) Serve immediately.

1¹/₂ cups whole milk

6 tablespoons (³/₄ stick) unsalted butter

¹/₄ cup all-purpose flour

5 ounces grated red Leicester or a farmhouse cheddar

2 ounces crumbled Stilton, Gorgonzola, or Maytag blue cheese

4 large egg yolks

1 cup fresh or thawed frozen corn kernels

1 teaspoon spicy brown mustard

Kosher salt and freshly ground black pepper

6 large egg whites, at room temperature

THE NUTTINESS OF IRISH STOUT OR PORTER WOULD STAND UP TO THE STRONG CHEESE AND SET OFF THE DELICATE EGGS.

TRY OFF-DRY RIESLINGS WITH GOOD ACIDITY FROM WASHINGTON STATE OR THE MOSEL.

Spinach and Jack Cheese Omelet

SERVES 4

When we first traveled in France, we were interested to see that a perfectly made omelet is accorded as much respect as the most elegant dish on any menu. We never managed to learn whether each pleat in a tall chef's toque really stands for a method of cooking eggs, but we did learn to treat eggs with more respect. That included breaking away from the eggs-are-for-breakfast idea. A fluffy omelet filled with vegetables is the perfect Sunday supper: easy and undemanding but comforting and delicious. Cooking the spinach right into the egg mixture makes this easier to fold than a filled omelet, and a topping of ratatouille adds deep, savory flavor contrast. You can also serve this with a mesclun salad tossed with lemon vinaigrette and sprinkled with diced tomato, and crisped toast rounds spread with a little fresh goat cheese.

Serve with warm Ratatouille (page 198).

12 large eggs, at room temperature

1/4 cup heavy cream or half-and-half

8 tablespoons (1 stick) unsalted butter, melted

8 ounces spinach, stems removed, well washed and dried

4 ounces Monterey Jack cheese, grated

Kosher salt and freshly ground black pepper

2 tablespoons chopped fresh chives

1) In a mixing bowl, whisk the eggs with the cream until smooth. Put 4 serving plates to heat in a low oven.

2) Heat a 10-inch nonstick skillet over medium heat. Add 2 tablespoons of the butter and swirl to coat the pan. Add a quarter of the spinach and cook, stirring, until just wilted, about 1 minute. Pour in about a quarter of the egg mixture. With a rubber spatula, gently nudge the eggs and spinach around in the pan just until combined.

3) Let cook, undisturbed, until the eggs congeal and begin to look cooked, 2 to 3 minutes. Sprinkle a quarter of the grated cheese and salt and pepper to taste on top of the omelet and cook just until the cheese melts, about another 1 to 2 minutes. The eggs should still be a bit runny.

4) Use the rubber spatula to loosen the omelet from the pan; it should be golden on the bottom. Use the spatula to fold the omelet toward you from the far edge, lifting from underneath and tilting the pan away from you to slide the omelet down as you fold. When the omelet is folded, remove a plate from the oven and tilt the pan to slide the omelet onto it.

5) Sprinkle with chives and serve immediately.

6) Repeat with the remaining ingredients.

DRINK A WELL-CHILLED DRY PROVENÇAL BANDOL OR CASSIS ROSÉ.

Pan-Roasted Salmon with Coriander Seed and Wilted Spinach

SERVES 4 TO 6

This entree from Brasserie T combines some of our favorite food ideas of the last ten years: quickly cooked fish, lightly wilted greens, sweet roasted garlic, and soothing mashed potatoes. Of course, none of these trends are really new—fish and vegetables have always been lightly cooked in Asia; Mediterraneans have been baking and boiling sweetness into garlic for centuries; and mashed potatoes could hardly be more traditional in Ireland as well as in America—but recombining ideas from different regions and different times is the essence of creative cooking.

The coriander here strikes a very Alsatian flavor note. One of the distinguishing features of Alsatian cooking is its use of fragrant Asian spices like cumin and coriander, otherwise little used in French cooking. The unusually warm climate that makes Alsace wonderful for wines also invited the long-ago spice trade between Venice and Paris to detour through its temperate valleys. This legacy persists in the region's cooking: today these spices are often paired with fish and vegetables, and ripe local muenster cheese is served with a pile of toasted cumin seeds alongside. In this recipe the spinach and salmon should be cooked as close to serving as possible and as briefly as possible.

Serve with Roasted Garlic Mashed Potatoes (page 210).

For the salmon:

1 teaspoon coriander seeds, crushed in a mortar

¹/₄ cup plus 2 tablespoons olive oil

2 tablespoons freshly squeezed orange juice

1) Make the marinade: whisk together the coriander, ¹/₄ cup of the olive oil, the orange juice, and salt and pepper to taste.

2) Arrange the salmon fillets in a nonreactive dish large enough to hold them in one layer. Reserving two tablespoons to use as a

dressing, pour the marinade over the fillets, cover, and refrigerate at least 1 hour or as long as overnight. Gently turn the fillets every so often.

3) When ready to serve, remove the salmon from the marinade and drain briefly. Season on both sides with salt and pepper.

4) Put 4 large ovenproof plates to warm in a low oven. Toss the orange, lemon, and lime sections with the two tablespoons of reserved marinade.

5) Cook the spinach: melt the butter in a skillet over medium heat. Add the shallots and garlic and cook, stirring, until softened, about 3 minutes. Add the spinach and water and cook, stirring, until wilted, about 1 minute. Add the nutmeg, lemon juice, and salt and pepper to taste and mix to combine. With a slotted spoon, transfer to a serving bowl, cover, and keep warm while you cook the salmon.

6) Heat the remaining 2 tablespoons of olive oil in a large skillet (preferably nonstick) over high heat, until the oil is very hot but not smoking. Add the salmon fillets, skin side down, and sear. (Do not crowd the pan; cook in batches if necessary.) When browned, turn carefully, then reduce the heat to medium and cook until done to your liking—about 4 minutes total. Do not turn the fish more than once.

7) Serve the dish: put a salmon fillet on each plate and garnish with the spinach. Scatter the plate with fresh herbs, citrus sections, and chopped tomato.

Kosher salt and freshly ground black pepper

1^1/2 to 2 pounds salmon fillets, cut into 4 to 6 serving pieces

1 orange or clementine, peeled and divided into sections

1 lemon, peeled and divided into sections

1 lime, peeled and divided into sections

2 tablespoons chopped fresh chives, parsley, cilantro, chervil, or a combination

1 plum tomato, chopped (optional)

For the spinach:

2 tablespoons unsalted butter

2 shallots, thinly sliced

2 garlic cloves, minced

1 pound spinach, well washed, tough stems removed

2 tablespoons water

^{1}/4 teaspoon ground nutmeg (optional)

1 tablespoon freshly squeezed lemon juice, or to taste (optional)

Kosher salt and freshly ground black pepper

A HOPPY PALE ALE DRINKS WELL WITH SALMON AND SPICES, BUT THE DRY CHARACTER OF DORTMUNDER WOULD BE ANOTHER GOOD CHOICE.

WHITE AND RED ARE EQUALLY GOOD HERE. TRY A FRENCH CHABLIS OR WHITE BURGUNDY, OR FOR RED CHOOSE A SIMPLY, FRUITY PINOT NOIR.

Salmon Paillards with Mustard-Dill Sauce and Creamy Cucumber Salad

When you're searching for an easy, elegant summer entree, look no further. To make this lush but light dish, put the cucumber salad together and make the mustard-dill sauce the night before. Bring home chewy brown bread and the freshest salmon you can find and dinner will come together in minutes. Cooking the dish right on the serving plates eliminates a lot of fuss.

For the mustard-dill sauce:

2 tablespoons Dijon mustard

2 tablespoons cider vinegar

2 tablespoons sugar

1 cup olive oil

1 tablespoon chopped fresh dill

For the salmon:

3 pounds boneless, skinless salmon fillets, cut into 6 serving pieces

1 tablespoon olive oil

Kosher salt and freshly ground black pepper

1 recipe Creamy Cucumber Salad (page 196)

1 tablespoon chopped chives

1) Make the sauce: in a small bowl, whisk together the mustard, vinegar, and sugar. Whisking, pour in the oil in a thin stream and whisk vigorously until the dressing is thick and smooth. Add the dill and stir to combine. Set aside.

2) Make the salmon: preheat the broiler.

3) Place each salmon piece between 2 sheets of plastic wrap. With the smooth end of a meat tenderizer or a rolling pin, pound the salmon slowly until very thin—about 1/4 inch thick—being careful not to break it up too much.

4) Peel the plastic wrap away from one side of each fillet and arrange them, skin side down, on ovenproof plates and arrange the plates on 1 or 2 baking sheets. Peel the remaining plastic wrap off the fillets. Brush the fillets with the olive oil and season with salt and pepper to taste.

5) Working in 2 batches if necessary, place the baking sheet very close to the heat and broil the salmon for about 2 minutes, or just until it begins to turn opaque.

6) Drizzle the fillets with the mustard-dill sauce and place a spoonful of cucumber salad in the center of each.

7) Sprinkle with chopped chives and serve, passing the remaining cucumber salad at the table.

GO FOR A CHARDONNAY WITH GOOD ACIDITY OR AN OREGON PINOT GRIS.

Sicilian Tuna with Braised Fennel, Tomato, and Capers

SERVES 4 TO 6

Fresh tuna is a specialty of the sun-soaked Italian island of Sicily and wow, how we love it! So are other key flavor elements of this summery dish: capers, fennel, and green olives. Every year when immense schools of tuna pour past the port of Trapani on their way from the deep Atlantic Ocean to their warmer Mediterranean spawning grounds, the fishermen take their boats far out to sea for the centuries-old tonnara. *In a strictly orchestrated ritual, the nets are waved in rhythm and the fishermen begin a chant that will not end until the boats are full.*

The only secret to this dish is to buy fish steaks that are at least an inch thick so that the flesh will not dry out during the cooking. If you prefer to use swordfish or to grill the fish skewered, in cubes, that will work equally well. The braised vegetables would make an excellent accompaniment to almost any grilled fish, meat, or poultry, or a simple pork or lamb roast. If you'd like to serve a grain dish alongside, Vegetable-Citrus Couscous (page 199) would complete the Sicilian theme. Couscous came to Sicily from nearby Africa many centuries ago and is used in many dishes there.

For the marinade:

¹/₂ cup olive oil

2 garlic cloves, finely minced

¹/₄ teaspoon freshly ground black pepper

1 tablespoon chopped fresh dill or fennel fronds, plus whole fronds for garnish

1) Whisk together the marinade ingredients. Arrange the fish in one layer in a glass or ceramic dish, then pour the marinade over. Turn to coat, cover with plastic wrap, and marinate, refrigerated, at least 2 hours or as long as overnight.

2) Make the vegetables: preheat the oven to 350°F.

3) In a large bowl, toss the garlic and shallots with the olive oil. Add the thyme, salt and pepper to taste, tomatoes, and fennel and toss gently to coat. On a baking sheet with sides, arrange the tomato halves cut side down, then arrange the rest of the mixture around them. Cover the pan with foil.

4) Bake 30 to 40 minutes, then uncover and bake 10 minutes more. Remove the tomatoes and fennel from the pan and keep warm, covered, in the turned-off oven. Transfer the juices and seasonings remaining in the pan to a saucepan. Bring to a boil, adding stock if needed to moisten the mixture. Stir in the capers, olives, and raisins. Whisk in the butter. Stir in the cilantro and reseason with salt and pepper to taste. (The vegetables can be prepared to this point up to 1 day in advance.)

5) Meanwhile, preheat a charcoal grill, grill pan, or broiler until very hot. Remove the fish from the marinade and drain briefly on a rack. Discard the marinade. Season the fish on both sides with salt and pepper. Grill or broil 2 to 3 minutes on each side, until done to your liking. Try not to turn the fish more than once. Tuna can be served quite rare, but swordfish should be cooked more (though not dry) for the best texture.

6) Put a tomato half and a fennel quarter on each plate, then rest the fish on top. Spoon the sauce on top and sprinkle with cilantro and pine nuts. Serve immediately with lemon wedges.

Grated zest of **1** orange

Juice of **1**/2 orange

2 tablespoons dry red wine

1/4 teaspoon crushed fennel seeds

1/2 teaspoon red pepper flakes (optional)

For the fish:

4 to 6 tuna or swordfish steaks, **7** ounces each, at least **1** inch thick

For the vegetables:

4 garlic cloves, minced

2 shallots, minced

1/2 cup olive oil

1 teaspoon fresh thyme leaves

Kosher salt and freshly ground black pepper

3 large ripe beefsteak tomatoes, cored and quartered lengthwise, with their juices

2 medium bulbs fennel, quartered

1/2 to **1** cup Chicken Stock (page 307) or low-sodium canned broth

2 tablespoons small capers in vinegar, drained

2 tablespoons halved pitted green olives, such as Cerignola, Atalanti, or another fleshy dark green olive

2 tablespoons halved pitted black olives, such as Kalamata

1/4 cup golden or other raisins

2 tablespoons cold unsalted butter

1 tablespoon chopped fresh cilantro, plus extra for garnish

1/4 cup pine nuts, toasted in a skillet just until golden

Lemon wedges

LOOK FOR A FULL-BODIED, RICH SAUVIGNON BLANC OR SICILIAN CHARDONNAY.

Sautéed Red Snapper with Tarragon Sauce

SERVES 4 TO 6

Perfectly cooked fish fillets atop subtle creamy sauces are frequently spotted at elegant French restaurants, but arm yourself with a nonstick skillet and a sieve and you'll be surprised how elegantly you can cook in your own kitchen. Whenever our work has taken us into regimented French kitchens where classic cuisine is the rule, we have noticed a dish like this on the menu: light, simple, and yet completely infused with flavor.

Tarragon is a quintessentially French flavoring: subtle, elegant, and delicious—but demanding. Unlike easygoing basil and parsley, which can be scattered freely into and over food, tarragon should be used carefully so that its anise flavor doesn't overwhelm the dish. Tarragon is usually paired with white wine and cream in France: the use of red wine here comes from another source. It was in Barcelona that we first tasted this peppery combination.

Serve with Vegetable-Citrus Couscous (page 199).

4 to 6 red snapper fillets, with skin, about 7 ounces each

2 tablespoons olive oil

Kosher salt and freshly ground black pepper

Pinch of cayenne pepper or to taste

2 garlic cloves, minced

1 shallot, minced

1 stalk celery, diced

1 small carrot, sliced

1) With the tip of a sharp knife, cut the skin side of the fillets with a pattern of X's. Rub with 1 tablespoon of the oil and season generously with salt and pepper. Sprinkle with cayenne. Spread the fillets out on a baking sheet and set aside.

2) Make the sauce: heat 2 teaspoons of the oil in a skillet over medium-high heat. Add the garlic, shallot, celery, and carrot and cook, stirring, until softened, about 5 minutes. Do not let the vegetables brown; reduce the heat if necessary.

3) Add the wine and cook, stirring, until reduced to a light syrup. Add the vinegar and chopped tarragon and cook, stirring, until reduced by half. Add the cream and sugar and bring to a boil. Reduce by one-third, until it coats a spoon.

4) Strain the mixture through a chinois or fine sieve into a saucepan. Immediately whisk in the butter. Add salt and pepper to taste and keep warm. Add some water if it gets too thick.

5) Working in batches if necessary to avoid crowding the pan, cook the fish: heat a teaspoon of olive oil in a nonstick skillet over high heat. Add the fillets, skin side down, and cook 3 minutes or until the skin is crispy. Turn, reduce the heat to medium, and cook on the other side until cooked through, about 3 minutes more or to your liking.

6) To serve, spoon the sauce over the fish. Sprinkle with chopped parsley and rest a sprig of tarragon across each plate.

1 cup dry red wine, preferably Pinot Noir
$^1/_2$ cup best-quality red wine vinegar
1 tablespoon chopped fresh tarragon, plus whole sprigs for garnish
1 cup light cream
Pinch of sugar
2 tablespoons unsalted butter
Chopped fresh parsley

DRY RIESLING OR RICH CHARDONNAY WITHOUT OAK COMPLEMENT THE DELICATE, RICH FLAVORS.

Brown-Butter Scallops with Braised Leeks

SERVES 4 OR 5

The French have a pretty name for what we call brown butter: beurre noisette, hazel-nut butter, a term that perfectly captures the nuttiness and toasted color of the mix-ture. Although brown butter is simple to execute, it is quite impressive and extremely delicious. Drizzled over seafood at the last minute, a hot lemon-spiked brown butter makes simple sautés taste new and fresh, and the way it "cooks" a parsley garnish can be very dramatic at the table. We've added another classic French preparation to this entree: braised leeks, which are rarely eaten as a vegetable in this country despite their delicate onion flavor. Braising in stock brings out it character perfectly.

Serve with Brown Basmati Pilaf (page 201).

2 large leeks, cut in half lengthwise, well washed, and cut into 2-inch lengths including 3 inches of the green

8 tablespoons (1 stick) unsalted butter

Kosher salt and freshly ground black pepper

2 cups Chicken Stock (page 307) or low-sodium canned broth

20 large sea scallops

1 tablespoon olive oil

Chopped fresh parsley

$1/2$ lemon, seeds removed

1) Divide the leek pieces into 4 or 5 bundles and tie each bundle with kitchen twine. Rinse the bundles under cold running water.

2) In a skillet with a lid, melt 2 tablespoons of the butter over medium heat. Add the leek bundles and sprinkle with salt and pepper. Cook, stirring occasionally, until softened, about 6 minutes. Pour in the stock, bring to a simmer, cover, and cook 20 to 30 minutes, until tender but not limp. Remove the bundles and keep warm.

3) Meanwhile, in a heavy-bottomed saucepan, melt 4 tablespoons of the butter over medium heat. When the foam subsides and small white flecks appear (these are the milk solids), reduce the heat to low. Cook gently until the specks turn pale brown, about 3 minutes. Turn off the heat.

4)   Toss the scallops with the olive oil and season generously with salt and pepper. Spread them out on a baking sheet and set aside.

5)   Melt the remaining 2 tablespoons butter in a skillet (preferably nonstick) over high heat. When the foam subsides, add the scallops, placing them upright in the pan. Brown about 2 minutes, then turn with tongs and cook on the other side just until cooked through, about 2 minutes more. The scallops should be medium-rare to medium, not dry.

6)   Arrange the scallops in a circle on your serving plates. Place a leek bundle in the center, and cut and remove the string. Sprinkle parsley over the scallops. Quickly reheat the browned butter, swirling it in the pan over medium heat until bubbly. Squeeze the lemon juice into the pan, swirl to combine, then pour the hot butter over the scallops. The parsley will sizzle and crackle. Serve immediately.

AN IRISH ALE WITH TRADITIONAL BUTTERY, ROUND FLAVOR DRINKS WELL WITH THE GENTLE FLAVORS AND TEXTURES HERE.

A RICH FRENCH CHABLIS OR POUILLY-FUISSÉ WITH GOOD ACIDITY MATCHES BEAUTIFULLY.

Chicken Pot Pie

A great American classic and now a very easy dinner, thanks to the miracle of good commercial puff pastry. The French version of this dish, made in individual pastry shells, has a much more aristocratic name: bouchée à la reine, *the "mouthful of the queen." Like many chicken dishes, this can be dressed up or down depending on what you serve with it: a Chilled Asparagus, Shaved Fennel, and Pecorino with Lemon-Basil Vinaigrette salad (pages 8–9) beforehand and Tangerine Angel Food Cake with Tangerine Glaze (pages 244–45) afterward make a light, elegant meal, but any green salad and a dessert of homemade cookies—may we suggest Cranberry Coconut Bars (page 273)?—will satisfy. If you are at all doubtful about serving humble chicken pot pie to guests, let us assure you that this is an enormously popular special at Brasserie T; many of our customers say that they've never before had a pot pie that wasn't frozen! You can't imagine what they have been missing.*

The simple filling can be made ahead through step 2 and reheated in the oven in step 5. Make a single big pie in a casserole dish or cast-iron skillet, or individual ones in ovenproof serving bowls or soufflé dishes.

For the filling:

- **¹/₄ cup canola oil**
- **2 garlic cloves, minced**
- **2 pounds boneless, skinless chicken breasts, cut into 1-inch pieces**
- **2 cups diced carrots**
- **1 cup diced parsnips**
- **2 cups thickly sliced cremini mushrooms**
- **1 cup diced celery**
- **1 small zucchini, cut into ¹/₂-inch cubes**

1) Make the filling: in a medium skillet, heat the oil over high heat. Add the garlic and chicken and sauté, stirring, until browned, about 5 minutes. Keep the heat high; the chicken should cook quickly or it will dry out. Add the carrots and parsnips and cook 2 minutes. Add the mushrooms and cook 1 minute. Add the celery and cook 1 minute. Add the zucchini, onions, peas, thyme, and basil and cook 1 minute.

2) Add the wine and 2 tablespoons of the stock to the pan and stir, scraping up the browned bits from the bottom of the pan.

3) Add the remaining stock and the cream and cook until thickened, about 10 minutes. Add salt and pepper to taste.

4) Meanwhile, preheat the oven to 375°F. Line a baking sheet with parchment paper.

5) On a lightly floured surface or a piece of parchment paper, unfold or unroll the puff pastry. If you plan to make one large pie, use a very sharp knife to cut one piece of pastry to fit the top of your baking dish but slightly smaller in size. If making smaller individual pies, cut a top pastry for each pie, again slightly smaller than the dishes. With a spatula, transfer the pastry to the baking sheet, making sure the individual pieces are not touching. Brush the surface with beaten egg, and bake 10 to 15 minutes, until lightly browned and puffy.

6) Meanwhile, turn the filling into an ovenproof serving dish or dishes. Each dish should be filled to within 1/2 inch of the top, so that the pastry will be higher than the rim of the dish.

7) When the pastry is done, remove from the oven and set aside. Raise the oven temperature to 400°F. Bake the filling 15 to 20 minutes, until bubbly and heated through.

8) Carefully place the pastry on top and return to the oven just to heat through, about 2 minutes.

9) Sprinkle with the parsley and serve immediately.

1 cup pearl onions, blanched, peeled, and trimmed

$1/2$ cup small green peas, fresh or frozen

2 teaspoons fresh thyme leaves

2 tablespoons shredded fresh basil

2 tablespoons white wine

$1/2$ cup plus 2 tablespoons Chicken Stock (page 307) or low-sodium canned broth

$1/2$ cup heavy cream

Kosher salt and freshly ground black pepper

To complete the dish:

1 or 2 sheets store-bought puff pastry, kept chilled

2 large eggs, beaten

Chopped fresh parsley or chives or a combination

A CLASSIC MALTY DARK LAGER WOULD BE GREAT WITH THIS UPDATED CLASSIC.

PERFECT WITH A YOUNG CALIFORNIA CHARDONNAY.

Coq au Vin Rouge

SERVES 4

Once you've made it at home, it's easy to understand why this simple dish of chicken marinated and then braised in wine is still a weekly specialty at so many bistros and brasseries in France. You don't need the finest, plumpest chicken, a pricey bottle of wine, a lot of time at the stove, or even the special mushrooms we suggest to come up with a great stew. In fact, the lineage of the dish suggests that it was invented as a way to tenderize and flavor the tough old barnyard birds that had outgrown their plumpness. Today's supermarket chickens, while tender, need all the flavor help they can get. Dress this entree up for company with a side dish of fresh pasta tossed with butter and chopped herbs or Roasted Garlic Mashed Potatoes (page 210), or serve with plain boiled potatoes or rice.

One 3^1/$_2$- to 4-pound chicken, quartered

Kosher salt and freshly ground black pepper

One 750 ml bottle dry red wine, such as a good Pinot Noir, Côtes-du-Rhone, or Zinfandel

2 bay leaves

2 sprigs fresh thyme

4 large garlic cloves, minced

^{1}/$_2$ cup plus 1 tablespoon olive oil

2 cups diced celery

2 cups diced carrots

2 cups diced onions

3 tablespoons tomato paste

2 cups Chicken Stock (page 307) or low-sodium canned broth

2 cups Beef Stock (pages 308–9) or low-sodium canned broth

1) The day before you plan to serve the stew, season the chicken pieces on all sides with salt and pepper. Put the chicken in a glass or ceramic bowl. Add 2 cups of the wine, 1 bay leaf, 1 thyme sprig, and half of the minced garlic and gently mix until the chicken is completely coated. Refrigerate, covered, turning the chicken occasionally, for at least 24 hours and at most 48 hours.

2) Heat ^{1}/$_4$ cup of the oil in a large skillet over high heat until it is hot but not smoking. Working in batches if necessary to avoid crowding the pan, remove the chicken from the marinade, shaking off any excess, and brown the chicken pieces on both sides (about 6 minutes on each side).

3) When all the chicken is browned, heat ^{1}/$_4$ cup of the oil in a large heavy pot over medium-high heat. Add the celery, carrots,

onion, and remaining garlic and sauté until softened, 5 to 8 minutes. Do not let the vegetables brown; reduce the heat if necessary. Add the tomato paste and remaining bay leaf and thyme sprig and sauté 2 minutes more.

4) Pour the remaining wine into the pot, stir, and cook, uncovered, over medium heat until the liquid is reduced by half. Add both stocks and bring to a boil. Add the chicken leg pieces and simmer 15 minutes. Add the breast pieces and pearl onions and simmer another 15 minutes.

5) Meanwhile, heat the remaining tablespoon of olive oil in a small skillet over medium-high heat and sauté the bacon until browned. Pour off any excess fat from the pan. Add the mushrooms and sauté until softened. Add the mushroom-bacon mixture to the chicken.

6) When the chicken is cooked through, add the butter, orange zest, and parsley. Taste and adjust the seasonings. Serve immediately. (Or let cool and refrigerate, covered, up to 2 days. Reheat over low heat and adjust the seasonings before serving.)

8 ounces pearl onions, blanched, peeled, and trimmed, or frozen pearl onions

1 cup diced slab bacon

1 pound cremini mushrooms, sliced $1/4$ inch thick

1 pound shiitake mushrooms, stems removed, sliced $1/4$ inch thick

4 tablespoons ($1/2$ stick) cold unsalted butter, cut into pieces

1 tablespoon finely chopped orange zest

1 cup finely chopped fresh parsley, chives, or a combination

A CLASSIC CHOICE WOULD BE A LIGHT BURGUNDY SUCH AS MERCUREY OR GIVRY, OR A CALIFORNIA PINOT NOIR.

Coq au Riesling

In Alsace the loyalty to the excellent local wines is so strong that Riesling is proclaimed to go with all foods, from pizza to foie gras—and it's almost true. Alsatian Rieslings have lots of full flavor without much sweetness, and this makes them ideal wines for cooking as well as drinking. Coq au Riesling is a favorite dish up and down the Alsatian wine route and at brasseries lucky enough to have an Alsatian pedigree. For the curious this sauce can also be poured over sautéed frog's legs, or bras de grenouille, as it might be in a particularly elegant Alsatian auberge by the pretty river Ill, a tributary of the Rhine.

With fresh cream and mushrooms contributing their deep flavors to the thick sauce, the fresh herbs sprinkled on at the end are a must.

Serve with Mustard Spaetzle (pages 204–5).

For the marinade:

3 garlic cloves, minced

1 teaspoon crushed juniper berries

¹/₂ cup dry white wine, preferably Alsatian

¹/₄ cup olive oil

6 whole chicken legs (drumsticks and thighs), with skin

To finish the dish:

¹/₄ cup all-purpose flour

¹/₂ teaspoon kosher salt

¹/₄ teaspoon freshly ground black pepper

¹/₄ teaspoon cayenne pepper

1) Marinate the chicken: combine the garlic, juniper, wine, and oil in a large shallow dish. Rinse the chicken legs under cold running water, drain on paper towels, and add to the marinade. Cover with plastic wrap and marinate, refrigerated, from 4 up to 24 hours. Turn the chicken legs over occasionally.

2) In a shallow bowl, combine the flour, salt, pepper, and cayenne..

3) In a large skillet, melt 2 tablespoons butter over medium-high heat. Working in batches if necessary to avoid crowding the pan, lift the chicken pieces out of the marinade, dredge them lightly with the flour mixture, and place them in the skillet. Sauté until golden brown on both sides. If needed, add more butter to the pan between batches. As you finish browning each chicken piece, remove to a platter and cover with foil to keep warm.

4) When all the chicken is browned and transferred to the platter, add the shallots and garlic to the skillet. Cook over medium-high heat, stirring, until softened, about 2 minutes. Add the mushrooms and cook, stirring, until softened and beginning to brown around the edges, 3 to 5 minutes more.

5) Add the parsley and wine and bring to a simmer. Return the chicken to the pan, cover, and simmer until the chicken is cooked through, about 30 minutes.

6) Remove the chicken to a serving platter and keep warm. In a bowl, whisk the cream and egg yolk together. Turn off the heat under the skillet, let cool 1 minute, and whisk in the cream mixture. Over low heat, cook to thicken slightly. Add the nutmeg and salt and pepper to taste. Pour the sauce over the chicken legs, sprinkle with the chervil, and serve.

2 to 4 tablespoons unsalted butter

2 shallots, minced

2 large garlic cloves, minced

1 cup sliced fresh mushrooms, such as porcini (cèpes), shiitakes (caps only), creminis, or oysters (pulled apart)

1 tablespoon finely chopped fresh parsley

1^1/2 cups Alsatian Riesling or another full-bodied white wine

^{1}/2 cup heavy cream

1 large egg yolk

Pinch of ground nutmeg

Chopped fresh chervil or parsley

A LIGHT, CRISP ALE WILL ALLOW THE SUBTLE FLAVORS HERE TO SHINE.

ALSATIAN OR AUSTRIAN RIESLING IS THE NATURAL CHOICE.

Sautéed Calf's Liver with Caramelized Onions and Balsamic Sauce

SERVES 4

When we were planning the menu for Brasserie T, we decided it was time to polish up the classic liver and onions. Since then, this boldly flavored, aromatic main dish has made plenty of converts of people who thought they didn't like liver. Is it the sweetness of the balsamic vinegar and the caramelized onions that convinces them? The fact that the liver is cut into strips and crisped beforehand? Or the fresh accent of soft yellow, buttery polenta and a sprinkle of green herbs? We don't know for sure, but we do know that this tasty, economical main course has become a fixture on the Brasserie T menu: our regulars won't let us take it off! If possible, buy your liver fresh from a butcher rather than from a supermarket case. Using the freshest liver possible is the key to this dish.

Serve with Soft Polenta (page 202).

For the liver:
1¹/2 pounds very fresh calf's liver
Whole milk

For the caramelized onions:
2 tablespoons unsalted butter
2 large yellow onions, halved and thinly sliced
Kosher salt and freshly ground black pepper

To finish the dish:
1¹/2 cups diced slab bacon
1 cup all-purpose flour

1) The day before you plan to serve the dish, put the liver in a glass or ceramic dish and pour in milk to cover. Refrigerate, covered, overnight.

2) Make the caramelized onions: In a large skillet, melt the butter over medium heat. Add the onions and salt and pepper to taste; reduce the heat to low, and cook, stirring often, until soft and sweet, about 25 minutes.

3) When ready to serve, clean the liver, removing any remaining membrane or veins. With a sharp knife, cut the liver lengthwise into ¹/2-inch-thick slices, then crosswise into 2-inch strips.

4) When the onions are cooked, remove them from the pan and add the diced bacon. Cook over medium-high heat until lightly browned and most of the fat has been rendered, about 5 minutes. Drain the bacon on paper towels and set aside. Save the fat from the skillet and wipe it out with paper towels.

5) Combine the flour, salt, and pepper in a bowl.

6) In the skillet, heat the bacon fat over medium-high heat until hot but not smoking. Dredge the liver strips, a few at a time, in the flour mixture, shake off any excess, and place them in the hot fat. If needed, add some olive oil to the pan. Repeat until all the liver is in the pan.

7) Sear the liver strips on all sides until browned but still pink inside, 3 to 5 minutes. (They will cook a little more later in the recipe.) Remove them from the pan. Add the balsamic vinegar and stock to the pan and deglaze over medium heat, stirring to scrape up the browned bits from the bottom of the pan. Cook until reduced by half, then add the onions and bacon and stir to combine.

8) Increase the heat to high. Stir in the butter. Add the liver back to the pan and cook, stirring, until well combined and heated through, 1 to 2 minutes. Taste for salt and pepper.

9) Serve immediately sprinkled with fresh parsley and chives.

1 1/2 teaspoons kosher salt
1 teaspoon freshly ground black pepper
Olive oil
1/2 cup balsamic vinegar
**1/3 cup Chicken Stock (page 307)
   or low-sodium canned broth**
**4 tablespoons (1/2 stick) cold unsalted
   butter**
**Finely chopped fresh parsley or chives
   or a combination**

A BRITISH OLD ALE WITH RICH FLAVOR AND SLIGHT SWEETNESS WOULD ECHO THE FLAVOR OF THE SAUCE BUT STILL REFRESH THE PALATE.

LOOK·FOR LIGHT, FRUITY ITALIAN MERLOT OR A YOUNG, SLIGHTLY CHILLED BEAUJOLAIS.

Individual Veal Meat Loaves
with Tomato-Basil Sauce

SERVES 4 TO 6

The essence of brasserie cuisine is its lack of pretension, and American food doesn't get much less pretentious than meat loaf. At lunchtime Paris brasseries sometimes serve the French version of meat loaf and mashed potatoes in a humble, tasty dish called hachis Parmentier. *In French cuisine the name Parmentier always means potatoes. Augustin Parmentier (1737–1813) was the first French agronomist to realize the culinary potential of potatoes: before his work, potatoes in France were fed only to cows and pigs! Parmentier persuaded Louis XVI to lead the fashion for the important new food; the king obliged, even going so far as to sport a potato flower in the royal buttonhole, and the court and then the country followed suit. When Parmentier hosted a dinner for Benjamin Franklin in which every course was based on potatoes, the tuber's transatlantic destiny was sealed. France acknowledges Parmentier's contribution to the nation's gastronomy on his large and graceful tombstone in Paris's Père Lachaise cemetery, decorated with delicate carved potato vines.*

When we think of meat loaf we think of comfort food. The flavor of our meat loaf is sparked with fresh ginger and highly seasoned breadcrumbs; with a quick tomato sauce on top and a pillow of aromatic mashed potatoes underneath, this down-home dinner goes uptown. Be careful not to overcook the meat; even the best meat loaf can't overcome a gray color and toughened texture.

3 tablespoons olive oil
¹/₄ cup diced carrot
¹/₄ cup diced celery
¹/₄ cup chopped onion
¹/₂ cup sliced button mushrooms, about ¹/₄ inch thick

1) Preheat the oven to 350°F.

2) In a large skillet, heat 2 tablespoons of the oil over medium heat. Add the carrot, celery, and onion and cook until softened but still firm; but do not let them brown. Turn the vegetables out onto

146

a baking sheet, spread them out evenly, and set aside to cool (this process will cool the vegetables quickly and stop the cooking, so that they stay firm).

3)   Put the skillet back on the stove and heat 1 tablespoon of the oil over medium-high heat. Add the mushrooms and ginger and sauté until the mushrooms start to release their juices, 3 to 4 minutes. Add the soy sauce and cook, stirring, 2 minutes more, until all the liquid has evaporated and the mushrooms are beginning to brown. Turn out onto the baking sheet with the other vegetables and let cool 15 minutes.

4)   In a bowl, combine all the vegetables with the eggs, egg white, breadcrumbs, Worcestershire sauce, salt, pepper, and ground veal. Use your hands to mix just until combined. Do not overmix.

5)   Form the veal mixture into oval loaves about 4 inches across and 2 inches thick, flat on the bottom but with curved tops. Line a baking sheet with parchment paper or grease it with olive oil. Arrange the loaves on the sheet and bake 45 minutes, until the loaves are crusty and brown on the outside but still somewhat pink inside. Do not overcook.

6)   To serve, heat the tomato-basil sauce. Slice each loaf into 4 to 5 pieces.

7)   Mound a large spoonful of Pesto Mashed Potatoes or other mashed potatoes in the center of each plate and lean the slices of meat loaf against it. Spoon the tomato-basil sauce around the edge of the plate (not over the meat loaf), then sprinkle the plate with parsley and cheese.

$1^1/2$ teaspoons grated fresh ginger

1 teaspoon soy sauce

2 large eggs

1 large egg white

$^1/2$ cup Seasoned Breadcrumbs (page 306)

$1^1/2$ teaspoons Worcestershire sauce

$^1/4$ teaspoon kosher salt

$^1/8$ teaspoon freshly ground black pepper

$2^1/2$ pounds ground veal

2 cups Quick Tomato-Basil Sauce (see Spaghettini with Quick Tomato-Basil Sauce, pages 94–95)

1 recipe Pesto Mashed Potatoes (pages 208–9)

Chopped fresh parsley

Grated Parmesan cheese

A LIGHTLY MALTY VIENNA-STYLE LAGER HAS THE RIGHT BALANCE OF SWEET AND BITTER.

MATCH THIS WITH A FRESH DOLCETTO OR WASHINGTON STATE MERLOT.

Chicago Choucroute

Choucroute garnie, or "garnished sauerkraut," is the defining brasserie dish, so we knew from the outset that ours had to be perfect. Choucroute is one of the very few truly Alsatian dishes always found on brasserie menus in Paris and the provinces. Chez Jenny, a very Alsatian brasserie near Paris's Place de la République, has built an entire menu around the dish. When we first had choucroute there, we couldn't quite believe it was a French dish: sausages and sauerkraut seemed so . . . American! That first choucroute really opened our eyes to the many different ways in which one nation's cuisine can be expressed.

Alsatian sauerkraut is very different from the soft, salty product we eat on hot dogs at the ball park. For one thing, it has a strong flavor, whether from the fresh local cabbage it is made from, the many spices—cumin, coriander, juniper, and fresh herbs—it is preserved with, or the wine it is ultimately simmered in to remove the excess salt. Traditionally home-fermented in large wooden trunks, the annual making of choucroute is still an event in Alsace; this may explain why the dish is named after the cabbage and not the meat. Shredded cabbage is combined with salt (no water is added) and is gradually pressed down into the trunk as it softens, with the liquid running out at the bottom. Each autumn, signs advertising "nouvelle choucroute" line the roads, and it is eaten all winter as a crunchy, fragrant accompaniment to any number of meat dishes. In fact, we quickly got used to eating it every day.

When we opened Brasserie T, we found that we couldn't improve on the classic Alsatian combination of sauerkraut, onions, juniper berries, pork, and potatoes. We do eliminate the traditional thick slices of fresh fatty belly bacon, which the Alsatians call "lard." You'll find the various meats and sausages we suggest at any German, Polish, or Czech butcher shop, but there are also perfectly acceptable substitutes at your supermarket. Just aim for a combination of mild, smoked, and spiced cured (cooked) sausages. In a pinch, any good smoked ham can substitute for the pork butt and *Kässler rib. We are fortunate to have a truly dazzling array of mustards at our supermarkets these days. Hot French Dijon mustard (the domestic Dijons don't have the same bite) is the most authentic—but we also like green peppercorn mustard, coarse-grain French mustard, and brown Polish mustard like Kosciusko. This is an easy and impressive dish for a winter dinner party; the recipe can easily be doubled or made ahead and reheated in the pot. For a complete Alsatian dinner, start with either Caramelized Onion Tart (pages 18–19) or Escargots with Lots of Garlic (pages 26–27), followed by choucroute and then Tarte Flambée aux Pommes (pages 236–37).*

1) In a large heavy saucepan with a lid, heat the olive oil over medium-high heat. Add the onion and cook 3 to 5 minutes, until translucent. Add the sauerkraut, wine, stock, juniper berries, bay leaf, peppercorns, rosemary, thyme, and pork butt and cover. Simmer 20 minutes to let the flavors blend.

2) Add the remaining meats and the potatoes and cover. Let simmer, undisturbed, another 15 to 20 minutes or until meats are hot.

3) Add the butter, mix gently, then add salt and pepper to taste.

4) To serve, cut the sausages in half and slice the pork butt 1/2 inch thick. Spoon the sauerkraut into the center of a large platter and arrange the meats and potatoes around it. Garnish with a drizzle of extra-virgin olive oil, additional grinds of the peppermill, and a sprinkling of fresh parsley.

2 tablespoons olive oil

1 large onion, chopped

6 cups sauerkraut, as fresh as possible (not canned), well rinsed and drained in a colander

1 cup dry white wine, such as Alsatian Riesling or Pinot Blanc

2 cups Chicken Stock (page 307) or low-sodium canned chicken broth

6 juniper berries

2 bay leaf

6 black peppercorns

2 sprigs fresh rosemary

2 sprigs fresh thyme

8 ounces smoked pork butt, in one piece

4 Thuringer sausages (coarse-ground, smoky kielbasa-like sausages)

4 Kässler ribs (smoked pork chops)

4 knockwurst sausages

12 small red potatoes, boiled in salted water 15 minutes or until tender

2 tablespoons unsalted butter

Kosher salt and freshly ground black pepper

Extra-virgin olive oil

Chopped fresh parsley

A TRADITIONAL AMBER ALE WITH MEDIUM BODY AND LIGHTLY BITTER FINISH WOULD BOTH COMPLEMENT AND CONTRAST THE RICH MEATS AND PIQUANT SAUERKRAUT.

THIS CLASSIC DISH CALLS FOR NOTHING BUT A RICH ALSATIAN RIESLING, A LIGHT GEWURZTRAMINER WITH GOOD ACIDITY, OR A YOUNG PINOT NOIR.

Saucisson with Green Lentils and Potato-Onion Ragoût

SERVES 4 TO 6

"It was a quick walk to Lipp's and every place I passed that my stomach noticed as quickly as my eyes or my nose made the walk an added pleasure. There were few people in the brasserie and when I sat down on the bench against the wall with the mirror in back and a table in front and the waiter asked if I wanted beer I asked for a distingué, the big glass mug that held a liter, and for a potato salad. The beer was very cold and wonderful to drink . . . After the first heavy draught of beer I drank and ate very slowly. When the pommes a l'huile were gone I ordered another serving and a cervelas. This was a sausage like a heavy, wide frankfurter split in two and covered with a special mustard sauce. I mopped up all the oil and all of the sauce with bread and drank the beer slowly until it began to lose its coldness and then I finished it and ordered a demi and watched it drawn. It seemed colder than the distingué and I drank half of it."
—*Ernest Hemingway,* A Moveable Feast

The simple sensuality of this passage awakens powerful thirsts and hungers that can be satisfied by the following dish—and a cold, robust golden lager alongside. Years later, Rick had his first French garlic sausage in the very same brasserie, one of the city's busiest. The pommes à l'huile *are still on the Lipp menu as well; you'll find our recipe on page 215.*

For a quicker dinner, you can make this dish without the ragoût. In step 4, just add the sliced sausage to the lentils and heat through.

1) Cook the lentils: heat the olive oil in a medium saucepan over medium-high heat. Add the carrot, celery, and onion, reduce the heat, and cook, stirring, until the onion is translucent, about 5 minutes. Do not let the vegetables brown.

2) Add the lentils, stir to coat, and add the water, salt, and pepper. Bring to a boil. Remove the cover, reduce the heat, and simmer just until the lentils are tender, 20 to 25 minutes. Drain and spread out on a baking sheet to cool.

3) When you are ready to complete the dish, reheat the lentils in a saucepan with the wine and stock. Simmer until the liquid is reduced by half and season to taste with salt and pepper. Stir in the butter.

4) Meanwhile, slice the sausage 1/4 inch thick. Place in a pot with the Potato-Onion Ragoût for the last 20 minutes of cooking, to heat through.

5) To serve, spoon the lentils on one side of a plate and the ragoût on the other side, with slices of sausage down the middle. Sprinkle with parsley and serve. Pass the mustard at the table.

For the lentils:

1 tablespoon olive oil

1 large carrot, chopped

1 large stalk celery, diced

1 small onion, chopped

1 1/2 cups green lentils, rinsed

4 cups water

1 teaspoon kosher salt

1/2 teaspoon freshly ground black pepper

To finish the dish:

1 cup red wine

1 cup Veal Stock (pages 308–9), Chicken Stock (page 307), or low-sodium canned broth

Kosher salt and freshly ground black pepper

1 tablespoon cold unsalted butter

1 1/2 to 2 pounds French, Polish, or other good-quality precooked sausage, preferably garlic

1 recipe Potato-Onion Ragoût (page 211; see step 4)

Chopped fresh parsley or chives or a combination

Dijon mustard

GOLDEN GERMAN-STYLE LAGER WORKS WELL WITH THE RICH SAUSAGE AND NUTTY LENTILS.

MATCH WITH A PUNCHY CHÂTEAUNEUF-DU-PAPE OR A CALIFORNIA ZINFANDEL.

Mediterranean Navarin of Lamb

Navarin of lamb is the kind of unpretentious and flavorful dish we never tire of—and we are certainly not alone. Most French bistros and brasseries have a selection of favorite dishes like this one that rotate on and off the menu with the seasons or appear weekly as a plat du jour. Since a neighborhood brasserie is the kind of restaurant you might eat in two or three times a week, you quickly learn to plan your week around the knowledge that Tuesday is navarin d'agneau, *Thursday* coq au vin, *Saturday a festive* couscous royale, *and so on.*

Navet is French for turnip, and without turnips your stew will not be a navarin, but parsnips or potatoes can be substituted if you prefer them. Fennel and rosemary add the scent of Provence to this satisfying stew.

Serve with Spiced Hummus (page 200).

¹/4 cup olive oil

4 pounds boneless lamb for stew, cut into 1-inch cubes

1 large bulb fennel, trimmed and diced

3 medium turnips, peeled and diced

4 medium carrots, cut into 1-inch chunks

2 stalks celery, cut into 1-inch chunks

1 medium onion, diced

3 garlic cloves, minced

1 pound mixed shiitake, cremini, and button mushrooms

1 cup brandy or Cognac

1) In a large heavy pot, heat the oil over medium-high heat until it is hot but not smoking. Add half of the lamb and sauté, stirring occasionally, until the meat is browned on all sides. Remove from the pot and repeat with the remaining lamb.

2) Add the fennel, turnips, carrots, celery, onion, and garlic. Cook, stirring, until the vegetables are softened, about 5 minutes.

3) Remove the stems from the shiitake mushrooms and slice all the mushrooms ¹/4 inch thick. When the vegetables have cooked 5 minutes, add the mushrooms to the pot. Cook 5 minutes more.

4) Add the brandy and cook until it is reduced by half. Add the wine, rosemary, thyme, salt, and pepper. Mix well and simmer for 5 minutes.

5) Add the stock, raise the heat, and bring the stew to a boil. Skim off any scum that rises to the top. Reduce to a simmer and cook, uncovered, skimming as necessary and stirring occasionally, about 2 hours, until the lamb is cooked through and extremely tender. Start tasting the meat after about 1 1/2 hours. When it is almost done, squeeze the oranges and add their juice to the stew. Keep cooking until the meat is tender and the sauce is thick enough to coat the back of a spoon.

6) At the last moment, add the butter and tomatoes and stir until all the butter is melted. Transfer the stew to a serving bowl or serve on individual plates. Sprinkle each serving with chopped and whole cilantro leaves.

2 cups dry red wine

2 tablespoons chopped fresh rosemary

2 tablespoons fresh thyme leaves

1 teaspoon kosher salt

1/2 teaspoon freshly ground black pepper

4 cups Veal Stock (pages 308–9), Chicken Stock (page 307), or low-sodium canned broth

2 large oranges

3 tablespoons cold unsalted butter, cut into pieces

6 plum tomatoes, diced

Fresh cilantro, chopped and whole leaves

DRINK A TOASTY STOUT WITH CARAMEL NOTES WITH THIS WARMING, HEARTY DISH.

LOOK FOR A CRU BEAUJOLAIS OR DOLCETTO.

Marinated Rib-Eye Steaks with Tobacco Onions

SERVES 4

When you run a restaurant in Chicago, you have to give some serious thought to steak. The city was built around stockyards that turned the West's cattle into beef for the rest of the country, and Chicagoans still consider themselves the best judges around of what makes a good steak. With competition from extraordinary steakhouses like Morton's, Gibson's, and Gene and Georgetti, where teams of butchers devote their full attention to cutting and aging the finest beef, how do you get brasserie customers to try your rib-eye?

Our favorite approach: marinating the meat in a savory, spicy mixture that infuses the finished steaks with more flavor and fire than plain grilling. This method works beautifully for home cooking. Steaks with this much going for them don't need any sauce at all, but the contrast from a nest of crunchy, salty-sweet onions on top is fantastic. At Paris's La Coupole and most other brasseries, a similar effect is achieved by serving the spitting-hot steaks on beds of fresh watercress: the cool pepperiness of the greens sets off the flavor and texture of the meat. Feel free to drop the onions and try that instead. When you buy your steaks, the butcher might use the term T-bone instead of rib-eye; the cut is identical.

Serve with Blue Cheese Double-Baked Potatoes (page 212).

For the steaks:
**One 12-ounce bottle brown or pale ale,
    such as Newcastle or Sierra Nevada**
1 cup olive oil
1 medium red onion, finely chopped
4 garlic cloves

1) The day before you plan to serve the dish, marinate the steaks: Combine the ale, oil, onion, garlic, rosemary, peppercorns, and pepper flakes in a blender and process until very smooth. Put the steaks in a nonreactive dish, pour the marinade over them, and mix to coat on all sides. Refrigerate, covered, overnight. Turn the steaks over occasionally.

2) When you are ready to cook, remove the steaks from the marinade and drain on a rack. Discard the marinade and season with salt and pepper to taste.

3) Make the onions: preheat the oven to 300°F and line an ovenproof plate with paper towels.

4) Heat the oil in a deep pot or deep-fryer to 350°F. In a large mixing bowl, combine the flour, paprika, cayenne, black pepper, and salt. Toss the shredded onions in the flour, then lift the onions out of the bowl with your hands, shaking to get rid of excess flour. Drop into the hot oil and fry until crisp and golden brown. Remove with tongs to the towel-lined plate and sprinkle with salt. Keep hot in the oven until ready to serve.

5) Meanwhile, preheat a charcoal grill, broiler, or cast-iron skillet until very hot. Working in batches if necessary to avoid crowding the pan, sear the steaks for 4 minutes on one side. Then turn and finish cooking on the other side, until done to your liking.

6) Drizzle steaks with olive oil. Serve with a mound of onions on top.

2 teaspoons fresh or dried rosemary

1 teaspoon cracked black peppercorns

$1/2$ teaspoon red pepper flakes

Four 10-ounce bone-in rib-eye steaks, about $1^1/2$ inches thick

Kosher salt and freshly ground black pepper

2 teaspoons extra-virgin olive oil (optional)

For the onions:

5 cups corn oil, for frying

1 cup all-purpose flour

1 teaspoon hot or sweet paprika or a combination

$1/2$ teaspoon cayenne pepper

1 teaspoon freshly ground black pepper

1 teaspoon kosher salt, plus extra for sprinkling

2 large onions, red or yellow, halved lengthwise and very thinly sliced

THESE INTENSE FLAVORS CALL FOR A FULL-FLAVORED PORTER.

MATCH WITH BORDEAUX OR A STRUCTURED CALIFORNIA CABERNET.

Weekend Cooking

Portofino Bouillabaisse

Spring Vegetable and Rabbit Fricassee

Fish and Chips in Peppery Amber Beer Batter

Lemon-Sage Roast Chicken with Sausage-Mushroom-Potato Stuffing

Cassoulet

Roast Pork Loin with Armagnac-Prune Stuffing

Pork Chops with Barley Ragoût, Apple Cabbage Compote, and Mustard Sauce

Veal Milanese with Red Wine Sauce, Artichokes, and Cremini Mushrooms

Osso Buco with Saffron Risotto and Orange Gremolata

Provençal Lamb Shanks with Roasted Vegetables, Roasted Garlic, and Tapenade

Hazelnut-Crusted Rack of Lamb

Pot-au-Feu

Civet of Venison and Wild Mushrooms

Mustard-Crust Sweetbreads with Madeira and Morels

Portofino Bouillabaisse

SERVES 4 TO 6

You never forget your first real bouillabaisse. That may sound like an awfully romantic thing to say about fish stew, but it's true. In our memory of that day, the brilliant Riviera sunshine blends with the golden saffron color of the dish, the salt air blowing off the Mediterranean becomes one with the briny scent of the stew, and in the middle of a midwestern January we haul out the photo album to reminisce about the classic bouillabaisse served to us at Le Tetou in the French resort town of Golfe-Juan.

Bouillabaisse is the kind of dish you build in your bowl, starting with a ladleful from a tureen of thick orange broth reddened with tomatoes. Next comes a bowl of glistening potatoes, boiled soft in fish stock, olive oil, and more saffron. The rouille, a thick emulsion bursting with olive oil and hot peppers, arrives with a bowl of crisp croutons to spread it on. The fish and shellfish are piled high on separate platters and placed in the center of the table within everyone's reach. And finally, when all your senses are unbearably stimulated by the feast in front of you, the eating begins.

That memorable bouillabaisse was served to us on the French side of the border, but as we pushed on into Italy we found the pescatores and ciuppins of the Ligurian coast very similar, except for the addition of—you guessed it—pasta. We think you'll appreciate the substance it adds, making the dish into a whole fish-pasta-soup meal. Our choice of shellfish and fish for this recipe is dictated by what is available to us, and it will yield excellent results; but feel free to add or subtract according to your taste. To experience a truly authentic bouillabaisse with Mediterranean seafood, your local fishmonger will not be much help; you'll have to call the travel agent instead, to book a trip to Portofino!

1) Make the rouille: in a food processor, combine the chile, soaking water, potato, and stock and pulse to a paste. Add the egg yolk, garlic, and saffron and pulse to combine. With the motor running, add the light olive oil in a thin stream until the mixture emulsifies. Transfer to a serving bowl and add cayenne, salt, black pepper, and lemon juice to taste.

2) Bring a large pot of salted water to a boil. Add the pasta, stir, and cook until tender but still firm, 8 to 10 minutes. Drain well, rinse with cold water, toss in the 2 tablespoons olive oil, and set aside.

3) Meanwhile, clean the mussels: put them in the sink and cover them with cold water. Swish them around vigorously in the sink, rubbing them against each other to remove sand and grit, then drain the water and rinse out the sand that remains. Repeat until no sand remains in the sink. Discard any mussels with cracked shells. Pull the beard from the side of each mussel with your fingers, or use your fingers and a paring knife for a better grip.

4) Rinse the clams and crab legs in cold water and set aside.

5) Cut the fish into 2-inch chunks and season on both sides with salt, black pepper, and cayenne.

6) In a large deep pot, heat the remaining oil over medium-high heat. Add the onion, garlic, carrots, celery, and fennel. Cook, stirring, until softened and the onion is translucent. Do not let the vegetables brown; lower the heat if necessary.

7) Add the lobster and crab legs, stirring gently. Add the orange juice and lemon juice and simmer 3 minutes.

8) Add the Pernod and wine and simmer 5 minutes to reduce by half. Add the tomatoes, bay leaf, thyme, and saffron and continue simmering, breaking up the tomatoes with a spoon.

For the rouille:

1 small dried red chile, stemmed and soaked in 2 tablespoons warm water until softened (reserve water)

1 medium Idaho potato, peeled, cut into chunks, and boiled in salted water until fork-tender

6 tablespoons Fish Stock (page 310) or clam juice

1 large egg yolk

4 garlic cloves, minced

Pinch of saffron threads

6 to 8 tablespoons light olive oil

Cayenne pepper

Kosher salt and freshly ground black pepper

Freshly squeezed lemon juice

To finish the dish:

8 ounces tubetti, ditalini, or other small chunky pasta

1/2 cup olive oil, plus 2 tablespoons

16 black mussels in their shells

8 littleneck clams in their shells

4 whole king crab legs in their shells

1 pound skinless monkfish or halibut fillets

Kosher salt and freshly ground black pepper

1/4 teaspoon cayenne pepper, or to taste

1 large onion, diced

4 large garlic cloves, minced

2 large carrots, cut into 1/2-inch cubes

2 large celery stalks, cut into 1/2-inch cubes

1 small or 1/2 large bulb fennel, cut into 1/2-inch cubes

1 lobster tail in the shell, sliced 1 inch thick

1/2 cup freshly squeezed orange juice

1/4 cup freshly squeezed lemon juice

1/2 cup Pernod, Ricard, or other anise liqueur

2 cups dry, light-bodied white wine

One 32-ounce can Italian plum tomatoes, drained

1 bay leaf

1 sprig fresh thyme

1/2 teaspoon saffron threads

6 cups Fish Stock (page 310) or clam juice

8 sea scallops

8 jumbo shrimp, peeled and deveined

8 tablespoons (1 stick) cold unsalted butter, cut into pieces

Chopped fresh parsley

3 boiled potatoes, quartered

1 thin baguette, sliced 1/4 inch thick and toasted

9) Add the stock to the bouillabaisse and bring to a boil. Add the scallops, shrimp, and fish and simmer 6 to 8 minutes, just until the fish is cooked through. Do not let it overcook.

10) Heat oven to 250°F and put the serving bowls in to heat them.

11) Lift the fish and shellfish from the pot and divide it among the hot serving bowls. Ladle a little bit of liquid over each and place in the oven while you finish the dish.

12) Raise the heat and boil the mixture until the liquid is reduced slightly. Whisk in the butter and stir in the pasta.

13) Remove bowls of fish from the oven and serve. Fill each bowl with soup and sprinkle with parsley. Pass the boiled potatoes; they should be dunked in the soup. Pass the toasted bread and rouille, spreading the rouille on the toasts and floating them in the soup.

TRY A PROVENÇAL CASSIS WHITE OR ROSÉ OR ANY FLOWERY, FRESH WHITE FROM A COASTAL REGION.

Spring Vegetable and Rabbit Fricassee

SERVES 4 TO 6

The word fricassee has an American ring to it, but the method of the dish is traditionally French; and to really confuse the issue, food expert Giuliano Bugialli contends that the name comes from the Italian word fracassare. *It means "to break things up into pieces," and certainly describes what happens to the rabbit or chicken you are planning to cook this way. French brasserie and bistro tradition includes plenty of hearty, satisfying rabbit stews, but some of our customers at Brasserie T have had to be persuaded to try rabbit. Young rabbit isn't gamy or tough, as they feared; instead, it has a mild flavor and meaty texture that can take strong flavors like bacon, thyme, cream, and mustard.* Cipolline *are Italian onions that are flat on the bottom and the top, with a delicate sweetness. They are sometimes available in particularly well-stocked supermarkets or Italian produce shops, but whole shallots are an excellent substitute.*

With so many overtenderized and flavorless chickens available in supermarkets today, a young rabbit is a better option than chicken for many stews. In a substantial fricasee like this one, where the meat is browned in bacon fat, floured, and napped with a fresh white sauce along with plenty of crisp-tender vegetables, rabbit makes an ideal spring dinner for guests and family. The rabbits can be bought already cut up.

1) Blanch the vegetables: bring a large pot of salted water (preferably one with a strainer insert) to a boil over high heat. Fill a large bowl or pot with ice cubes and cover with cold water.

2) When the water boils, add the *cipolline* and boil until crisp-tender, about 5 minutes. Lift the *cipolline* from the boiling water and plunge into ice water to stop the cooking. When cool to the

24 whole peeled *cipolline* or small shallots

3 medium carrots, sliced $1/4$ inch thick

18 medium asparagus stalks, cut into 2-inch lengths

$1^1/2$ cups fresh or best-quality frozen peas

1 tablespoon olive oil

8 ounces slab bacon, cut into $1/2$-inch cubes

1 cup all-purpose flour

$1/2$ teaspoon kosher salt

$1/4$ teaspoon freshly ground black pepper

Two 2- to $2^1/2$-pound rabbits, cut into serving pieces

2 stalks celery, sliced $1/4$ inch thick

1 medium onion, chopped

6 garlic cloves, minced

1 Bouquet Garni (page 297)

$1/4$ cup Cognac or brandy

1 cup dry white wine

3 cups Veal Stock (pages 308–9), Chicken Stock (page 307), or low-sodium canned broth

$1^1/2$ cups Mushroom Mix (pages 294–95)

1 cup heavy cream

$2^1/2$ tablespoons Dijon mustard

Pinch of sugar

Kosher salt and freshly ground black pepper

3 tablespoons cold cubed butter

Chopped fresh chives

touch, set aside to drain. Repeat with the carrots, boiling about 10 minutes. Repeat with the asparagus, boiling about 5 minutes. Repeat with the peas, boiling 2 to 4 minutes, depending on their size and freshness.

3) In a large skillet with a lid, heat the oil over medium-high heat. Add the bacon and cook, stirring, just until golden brown. Do not overcook. Remove the bacon pieces and drain on paper towels. Reserve the oil in the pan.

4) Meanwhile, in a shallow dish or plate, combine the flour, salt, and pepper. Rinse the rabbit pieces under cold running water and drain on paper towels.

5) Working in batches if necessary to avoid crowding the pan, dredge the rabbit pieces in the flour and add to the hot bacon fat in the pan. Cook over medium-high heat until golden on both sides. Remove from the pan and set aside. If necessary, repeat with remaining rabbit pieces.

6) If more than 2 tablespoons of fat remain in the pan, pour off the excess. Add the celery, onion, and garlic and cook over medium-high heat until the onion is translucent, 5 to 8 minutes. Do not let the vegetables brown; reduce the heat if necessary. Add the bouquet garni.

7) Add the Cognac. Return to the stove carefully to prevent flaming. Cook, stirring to scrape up the browned bits from the bottom of the pan with a wooden spoon.

8) Return all the rabbit pieces to the pan and add the wine. Simmer to reduce the liquid by half. Add the stock and bring to a simmer. Reduce the heat to low, cover, and cook 30 to 40 minutes.

9) Uncover and add the *cipolline*, carrots, asparagus, peas, bacon, and mushrooms. Cook over low heat, stirring occasionally, until the rabbit and vegetables are tender and cooked through, 10 to 15 minutes more. Remove the bouquet garni and stir in the cream. Bring to a boil. Whisk in the mustard and sugar. Add salt and pepper to taste and whisk in the butter.

10) Transfer to a large serving dish and sprinkle with chives.

TRY ROBUST, STRUCTURED REDS LIKE GIGONDAS OR CORNAS FROM FRANCE OR A FULL-BODIED RHÔNE-STYLE VIOGNIER FROM CALIFORNIA.

Fish and Chips in Peppery Amber Beer Batter

SERVES 6 TO 8

Fish fried in a crisp, golden beer batter and served with fried potatoes is a late-night classic, the British equivalent of a plat brasserie. We learned how good fish and chips can be on our very first night in England. Jet-lagged, we awoke ravenous at 2 A.M. Our new boss, Bob Payton, hustled us into the car and drove off into the dark, sleeping countryside. After so many years living in Chicago and New York City, we couldn't imagine what this silent farmland in the middle of nowhere could have in store as a late-night snack. Around a bend, suddenly we were in the midst of a crowd. The local pub had just pushed the last patrons out the door, and the "nippy chippy," a van with the apparatus for making fish and chips, had driven up to feed the hungry mob. We joined the line and were rewarded with warm bundles of fried fish and French fries sprinkled with malt vinegar and wrapped in newspaper. It was one of our best meals in England.

Fish and chips are no longer legally wrapped in newspaper, although we know of one posh restaurant that serves an upscale version wrapped in layers of parchment and a page from the Financial Times. *Our version adds cayenne to the batter, but if you are making this for kids, you may want to reduce it somewhat. The malt vinegar should accent, not soak, the dish; use it as you would a squeeze of lemon.*

Serve with Caraway Coleslaw (page 195).

For the batter:

One 12-ounce bottle amber beer, such as Murphy's Irish or New Amsterdam, at room temperature

1) Make the batter: combine the beer and yeast in a mixing bowl. One by one, whisk in the eggs. Stir in the flour, salt, black pepper, and cayenne and set aside until ready to use.

2) Fry the chips: heat at least 4 inches of oil in a large deep-fryer or deep kettle to about 325°F. Make sure the oil does not come too close to the top of the pot; it will bubble up as the fish and chips are added. Line a baking sheet with paper towels and preheat the oven to 250°F.

3) Test the oil with one piece of potato to make sure it cooks evenly and does not burn. Working in batches to make sure the oil remains very hot at all times, fry the potatoes about 4 minutes, until golden brown outside and tender within. With a slotted spoon or tongs, remove to the baking sheet to drain, then sprinkle lightly with salt and pepper. Place the baking sheet in the oven (leave the door ajar) to keep warm while you repeat the process with the remaining potatoes.

4) Fry the fish: make sure the frying oil is heated to 325°F, and line another baking sheet with paper towels.

5) Toss the flour with the salt and pepper and spread out on a plate. Working in batches, lightly dredge the cod in the flour and shake off any excess flour. Dip the cod in the batter and shake off any excess batter. Fry about 4 minutes, until golden brown. With a slotted spoon or tongs, remove to the lined baking sheet to drain, then sprinkle lightly with salt and pepper. Place the baking sheet in the oven (leave the door ajar) to keep warm while you repeat the process with the remaining fish.

6) When all the fish is cooked, remove everything from the oven. Arrange the fish pieces in the center of a platter, then arrange the potatoes around them. Sprinkle with parsley, then place the lemon wedges around the platter.

7) Serve immediately, passing vinegar at the table.

1 package (^{1}/4 ounce) active dry yeast

3 large eggs

2 cups all-purpose flour

1^1/2 teaspoons kosher salt, plus extra for sprinkling

1 teaspoon freshly ground black pepper, plus extra for sprinkling

1 teaspoon cayenne pepper, or to taste

For the chips:

Oil for deep-frying (we recommend half peanut, half corn)

3 pounds Idaho potatoes, scrubbed and cut lengthwise into ^{1}/4-inch-thick batons

Kosher salt and freshly ground black pepper

For the fish:

1 cup all-purpose flour

1 teaspoon kosher salt

^{1}/2 teaspoon freshly ground black pepper

3 pounds boneless cod fillets, cut into large "fingers"

Chopped fresh parsley, chives, or a combination

Lemon wedges

Malt vinegar

A TRADITIONAL, FULL-BODIED MALTY BRITISH BITTER ALE IS A MUST WITH THIS DISH.

Lemon-Sage Roast Chicken with Sausage-Mushroom-Potato Stuffing

SERVES 6 TO 8

We love all kinds of great roasted chicken and eat it at least three to four times a week. There's something elementally satisfying about any well-roasted chicken, but we are especially proud of our version. We love to watch our customers lean over their plates to inhale the heady fragrance of fresh sage, savory sausage, bosky mushrooms, and sharp lemon. This is a grand but still friendly dish that is perfect for guests, and it's easy on you because there's no carving involved. Your only challenge is trying to save some stuffing for the next day—we never have any leftovers!

It's very important to slice the lemons as thinly as possible so that they don't overpower the dish.

For the chicken:

Two 3^{1}/$_2$- to 4-pound chickens, quartered

20 whole fresh sage leaves

2 lemons, very thinly sliced

^{1}/$_4$ cup Garlic Oil and Puree (page 292), or ^{1}/$_4$ cup olive oil mixed with 3 minced garlic cloves

Kosher salt and freshly ground black pepper

3 cups Chicken Stock (page 307) or low-sodium canned broth

For the stuffing:

12 ounces (6 cups) shiitake, cremini, or oyster mushrooms, or a combination, wiped clean

1) Preheat the oven to 400°F.

2) Under the skin of each chicken quarter, tuck 2 sage leaves and 1 lemon slice. Arrange the quarters on a wire rack in a large roasting pan, brush with the garlic oil, and season generously with salt and pepper. Roast without basting until the skin is golden brown and the flesh is almost cooked through—about 30 minutes.

3) Pour the chicken stock around, not over, the chicken quarters into the roasting pan. Place 1 slice of lemon on top of each chicken quarter and continue roasting until the juices run clear and a leg moves easily in its socket, about 20 minutes more.

4) Meanwhile, make the stuffing: remove and discard the stems of the shiitakes. Cut the shiitake caps and the creminis in quarters.

With your hands, pull the oyster mushrooms apart into bite-size pieces. In a large skillet, melt the butter over medium-high heat. Add the mushrooms and sauté until tender and mushrooms start to give off their liquid, about 5 minutes. Transfer to a bowl with their liquid and set aside.

5) Add the pure olive oil to the skillet and heat over medium-high heat. Add the potatoes and pan-fry, stirring occasionally, until golden brown and cooked through, about 15 minutes. Remove the potatoes from the pan and set aside.

6) Wipe out the skillet, then crumble the sausage into it and cook, stirring, over medium-high heat until the sausage is just beginning to brown, about 5 minutes. Add the onions and garlic and cook until the sausage is thoroughly browned, about 5 minutes more.

7) Add the sage, basil, bread cubes, tomatoes, potatoes, and mushroom mixture to the pan and mix to combine, adding a ladleful of stock if needed to moisten the mixture. Season to taste with salt and pepper. Cook, stirring, until heated through.

8) When the chicken is done, remove from the oven and set aside to rest on a carving board or platter, covered with foil, at least 10 minutes.

9) Meanwhile, make the sauce: strain the juices from the roasting pan into a saucepan and skim off any fat floating on the top. Bring to a boil over high heat, reduce by one-third, then add the garlic and salt and pepper to taste. Turn off the heat and immediately whisk in the butter.

10) Serve the dish: divide the stuffing on plates. Place a chicken quarter on each plate and then drizzle with a spoonful of sauce. Sprinkle with the chives and serve immediately.

6 tablespoons unsalted butter

$1/4$ cup pure olive oil

4 large Idaho potatoes, peeled and cut into $3/4$-inch cubes

$1^1/2$ pounds bulk sweet or hot Italian sausage

4 medium red onions, halved and thinly sliced lengthwise

4 garlic cloves, minced

2 tablespoons minced fresh sage

$1/3$ cup minced fresh basil

4 cups $1/2$-inch cubes sourdough bread

1 cup chopped sun-dried tomatoes, packed in oil or reconstituted

1 cup Chicken Stock (page 307) or low-sodium canned broth

Kosher salt and freshly ground black pepper

For the sauce:

1 large garlic clove, minced

Kosher salt and freshly ground black pepper

4 tablespoons ($1/2$ stick) unsalted butter

1 tablespoon chopped fresh chives, parsley, chervil, or a combination

DRINK A DARK LAGER OR BRITISH-STYLE BROWN ALE WITH THIS ROBUST DISH.

TRY A FRUITY DOLCETTO OR A YOUNG SPANISH RIOJA.

Cassoulet

After all these years, the southwestern towns of Toulouse, Carcassonne, and Casteldnaudary are still fighting over who makes the real, authentic cassoulet, and there's no decision in sight. The most famous brasserie in the region, Le Bibent of Toulouse, makes their famous cassoulet Toulousain *with preserved duck, sausages, pork shoulder, and pork rind, but some would say that a cassoulet without mutton is no cassoulet at all. Other locals protest against the use of duck, insisting that the region's celebrated geese must appear in the dish. In other parts of France, cassoulet is likely to appear as a much-loved winter special, as at the welcoming art nouveau Paris brasserie called Julien—also famous for its magnificent painted-glass panels of young women representing the four seasons.*

Our cassoulet is a bit lighter and less fatty than the original. We've cut way down on the amount of meat in the dish and lightened the texture with a big dose of bright-flavored tomatoes. Our seasoned breadcrumbs make a savory crust, traditionally broken and pushed down into the stew at the table to absorb the juices. (However, this step can be omitted if you like.) Making a confit, which effectively combines cooking and preserving, is virtually unknown in American cooking today. But in France, especially in the goose-raising lands of the Perigord and Alsace, enticing jars of luxurious con-fit d'oie (preserved goose) still draw passersby to every butcher's window. We prefer the meatier, more flavorful confit de canard *(duck) and encourage you to make it at home for the best flavor. Covered with its own fat and kept cool, confit lasts up to two months. When you make the cassoulet, do save the fat from the confit; it makes the most incredible fried potatoes. Your butcher can easily order duck legs for you; duck fat can be bought at gourmet stores, but fresh vegetable oil is fine. The cassoulet and confit can both be made well in advance, reheated, and combined at the last minute.*

1) At least 2 days and up to 2 weeks before serving the dish, begin the confit: thickly coat the duck legs with salt, pepper, orange zest, garlic, and juniper berries, massaging the seasonings into the skin and flesh. Press the thyme sprigs against the legs and place them on a plate or in a dish. Cover with a clean towel and refrigerate 48 hours.

2) Preheat the oven to 350°F.

3) Use your fingers to brush the seasonings off the duck legs, then dry them with a kitchen towel. Do not rinse the legs but do clean them well with your towel.

4) In an ovenproof heavy-bottomed pot, heat 1 tablespoon of the oil over medium-high heat. Working in batches to avoid crowding the pan, and adding the remaining oil if necessary, sear the duck legs on both sides until the skin is browned and crisp.

5) When all the duck pieces are browned, return them to the pot and cover with the duck fat. Cover and bake for at least 3 to 4 hours, until the meat is cooked, very tender, and almost falling off the bone. Carefully lift the legs out of the pot and let cool on wire racks, reserving the fat. When the legs are cool, put them in a bowl, cover them with the fat, cover tightly with plastic wrap, and refrigerate up to 2 weeks, until you are ready to make the cassoulet. This is a preserving technique.

6) A least one day before you plan to serve the cassoulet, soak the beans in a gallon of cold water.

7) The next day, drain the beans, put them in a pot, and cover with fresh unsalted water. Bring to a simmer and cook for about 30 to 40 minutes, adding water as needed, until almost completely soft (they will cook a little more later in the recipe). Drain the beans and refrigerate until ready to make the cassoulet.

8) When you are ready to make the cassoulet, heat the olive oil in a large heavy pot over medium-high heat. Add the garlic and

For the duck confit:

6 whole duck legs, including thighs

Kosher salt and freshly ground black pepper

Grated zest of 3 large oranges

2 large garlic cloves, minced

3 cups juniper berries, crushed in a mortar or grinder

1 bunch fresh thyme

2 tablespoons olive oil

5 cups duck fat, vegetable oil, or a combination

For the cassoulet:

1 pound dried cannellini, great Northern, flageolet, or other small white beans

$1/4$ cup plus 1 tablespoon olive oil

8 large garlic cloves, minced

2 large onions, chopped

1 pound slab bacon, cut into $1/2$-inch cubes

4 large carrots, cut into $1/2$-inch cubes

8 stalks celery, cut into $1/2$-inch cubes

2 pounds smoked pork butt, cut into 1-inch cubes

2 pounds smoked sausages such as Thuringer or kielbasa, sliced into 1-inch pieces

1 pound stewing lamb, cut into 1-inch cubes

2 quarts hot Veal Stock (pages 308–9), Chicken Stock (page 307), or low-sodium canned broth

4 bay leaves

6 sprigs fresh thyme, tied together with twine

One 28-ounce can Italian plum tomatoes

6 tablespoons tomato paste

Kosher salt and freshly ground black pepper to taste

About 2 cups Seasoned Breadcrumbs (page 306) (optional)

4 sprigs whole thyme

Chopped fresh parsley

onions and cook, stirring, for 2 minutes. Add the bacon and cook, stirring, until it begins to brown. Add the carrots, celery, pork butt, sausage chunks, and lamb cubes and cook for 10 minutes, stirring occasionally, until the vegetables have browned.

9) Add the stock, bay leaves, thyme, and tomatoes and stir to combine, breaking up the tomatoes with a spoon. Simmer, uncovered, stirring occasionally, for 40 minutes.

10) Meanwhile, preheat the oven to 450°F.

11) Lift the duck legs from the bowl (some fat will adhere to them) and place, fleshy side down, on a baking sheet with sides. Bake until hot and crispy, about 15 minutes, or until heated all the way through. Do not let them dry out.

12) Add the beans and tomato paste to the cassoulet and stir to combine. Add some boiling water if the mixture seems too thick.

13) Simmer until the beans are cooked through and soft, about 15 minutes more. Season to taste with salt and pepper. (The cassoulet can be prepared to this point up to 2 days in advance and reheated in the oven with the duck at serving time.)

14) Preheat the oven to 325°F. Spoon the cassoulet into individual ovenproof serving bowls or one large casserole dish and arrange the duck legs on top, pressing them lightly into the mixture. Sprinkle the breadcrumbs, if desired, on top and bake until the mixture is piping hot and the crust is golden brown on top, 10 to 15 minutes.

15) Serve with a sprig of thyme stuck into each serving and a sprinkling of parsley on top.

Roast Pork Loin with Armagnac-Prune Stuffing

SERVES 8 TO 10

Pork and prunes are a time-honored flavor combination in the Loire valley, and prunes and Armagnac have a natural taste affinity as well. Armagnac, like Cognac, is a strictly controlled French appellation; only certain brandies, all made in a certain region of Gascony and in a certain rich, aromatic style, can be called Armagnac on the bottle. Designed in 1919 to protect both producers and consumers, the French system of labeling wine has become big business, and the competition to secure AOC—appellation d'origine contrôlée—status is intense.

Today the system has been expanded to include food as well: the names of Bresse poultry, Le Puy lentils, Roquefort cheese, Charentes butter, even Grenoble walnuts are "owned" by producers who observe certain traditions, and are legally protected by the Institut National des Appellations d'Origine. In other words, just because you happen to live in the town of Bresse and raise chickens, it is not legal for you to sell them in the market as "Bresse chickens." The AOC system is one of the more tangible proofs that the French really do take food more seriously than the rest of the world.

Fortunately, even anonymous ingredients make wonderful food. The pork we find at butcher shops and supermarkets these days is so lean that it requires moist cooking and a lot of aromatics to give it extra flavor.

Serve with Sweet Potato–Apple Puree (page 207).

2 cups pitted prunes

1 cup Armagnac, Cognac, or port

One 4-pound boneless pork loin (not the tenderloin)

Kosher salt and freshly ground black pepper

2 tablespoons olive oil

1 garlic clove, minced

4 ounces cremini mushrooms, stems trimmed, sliced $^1/_4$ inch thick

4 ounces shiitake mushrooms, stems removed and discarded, sliced $^1/_4$ inch thick

10 ounces fresh spinach, thick stems removed, well washed and dried

Herb Oil (page 293) or Herb Mix (page 296)

1) The day before you plan to serve the roast, chop the prunes with a sharp knife, put them in a bowl, and pour the Armagnac over them. Marinate, stirring occasionally, at least 24 hours.

2) When ready to make the roast, drain the prunes and reserve the marinating liquid.

3) Preheat the oven to 425°F.

4) If using a rolled roast, untie it, lay it flat on a clean counter, and trim it of all fat and sinew. If there are sections that seem especially thick, cut slashes in them with a sharp knife. Proceed to step 6).

5) If using a whole loin, lay it parallel to the counter edge and cut a deep horizontal slash along the length of the loin, about halfway through to the back. You now have 2 long half-cylinder pieces that are joined along one long edge. Slash each of these halves in the same manner, again without cutting through to the back. Trim the roast of all fat and sinew and lay it down on the seam.

6) With a meat tenderizer, heavy rolling pin, or wine bottle, pound the pork into a large rectangle as evenly as possible. You should be able to get it to about $^1/_2$-inch thickness without breaking the meat. Don't be concerned if the shape is not very even. Season with plenty of salt and pepper and set aside while you make the stuffing.

7) Heat the oil and garlic in a skillet over high heat. Add the mushrooms and cook, stirring, until they release their juices and begin to brown. Add the spinach and toss, cooking just until slightly wilted. Immediately remove from the heat and set aside; the spinach will continue to cook as it cools.

8) Along one long edge of the pork, arrange the prunes. In a parallel line about 2 inches away, arrange the spinach and mushrooms.

Starting at the prune edge, firmly roll the pork up into a log. With kitchen twine, tie loops snugly around the log at 1-inch intervals. This will help keep the shape during the roasting.

9) Place the pork on a rack in a roasting pan and roast 15 minutes. Baste with the reserved prune marinating liquid, lower the heat to 350°F, and roast for 1 to 1^1/2 hours, until the internal temperature reaches 160°F.

10) Let rest 15 minutes, then cut into 1-inch-thick slices. Serve sprinkled with herb oil or herb mix.

A RICH WHITE IS YOUR BEST CHOICE HERE, SUCH AS FULL-BODIED ALSATIAN OR AUSTRIAN RIESLING OR PINOT GRIS.

Pork Chops with Barley Ragoût, Apple Cabbage Compote, and Mustard Sauce

SERVES 4

Pork and cabbage are constant companions on Alsatian restaurant menus, where a pork chop is considered a light snack: instead of just a chop, you're likely to be presented with an entire shoulder or shank of meat on top of several pounds of delicately steaming choucroute (sauerkraut) as lunch for one. The choucroute is made from the huge crinkly-leafed round cabbages that march in rows all over the region's farmland. If you fly into Strasbourg in September, as we did, the cabbages growing outside the city are so big that you can identify them from the air.

In the nearby wine center of Riquewihr, a perfectly preserved sixteenth-century town, the renowned wine producer Preiss-Zimmer runs a traditional Alsatian restaurant called Le Tire-Bouchon, "The Corkscrew." The friendly winstubs of Alsace, casual restaurants often owned by local winemakers or wine cooperatives, serve hearty rustic food that often reflects the combined German and French culture of the region. Here's our interpretation, in which a creamy grain ragoût provides substance and an elegant mustard sauce brightens the flavors.

For the mustard sauce:

1³/4 cups Chicken Stock (page 307) or low-sodium canned broth

³/4 cup heavy cream

1 tablespoon coarse-grain country mustard

Kosher salt and freshly ground black pepper

1 tablespoon cornstarch

2 tablespoons white wine or dry vermouth

1) Make the sauce: in a saucepan, combine the stock and cream over low heat. Bring to a simmer and reduce by half.

2) Whisk in the mustard and salt and pepper to taste and raise the heat to medium. In a small bowl, whisk together the cornstarch and wine. When the mustard mixture comes to a boil, whisk in the cornstarch mixture. Simmer the sauce for 5 minutes, then cover and set aside while you finish making the dish.

3) Rub each pork chop on both sides with 1 teaspoon olive oil and season generously with salt and pepper. Set aside.

4) Make the ragoût: in a saucepan, heat 2 tablespoons of the butter and the olive oil. Add the celery, carrot, onion, and garlic and cook, stirring, until softened, about 5 minutes. Add the stock, stir, and bring to a simmer. Add the barley, stir, and cook, covered, about 10 minutes. Add the lentils, stir, and continue cooking until both grains are tender, about 40 minutes more (about 50 minutes total). When the grains are cooked, stir in the remaining 2 tablespoons of butter and season with salt and pepper to taste.

5) Meanwhile, in a large skillet, cook the bacon until browned and almost crisp. Without turning off the heat, remove the bacon with a slotted spoon. To the fat in the pan, add the cabbage, onion, and garlic and cook over medium heat, stirring, until tender, about 8 minutes. If necessary, add a little water to the pan to prevent the cabbage from browning too much.

6) Add the apples, orange juice, and brown sugar and cook just until the apples are softened, about 3 minutes. Stir in the bacon and add salt and pepper to taste. Cover and keep warm while you cook the pork chops.

7) In a heavy skillet, heat the butter over medium heat until bubbling. Add the chops and cook until browned, then turn and brown the other side, 6 to 8 minutes per side, until done to your liking. Or grill the pork chops over high heat until done to your liking.

8) Reheat the mustard sauce over low heat, whisking to restore the texture. If necessary, add water or stock to thin it out.

9) To serve the dish, use a slotted spoon to place a mound of the barley ragoût on each plate. Lean a pork chop on it, then drizzle mustard sauce over the plate. Add a sprig of parsley and sprinkle the plate with chopped parsley. Serve immediately.

For the pork chops:

4 pork chops, at least 1 inch thick, 6 to 8 ounces each

4 teaspoons olive oil

Kosher salt and freshly ground black pepper

2 tablespoons unsalted butter

For the ragoût:

4 tablespoons (^{1}/2 stick) unsalted butter.

2 tablespoons olive oil

2 large stalks celery, diced

1 large carrot, diced

1 large onion, diced

4 garlic cloves, minced

6 cups Chicken Stock (page 307) or low-sodium canned chicken broth

1 cup pearl barley

1 cup green lentils

Kosher salt and freshly ground black pepper

To finish the dish:

1 pound slab bacon, diced

1 medium head green cabbage, preferably Savoy, finely shredded

1 large onion, diced

2 garlic cloves, minced

2 Granny Smith apples, cored and diced (do not peel)

Juice of ^{1}/2 orange

1 tablespoon light brown sugar

Kosher salt and freshly ground black pepper

Whole sprigs of rosemary for garnish

FESTBIER OR VIENNA-STYLE LAGER WOULD MAKE A CLASSIC MATCH
WITH THESE ALSATIAN INGREDIENTS.

PAIR WITH ALSATIAN OR GERMAN RHEINGAU RIESLING WITH AN OFF-DRY QUALITY.

Veal Milanese with Red Wine Sauce, Artichokes, and Cremini Mushrooms

SERVES 4 TO 6

Thin scallops of veal are the basis for some of the most-loved dishes of the Italian kitchen: Roman saltimbocca; the American favorite, veal parmigiana; and crisp-fried costolette alla Milanese. In most of Italy, as in America, veal scallops are very expensive, so they are most often served as festive holiday meals. This traditional dish of veal dipped in breadcrumbs and fried golden in butter is a reflection of Milan's northerly location near Germany and Austria, where Wiener schnitzel (Vienna cutlet) is practically an obsession. In his culinary memoir, Blue Trout and Black Truffles, *Joseph Wechsberg tells us that in Vienna before the wars, chefs were so preoccupied with making light, crisp Wiener schnitzel that a test was devised: if a man could sit on the schnitzel without leaving a grease stain on his pants, the schnitzel was pronounced excellent. (Whether the man then had to eat the schnitzel is unclear.)*

We nap our costolette *in a savory sauce of red wine that can be made well in advance. For crispness, the scallops must be cooked briefly over very high heat, then quickly drained and served. If made correctly, the coating will be crisped by the oil rather than absorb it. The veal must be cooked at the last minute, but the roasted potatoes can be made beforehand and added to the sauce with the artichokes and mushrooms in step 5. For an even simpler dish, eliminate the sauce altogether and serve the crisp cutlets with lemon wedges, fresh herbs, and a dusting of grated Parmesan cheese.*

Serve with Rosemary Roasted Potatoes (page 214).

2 tablespoons Garlic Oil and Puree (page 292), or 2 tablespoons olive oil mixed with 1 minced garlic clove

8 ounces cremini mushrooms, quartered

1 small onion, chopped

1) In a fry pan, heat 1 tablespoon of garlic oil and sauté the mushrooms until tender. Set aside.

2) In a large heavy saucepan, heat the remaining tablespoon of garlic oil over medium-high heat. Add the onions and cook until they start to sweat, about 3 to 5 minutes. Add the carrots, celery, and thyme and cook, stirring another 3 to 5 minutes.

3) Add 1/2 cup of wine and boil until syrupy and reduced by three-quarters. Add the stock and bring to a boil. Reduce the heat to a simmer and cook until reduced by three-quarters.

4) Whisk the cornstarch into the remaining 2 tablespoons of wine, then whisk the mixture into the sauce and vegetables. Simmer for 1 minute to thicken the sauce. Strain the sauce over the mushrooms. Add cooked artichokes and set aside. (The sauce and vegetables can be made the day before up to this point.)

5) Remove the veal from the refrigerator. The scaloppine should be about 1/4 inch thick. If necessary, place them between sheets of plastic wrap and pound thin with a tendering mallet or rolling pin.

6) Spread the flour out on a plate. In a wide bowl, whisk the eggs until beaten. Spread the breadcrumbs out on a plate. Dredge each scallop in flour, then egg, then breadcrumbs and place on a plate. Refrigerate until ready to cook and serve.

7) When ready to cook the veal, place a baking sheet in the oven and preheat to 200°F.

8) In a large skillet, heat 1/4 cup of the oil over medium-high heat until hot but not smoking. Place a few scallops at a time in the hot oil and sauté until golden, about 1 minute on each side. Repeat until all the scallopine are cooked, adding more oil to the pan between batches. Drain on paper towels then place in the oven to keep warm.

9) Warm the sauce and vegetables. Whisk in the cold butter to thicken. Taste for seasoning.

10) Place 2 veal scallopine on each serving plate. Spoon the sauce and vegetables around the veal and drizzle with herb oil, sprinkle with parsley and cheese, place a lemon wedge on the plate and serve immediately.

2 medium carrots, diced
2 stalks celery, diced
2 teaspoons fresh thyme leaves
1/2 cup plus 2 tablespoons red wine
8 cups Veal Stock (pages 308–9) or low-sodium canned chicken broth, beef broth, or a combination
1 tablespoon cornstarch
8 small fresh artichokes, cooked as directed on pages xxxii–xxxiii and quartered, or one 10-ounce package frozen artichoke hearts, thawed and quartered
8 large veal scaloppine, chilled
All-purpose flour
3 large eggs
1 cup Seasoned Breadcrumbs (page 306)
1/2 cup light olive oil
4 tablespoons (1/2 stick) cold unsalted butter, cut into pieces
Herb Oil (page 293) (optional)
Chopped fresh parsley
Freshly grated Parmesan cheese
1 lemon, quartered

A ROSSO DI MONTALCINO, FRUITY BARBERA, OR CARMIGNANO WILL COMPLEMENT THIS DISH BEAUTIFULLY.

Osso Buco with Saffron Risotto and Orange Gremolata

SERVES 6

The rich, deep flavors of this classic Milanese dish come not only from the simple ingredients but from the slow, moist cooking that gives them time to combine. The result is a dish that is delicate but suffused with flavor. The spark provided by the green, citric gremolata is a brilliant addition; almost like a Mexican salsa cruda, it cuts right through the richness and provides a new dimension of flavor. Osso buco means "hole in bone"; variations range from turkey osso buco to osso buco in bianco, cooked in a green herbal braise. Although it has the simple elegance of a classic, Giuliano Bugialli, a reigning expert on Italian food traditions, places the dish at no more than 150 years old.

Pale golden saffron risotto is the standard accompaniment, but Rosemary Roasted Potatoes (page 214) or any of our mashed potato recipes would also be lovely.

For the osso buco:

6 veal shanks, about 2 inches thick, tied around the middle with butcher twine

Kosher salt and freshly ground black pepper

1/2 cup all-purpose flour

1/2 cup olive oil

1 tablespoon fresh thyme leaves

1 tablespoon chopped fresh rosemary

1 teaspoon finely chopped lemon zest

1 teaspoon finely chopped orange zest

4 cups diced carrots

4 cups diced onions

1) Preheat the oven to 350°F.

2) Season the shanks with salt and pepper. Press firmly, working to rub the seasonings into the meat.

3) Put the flour in a shallow bowl and dredge the shanks in it, shaking off any excess.

4) Heat the oil in a large ovenproof pot over medium-high heat. Add 3 of the shanks and brown well on all sides. Remove from the pot and brown the remaining shanks. Remove from the pot.

5) In the same pot, combine the thyme, rosemary, lemon, orange, carrots, onions, celery, garlic, and bay leaf. Add the wine and cook for 3 to 5 minutes, scraping up the browned bits from the bottom of the pot with a wooden spoon.

6) Return the meat to the pot, laying it on top of the vegetables. Pour the stock over the meat and vegetables in the pot. Stir in the tomato paste. The meat should be covered; if necessary, add more stock or hot water.

7) Cover the pot and braise in the oven for about 3 hours, until the meat is very tender. (The shanks can be made through this step up to 2 days in advance and reheated.)

8) Make the gremolata: combine all the ingredients for the gremolata in a bowl, mix well, and set aside.

9) Make the risotto: about an hour before serving, combine the stock and saffron in a saucepan. Simmer, uncovered, for 10 minutes, until the stock takes on a rich golden hue. Keep warm.

10) Heat the oil in a heavy-bottomed saucepan over medium heat. Add the onion and garlic, and cook gently until the onion begins to turn translucent. Do not brown.

11) Add the rice and stir until each grain is evenly coated with oil. Add half of the wine and cook, stirring occasionally, until the wine is almost completely absorbed by the rice. Repeat with the remaining wine. Add about $1/2$ cup of hot stock and cook, stirring frequently, until the stock is almost completely absorbed by the rice.

12) Repeat with the remaining stock. Toward the end of the cooking process, the mixture will become thick and creamy, and you will have to stir it more frequently to keep it from sticking to the pan.

4 cups diced celery

6 garlic cloves, minced

1 bay leaf

$1/2$ cup dry white wine

4 cups Veal Stock (pages 308–9), Chicken Stock (page 307), or low-sodium canned chicken broth

3 tablespoons tomato paste

2 tablespoons cold unsalted butter, cut into small pieces

For the gremolata:

$1/2$ cup finely chopped fresh parsley

2 tablespoons finely chopped lemon zest

2 tablespoons finely chopped orange zest

$1/4$ cup extra-virgin olive oil

For the risotto:

8 cups Chicken Stock (page 307) or low-sodium canned broth

2 teaspoons saffron threads

2 tablespoons olive oil

1 large onion, finely chopped

2 large garlic cloves, finely minced

1 pound arborio rice

$1/2$ cup dry white wine

1 cup freshly grated Parmesan cheese

4 tablespoons ($1/2$ stick) unsalted butter

$1/2$ cup heavy cream, whipped stiff and kept chilled (optional)

3 tablespoons finely chopped fresh parsley, chives, basil, or a combination

Kosher salt and ground white pepper

13) After the risotto has been cooking for about 30 minutes, taste a few grains. The rice should be soft but still have a little firmness at the center. If it is done, cover and remove from the heat immediately. If not, continue cooking in the same manner until it is done. When it is done, remove from the heat and stir in the cheese, butter, parsley, and salt and pepper to taste. Cover until ready to serve. Just before serving, fold in the whipped cream.

14) Meanwhile, finish the osso buco: on top of the stove, simmer the stew, uncovered, until the liquid reduces and thickens to your liking. Transfer the shanks to serving plates and remove butcher twine. Whisk the butter into the sauce until it acquires a glossy sheen.

15) To serve, spoon risotto around each shank. Spoon the sauce over and around the shanks, then top with gremolata. Serve immediately.

A FIZZY PALE ALE WITH MALTY FLAVOR WOULD MARRY WELL WITH THIS SLOW-COOKED DISH.

THE IDEAL (AND CLASSIC) WINE HERE IS A BARBERA WITH ENOUGH ACIDITY
TO CONTRAST THE RICHNESS OF THE OSSO BUCO.

Provençal Lamb Shanks with Roasted Vegetables, Roasted Garlic, and Tapenade

SERVES 6

The olive-spiked, winy daubes of Provence were evolved to create tender stews from the tough local bull meat, and big meaty lamb shanks respond brilliantly to the same slow-cooking treatment. Shanks are big bones covered with powerful working muscles, so the meat has a great deal of flavor and very little fat. With a tapenade of black and green olives and roasted zucchini and peppers added at the end, this Provence-flavored dinner is complete. (The name of the sauce comes from the Provençal word for caper— tapeno).

You can serve the braised meat by itself, with or without the roasted vegetables, or for a very special meal, add a creamy, fragrant potato gratin. The savory tapenade can be made a day ahead and refrigerated, then brought to room temperature before serving. Be sure to read the recipe all the way through before starting to cook so that you understand how the different elements come together.

Serve with Garlicky Potato Gratin (pages 216–17).

1) Preheat the oven to 350°F.

2) Season the lamb shanks with salt and pepper, working to rub the seasonings into the meat.

3) Heat the oil in a large ovenproof pot over medium-high heat. Add 3 of the shanks and brown well on all sides. Remove from the pot and brown the remaining shanks. Remove from the pot.

For the lamb:

6 lamb shanks, about 1 pound each

Kosher salt and freshly ground black pepper

¹/4 cup olive oil

4 medium carrots, chopped

4 stalks celery, diced

2 medium onions, chopped

³/4 cup fruity red wine, such as Beaujolais or Merlot

7 cups Veal Stock (pages 308–9)
   or low-sodium canned chicken broth
2 bay leaves
6 black peppercorns
1 sprig fresh thyme
1 sprig fresh rosemary
4 large garlic cloves, crushed
2 tablespoons unsalted butter

For the tapenade:
1/2 cup pitted Kalamata olives
1/2 cup pimento-stuffed green olives
1/2 teaspoon freshly grated lemon zest
2 anchovy fillets (optional)
2 large garlic cloves, minced
1 teaspoon capers, drained
1/2 cup extra-virgin olive oil

For the roasted vegetables:
2 medium red onions, diced
2 medium carrots, sliced on the
   diagonal 1/2 inch thick
2 stalks celery, sliced on the diagonal
   1/2 inch thick
2 red bell peppers, seeded and cut into
   eighths
2 yellow bell peppers, seeded and cut
   into eighths
1/4 cup Garlic Oil and Puree (page 292),
   or 1/4 cup olive oil mixed with
   2 large minced garlic gloves
Kosher salt and freshly ground black
   pepper
2 medium zucchini, halved lengthwise
   and sliced on the diagonal 1/2 inch
   thick
2 medium yellow (summer) squash,
   halved lengthwise and sliced on the
   diagonal 1/2 inch thick
12 cremini mushrooms, quartered

For the roasted garlic:
6 whole heads garlic, with the skin
6 teaspoons olive oil

4) In the same pot, combine the carrots, celery, and onions and sauté over medium heat until softened, about 5 minutes. Add the wine and boil until reduced by half. Add stock, bay leaves, peppercorns, thyme, rosemary, and garlic. Bring to a boil, add the shanks, and push them down in the pot so that they are completely covered with liquid (add water if necessary).

5) Cover the pot and braise in the oven until very tender and the meat pulls away from the bone, about 3¹/2 to 4 hours. (The shanks can be made through this step up to 2 days in advance.)

6) Make the tapenade: put all the ingredients for the tapenade except the olive oil in a food processor. Blend briefly, pulsing, until the mixture is combined but still coarse. Scrape into a bowl, stir in the olive oil, and cover until ready to use. (The tapenade can be made up to 2 days in advance.)

7) About an hour and a half before the lamb is ready, make the roasted vegetables: combine the onions, carrots, celery, and red and yellow peppers in a bowl. Add the garlic oil and salt and pepper to taste and toss to coat. Spread out on a baking sheet or big roasting pan. Roast, uncovered, in the oven with the lamb until the carrots are tender but not mushy, about 30 minutes. Stir the vegetables, mix in the zucchini, yellow squash, and mushrooms, and return to the oven for another 15 minutes.

8) Meanwhile, make the roasted garlic: rub each head of garlic with your hands to remove the loose skin, then rub each head with a teaspoon of olive oil. Cut 1/4 inch off the top of the head to expose the cloves, then wrap all 6 heads together tightly in aluminum foil. Tuck them into the oven, next to the roasting pan or lamb. Roast for 45 to 60 minutes, until very soft (test one after 45 minutes with the point of a knife). Keep wrapped in foil until ready to serve.

9) When the vegetables are tender, transfer to a serving bowl and keep warm.

10) When the lamb is cooked, remove the shanks from the pot and place them on serving plates. Keep warm, covered with aluminum foil, in the oven.

11) Strain the pan juices into a saucepan; skim any fat, then bring up to a boil. Whisk in the butter until the sauce acquires a glossy sheen.

12) To serve, remove the serving plates from the oven. Place roasted vegetables and an unwrapped roasted garlic bulb alongside each shank, and top with lamb sauce and a generous spoonful of the tapenade.

A CLASSIC INDIA PALE ALE WITH HIGH CARBONATION WILL STAND UP TO THIS HEARTY DISH.

LAMB IS VERY VERSATILE WITH BIG REDS. THE TAPENADE PUSHES THIS DISH TOWARD A SPICY NORTHERN RHONE WINE LIKE CÔTE RÔTIE OR SAINT JOSEPH.

Hazelnut-Crusted Rack of Lamb

SERVES 4

Hazelnuts have such an extraordinary toasty flavor, despite their intractable skins, that we always look forward to cooking with them. A special holiday dinner like this one is the ideal opportunity. Combined with vibrant orange, fresh herbs, and piquant mustard, the hazelnuts' rich crunch is perfect. And when pressed into tender roast lamb, the effect is extraordinary. Feel free to use this marinade and crust on a roast leg of lamb if racks are not available or seem prohibitively expensive. "Frenching" a rack of lamb involves trimming the extra fat and meat scraps from the ribs to expose the bones, leaving the chop whole. Any good butcher will be able to do this for you.

A whole hazelnut has a smooth mahogany shell and a thin brown skin underneath, both of which must be removed before making the crust. Many gourmet stores now stock shelled and peeled hazelnuts, but if only whole ones are available, remove the shells with a nutcracker, leaving the skins on. Taste the nuts to be sure they are fresh and sweet, not stale or rancid, then spread them on a baking sheet. Toast at 350°F until fragrant, about 20 minutes, then wrap them in a kitchen towel. Let them steam 10 minutes to loosen the skins, then rub hard to remove them. You won't get all the skins off, but don't worry about it.

In French, hazelnut oil is huile de noisette. It can be found at most gourmet stores, or you can use another nut oil like peanut or walnut if necessary.

For the marinade:
- 1 tablespoon finely chopped fresh rosemary
- 2 large garlic cloves, minced
- 1 cup olive oil
- Juice of 1 orange
- $^{1}/_{4}$ teaspoon freshly ground black pepper

1) Combine all the ingredients for the marinade in a glass or ceramic bowl or dish. Add the lamb racks, stir to coat, and marinate in the refrigerator overnight.

2) When ready to cook, remove the lamb from the marinade and drain slightly on a wire rack.

3) Make the crust: preheat the oven to 350°F.

4) Cut the bread into 1-inch cubes, spread out on a baking sheet, and bake until dry, about 10 minutes, depending on how stale your bread is. When dry, transfer to a food processor. Add the remaining ingredients for the crust and pulse until combined and crumbly.

5) Increase the oven temperature to 400°F.

6) Working in batches if necessary to avoid crowding the pan, heat the olive oil in a large skillet over high heat and brown the lamb on all sides, turning only when browned. Remove from the skillet and brush each rack with mustard, then pack on the crust with your hands.

7) Spread the carrots, celery, onions, and bouquet garni in the bottom of a roasting pan with a roasting rack. Arrange the lamb on the rack and place the rack on top of the vegetables in the pan.

8) Roast about 20 minutes for rare meat, 40 minutes for well-done. Remove from the oven and let rest at least 5 minutes, loosely covered with foil, while you make the sauce.

9) Pour the wine over the vegetables in the roasting pan and deglaze the pan with a wooden spoon, scraping up the bits from the bottom. Strain into a saucepan, add 1 sprig of rosemary, and bring to a simmer. Reduce by half, then whisk in the butter. Season to taste with salt and pepper.

10) To serve, spoon a bed of Tomato-Fennel-Olive Ragoût on each of 4 serving plates. Cut the lamb racks in half and place them, with the bones intertwined, on top of the ragoût. Spoon the sauce over and garnish with a rosemary sprig stuck vertically between the bones. Spoon Pumpkin Polenta alongside.

For the crust:

1 loaf 2- or 3-day-old Brioche (pages 82–83) or best-quality bakery white bread

$1/2$ cup hazelnuts, toasted and peeled (see headnote)

2 shallots

4 garlic cloves

Grated zest of $1/2$ orange

$1/4$ cup hazelnut, peanut, or walnut oil

$1/2$ cup chopped fresh parsley

1 teaspoon fresh thyme leaves

For the lamb:

4 racks of lamb (3 or 4 chops per rack), frenched (see above)

2 tablespoons olive oil

2 tablespoons Dijon mustard

$3/4$ cup diced carrots

$3/4$ cup diced celery

$1/2$ cup diced onions

1 Bouquet Garni (page 297)

$1^1/2$ cups red wine, preferably Barolo or Pinot Noir

5 sprigs rosemary

2 tablespoons cold unsalted butter, cut into pieces

Kosher salt and freshly ground black pepper

1 recipe hot Tomato-Fennel-Olive Ragoût (page 197) (optional)

1 recipe hot Pumpkin Polenta (page 203) (optional)

TRY RICH, SPICY REDS
SUCH AS BARBERA
FROM PIEDMONT,
CHÂTEAUNEUF-DU-PAPE,
OR CALIFORNIA ZINFANDEL.

Pot-au-Feu

SERVES 6 TO 8

In The Food of France, *culinary explorer Waverly Root observes: "No city restaurant can match the pot-au-feu of the French farmhouse, where the kettle has been simmering on the back of the stove for years, never being allowed to cool off, constantly being replenished with new ingredients, changing with the seasons." Sadly, few of us today can boast of having tasted such a well-ripened pot-au-feu. But the dish is often spotted on brasserie menus, where it is right at home among the other straightforward dishes that are easy to make, flexibly timed, and festive to eat.*

The very first restaurants in France were created around pot-au-feu; called "bouillons," they were simple storefronts where Parisian workers could sup on a piece of boiled beef, or poorer ones on just a cup of broth flavored with the meat and vegetables that constantly circulated through the never-emptied pot. While boiled beef has almost disappeared from the American scene, pot-au-feu is a wintry French classic, so basic to that country's cooking that it is not claimed by any one region but made by all.

Making pot-au-feu takes patience and a large cooking pot but not a great deal of work. Be sure to simmer rather than boil, or your meat will completely lose its flavor to the broth. At the last minute, there's nothing to do but get your biggest serving platter ready to hold the steaming piles of tender beef, poached vegetables, and rich marrow bones. If you wish to serve this in the most traditional way, make a separate first course of the broth, degreased and served with toasted bread rounds spread with the marrow from the beef bones. This dish should be very interactive, with lots of passing of garnishes, ladling of stock, and digging into bones to extract the delicate marrow. Pot-au-feu is the perfect opportunity to appreciate the flavor and crunch of real coarse sea salt, or gros sel.

1) The day before making the dish, put the marrow bones and oxtail in a bowl, cover with cold tap water, and refrigerate overnight.

2) The next day, drain the water off and tie up the marrow bones in cheesecloth. Set aside.

3) Put the oxtail, ham hock, and beef short ribs in a very large pot. Add 5 quarts cold water and the salt, cover, and bring just to a simmer over high heat. Do not boil; reduce the heat as soon as a simmer is reached.

4) Uncover and use a ladle to skim off any foam that has risen to the surface. Adjust the heat so that the mixture stays at a simmer. Add the bouquet garni, clove-studded onion, peppercorns, and cinnamon stick.

5) Simmer, uncovered, 2^1/2 to 3 hours, skimming frequently, until the meat is almost tender. (The dish can be made through this step up to 1 day in advance.)

6) Add the marrow bones and remaining pot-au-feu ingredients and simmer an additional 45 minutes.

7) Meanwhile, make the garnishes: combine the horseradish with the cream in a small bowl. Put the other garnishes in small bowls for passing at the table.

8) Heat a large platter in a 200°F oven. When the meat and vegetables are cooked through, lift them out of the pot and arrange on the platter, leaving the seasonings in the pot. Unwrap the marrow bones and place them on the platter. Taste the stock and add salt if necessary. If the stock seems weak, boil to reduce while keeping the pot-au-feu hot in the oven.

9) Serve in soup plates, ladling the stock into each plate and passing the meat and vegetables around the table. If possible, provide small spoons for scooping out the marrow from the bones (spread it on the baguette slices for a treat). Pass the garnishes separately.

For the pot-au-feu:

6 beef marrow bones, 1^1/2 inches thick

1 pound oxtail or beef shank, cut 1^1/2 inches thick (have the butcher do this)

1 large ham hock

2 pounds beef short ribs or lamb shank, cut 1 inch thick

1 tablespoon kosher or sea salt, or to taste

1 Bouquet Garni (page 297)

1 whole onion, peeled and studded with 6 cloves

10 black peppercorns

1 cinnamon stick

3 large potatoes, peeled and quartered

3 medium carrots, cut into 2-inch lengths

2 medium onions, halved

2 medium parsnips, cut into 2-inch lengths

1 large turnips, cut into ^{1}/8-inch wedges

4 small leeks, including 3 inches of green, trimmed, well washed, and left whole

2 stalks celery, cut into 2-inch sections

6 garlic cloves, crushed

For the garnishes:

1 cup prepared horseradish, drained

^{1}/4 cup heavy cream

Coarse salt

Cracked black pepper

Cornichons

Dijon or grainy mustard

Toasted baguette slices

A TRADITIONAL BRITISH BITTER ALE IS PERFECT FOR THIS SIMPLY FLAVORED BUT HEARTY DISH.

THE IDEAL MATCH IS A YOUNG, SIMPLE BEAUJOLAIS OR CHIANTI.

Civet of Venison and Wild Mushrooms

SERVES 6 TO 8

In the autumn wild venison (chevreuil) and boar (sanglier) from Alsace's Vosges Mountains begin to appear on the region's menus. Although Alsace is traditionally the domain of white wine, red wine is the local choice for tenderizing and flavoring the chunks of meat used for a civet, or stew. Ottrott-le-Haut is a tiny town draped on a gentle slope, where Rouge d'Ottrott, the region's only red wine, is made from Pinot Noir grapes. From the top of the hill, the Rhine River and Germany's Schwarzwald— the Black Forest—can be spotted on sunny days.

Ottrott is also memorable for its eaux-de-vie, fruit brandies, and extraordinary concentration of good restaurants. One of the best is the Hôtel Restaurant L'Ami Fritz, where the dark, deep civet is preceded by house-preserved duck foie gras and followed by ripened local Muenster cheese and roasted fruit with honey. Follow Alsatian tradition by making a meal of this stew with your own Truffled Chicken Liver Mousse (pages 20–21) and Roasted Fruits with Cinnamon–Red Wine Glaze and Toasted Almonds (pages 232–33).

Serve with Parsnip-Celeriac Puree (page 206).

---

1 cup all-purpose flour

2¹/₂ teaspoons kosher salt

1¹/₂ teaspoons freshly ground black pepper

3 pounds boneless venison stewing meat, cut into 1-inch cubes

3 tablespoons olive oil

3 large carrots, diced

3 stalks celery, diced

1) Combine the flour, 1 teaspoon of the salt, and ¹/₂ teaspoon of the pepper and sprinkle over the venison, tossing to coat.

2) In a large heavy pot, heat the oil over high heat. Add half the venison and brown on all sides, turning only when browned. Remove from the pot with a slotted spoon and brown the remaining venison, adding more oil to the pot if necessary. Remove the meat from the pot.

3) In the same pot, combine the carrots, celery, onion, and garlic and cook, stirring, just until softened, about 5 minutes. Add the mushrooms and cook 2 minutes more.

4) Return the meat to the pot, add the wine, and cook until reduced by half. Stir in the rosemary, thyme, bay leaf, remaining 1½ teaspoons salt, and remaining 1 teaspoon pepper. Add the stock, cover, and bring to a boil. Skim off any scum that has risen to the top. Reduce the heat to a simmer, cover, and cook at least 2 hours, until the meat is very tender. Remove.

5) About 15 minutes before the stew is done, stir in the pearl onions.

6) If necessary, raise the heat to reduce and thicken the stew liquid. When it reaches stew consistency, whisk in the butter, check for seasoning, and serve.

1 large onion, diced

4 garlic cloves, minced

8 ounces cremini mushrooms, sliced ¼ inch thick

8 ounces shiitake mushrooms, stems removed and discarded, sliced ¼ inch thick

8 ounces oyster mushrooms, pulled apart into bite-size pieces

3 cups red wine, preferably a French Burgundy or American Pinot Noir

1 tablespoon finely chopped fresh rosemary

1 tablespoon fresh thyme leaves

1 bay leaf

4 cups Veal or Beef Stock (pages 308–9), Chicken Stock (page 307), or low-sodium canned broth

2 cups frozen pearl onions, thawed

2 tablespoons cold unsalted butter, cut into pieces

A PLEASING PARTNER WOULD BE A FLEMISH BROWN ALE, ESPECIALLY ONE WITH THE DRIED-FRUIT FLAVOR OF THE OUDENAARDE STYLE.

CHOOSE A YOUNG, FRESH FRENCH BURGUNDY OR CALIFORNIA PINOT NOIR, OR TRY TO FIND A RARE ALSATIAN PINOT NOIR.

Mustard-Crust Sweetbreads
with Madeira and Morels

Of the 120,000 recorded species of fungi and mushrooms in the world, only about 1,800 are edible, and of these, only the truffle is more prized than the juicy, woodsy morel. Louis XIII of France is said to have adored their scent so much that he decorated his bedroom with them, and we can understand how he felt. Morels have only recently been domesticated but are found wild in many regions. Morels are known to prefer ashy soil, and the years following the eruption of Mount St. Helens produced a bumper crop of wild morels in the Northwest. If you can't wait until the next eruption, both the fresh and dried cultivated morels you can buy at gourmet stores are very good.

This recipe includes two other ingredients that qualify as delicacies in our kitchen: sweetbreads and Madeira wine. The term sweetbreads refers to the thymus gland of veal, lamb, or pork, but the ones you are most likely to find will be veal, and those are our favorites. The creamy meat has a delicate flavor, with none of the gaminess associated with other specialty meats, like kidneys or livers. The fresh sweetbreads are soaked, poached, and then compressed until the meat is firm. Madeira is a lightly sweet Portuguese wine with lots of wood flavor that reminds us of aged Spanish Amontillado sherry. The best ones for this dish will be labeled Sercial, Verdelho, or Bual to indicate the grape used. Like port, Madeira can be aged for an incredibly long time, up to a century. Try to buy one that is at least three years old or you won't get as good a sense of the special flavor.

Serve on top of Potato Galettes (page 213).

1) Two days before you plan to serve the dish, rinse the sweetbreads well under cold running water. Put the sweetbreads in a dish, add water to cover by 1 inch, and stir in the salt. Refrigerate 8 to 24 hours, changing the salt water every 8 hours or so.

2) The next day, drain the sweetbreads well in a colander while you prepare the court bouillon. In a large pot, combine the water, wine, carrots, celery, onions, thyme, bay leaves, parsley, peppercorns, and salt. Bring to a simmer and simmer 10 minutes, then add the sweetbreads and poach 30 minutes. Remove the sweetbreads from the court bouillon and arrange on a baking sheet. When cool enough to handle, trim the sweetbreads, removing any membranes, fat, or sinew. Put another baking sheet on top and place about six 1-pound weights on it (cans of food work well) to compress and firm the meat. Refrigerate overnight.

3) When ready to finish, cut the sweetbreads into 1-inch slices and season generously with salt and pepper. Put the mustard in a bowl and coat the pieces lightly but thoroughly by rolling them in the mustard and then dredging them in flour.

4) Preheat the oven to 200°F.

5) In a skillet, melt 2 tablespoons of the butter over medium-high heat. Working in batches if necessary to avoid crowding the pan, and adding more butter between batches, sauté the sweetbreads on both sides until golden brown, about 2 minutes on each side. Remove from the pan and keep warm, covered with foil, in the oven.

6) Add the Madeira to the pan and stir, scraping up the browned bits from the bottom of the pan with a wooden spoon. Add the morels and the stock and simmer until the morels are tender, about 5 minutes. Whisk in the remaining 2 tablespoons of butter and the herbs.

7) Spoon the morels and sauce over the sweetbreads and serve immediately.

2 pounds veal sweetbreads
1 teaspoon kosher salt

For the court bouillon:
12 cups water
One 750 ml bottle light white wine
2 large carrots, sliced
4 stalks celery, sliced
2 medium onions, coarsely chopped
1 teaspoon dried thyme
2 bay leaves
6 sprigs fresh parsley
6 black peppercorns
1 teaspoon kosher salt

To finish the dish:
Kosher salt and freshly ground black pepper
1 cup whole-grain Dijon mustard
1 cup flour
4 tablespoons unsalted butter
1/4 cup Madeira (see headnote)
6 ounces fresh morels, brushed clean, or 1 1/2 ounces dried morels soaked 15 minutes in warm water and drained (about 30 morels)
2 1/2 cups Chicken Stock (page 307) or low-sodium canned broth
1 tablespoon chopped fresh parsley
1 tablespoon chopped fresh chervil
1 tablespoon chopped fresh tarragon

MATCH WITH A VOUVRAY, CALIFORNIA VIOGNIER, OR LIGHT PINOT NOIR.

Side Dishes

Endive-Walnut Salad

Caraway Coleslaw

Creamy Cucumber Salad

Tomato-Fennel-Olive Ragoût

Ratatouille

Vegetable-Citrus Couscous

Spiced Hummus

Brown Basmati Pilaf

Soft Polenta

Pumpkin Polenta

Mustard Spaetzle

Parsnip-Celeriac Puree

Sweet Potato–Apple Puree

Pesto Mashed Potatoes

Roasted Garlic Mashed Potatoes

Potato-Onion Ragoût

Blue Cheese Double-Baked Potatoes

Potato Galettes

Rosemary Roasted Potatoes

Pommes à l'Huile
(French Potato Salad)

Garlicky Potato Gratin

Endive-Walnut Salad

Both sherry vinegar and walnut oil add instant interest to basic vinaigrettes; together, the effect is dramatically flavorful. Try to find genuine Spanish sherry vinegar from the region of Jerez de la Frontera, the Andalusian town that gave its name to the wines it crafts with such remarkable results. Sometimes labeled "vinagre de Jerez," sherry vinegar is a flavoring of great character, with sweet, winy, and woody notes mingling together much as they do in the great balsamic vinegars of Modena. If you're a balsamic vinegar fan (or addict), do make the effort to seek out some genuine sherry vinegar.

Endive is an easy way to add elegance and a crisp, bitter note to a salad, especially good before, with, or after any rich entree. Walnuts supply a different kind of crunch; be sure the ones you use taste fresh and sweet, not stale or rancid.

$^{1}/_{4}$ **cup sherry vinegar**

$^{1}/_{2}$ **cup extra-virgin olive oil, or $^{1}/_{4}$ cup each walnut oil and extra-virgin olive oil**

Kosher salt and freshly ground black pepper

4 medium Belgian endive, leaves separated

$^{1}/_{4}$ **cup roughly chopped walnuts**

1) Whisk together the vinegar and oil, then add salt and pepper to taste.

2) In a bowl, combine the endive and walnuts and toss with the vinaigrette.

Caraway Coleslaw

The combination of creamy and crunchy, sweet and tart elements is what gives a well-made coleslaw its classic appeal. Better give this at least a day to develop the flavors.

1)   In a large bowl, toss the cabbage, carrots, and onion together until well combined.

2)   In another bowl, mix together the mayonnaise and sugar, then use a rubber spatula to scrape into the bowl with the vegetables. Mix to combine, then add the half-and-half and caraway seeds. Mix well and add the lemon juice and salt and pepper to taste.

3)   Use immediately or refrigerate, tightly covered, up to 3 days. Before serving, taste and adjust the seasonings.

1 1/2 pounds green cabbage (about 1 small head), finely shredded

2 large carrots, finely grated

1 teaspoon finely chopped onion

2 cups Mayonnaise, homemade (page 299) or store-bought, or to taste

1/4 cup sugar

1 teaspoon half-and-half or heavy cream

3 tablespoons caraway seeds

Juice of 1/2 lemon, or to taste

Kosher salt and freshly ground black pepper

Creamy Cucumber Salad

The cool crunch and fresh green flavor of cucumbers are so unique that the vegetable would probably be considered a great delicacy if it weren't so easy to find and cook. This salad summons up our time in England, where poached salmon with cucumber salad is simple, elegant summer fare. Serve this atop Salmon Paillards with Mustard-Dill Sauce (pages 130–31), instead of coleslaw alongside Fish and Chips in Peppery Amber Beer Batter (pages 161–62), or with smoked fish and buttered pumpernickel bread for a no-cook summer dinner. The cucumber and cream cool off spicy and smoked flavors.

English or hothouse cucumbers are the extra-long ones that come wrapped in plastic at the supermarket. They have very few seeds, and those they do have are soft. If they are not available, use small kirby cucumbers instead.

1 English cucumber (about 1 pound), well washed (do not peel)

Kosher salt and freshly ground black pepper

$^1/_3$ cup Mayonnaise, homemade (page 299) or store-bought

Sugar

2 plum tomatoes, diced

1 small red onion, sliced into thin rings

2 tablespoons chopped fresh chives

1) Slice the cucumber very thin—about $^1/_8$ inch thick.

2) In a medium bowl, spread about a quarter of the cucumber slices. Sprinkle with salt and pepper, then dot with small spoonfuls of mayonnaise and sprinkle lightly with sugar. Repeat until all ingredients are used up, ending with a sprinkling of sugar. Cover with plastic wrap and refrigerate at least 3 hours or overnight.

3) When ready to serve, stir thoroughly. Add the tomatoes, onion rings, and chives and stir to combine. Taste and adjust the seasonings. Before serving, drain off as much liquid as you can.

Tomato-Fennel-Olive Ragoût

This quick, extremely flavorful stew gets its punch from the combination of Kalamata olives, hot pepper, sweet fennel, and fresh herbs. As an accent for any roast lamb or pork dish, or as a pasta sauce, it's unbeatable.

1) Heat the oil in a skillet over medium-high heat. Add the garlic, pepper flakes, and onions and cook, stirring, until the onions are softened, 5 to 7 minutes. Add the fennel and cook 3 minutes more. Add the tomatoes and reserved juice. Simmer 10 minutes, until the mixture has a stewlike consistency.

2) Add the olives, then stir in the butter. Add the basil and season with salt and pepper to taste. Serve immediately. (The ragoût can be made up to 3 days in advance.)

1 tablespoon extra-virgin olive oil

3 large garlic cloves, minced

1/2 teaspoon red pepper flakes

16 pearl onions, blanched, peeled, and trimmed, or frozen pearl onions

2 cups diced fennel (about 1 large bulb)

One 16-ounce can Italian plum tomatoes, drained, 1/2 cup juice reserved

1/2 cup Kalamata or Gaeta olives, pitted and quartered

1 tablespoon cold unsalted butter, cut into pieces

2 tablespoons chopped fresh basil, parsley, or a combination

Kosher salt and freshly ground black pepper

Ratatouille

The first Provençal restaurant in Paris opened its doors in 1786. The Trois Frères Provençaux, along with other Provençal fortune seekers, brought the tomato with them from the sunny south, where the pomme d'amour, *or love-apple, was widely known. Only recently, however, had the tomato made the transformation from decorative houseplant to delicious ingredient. At first Parisians greeted this new style of cuisine with suspicion, but by 1803 even the great gourmand Brillat-Savarin had to admit that "tomatoes are a great blessing to good cookery." We couldn't agree more.*

We don't know whether ratatouille was served by the Trois Frères, but this combination of eggplant, tomatoes, peppers, and squash always feels like Provence to us. For a quick vegetarian entree in the Provençal tradition, top a serving dish of ratatouille with fried eggs and serve with lots of bread. Salting the eggplant before cooking removes the excess moisture.

---

1 medium eggplant, halved lengthwise and diced medium

Kosher salt

¹/₄ cup Garlic Oil and Puree (page 292), or ¹/₄ cup extra-virgin olive oil mixed with 2 minced garlic cloves

2 medium onions, diced medium

3 small zucchini, diced medium

3 small yellow (summer) squash, diced medium

2 red bell peppers, diced medium

2 yellow bell peppers, diced medium

One 28-ounce can Italian plum tomatoes

¹/₂ bay leaf

Freshly ground black pepper

1 tablespoon sugar

¹/₄ cup finely shredded fresh basil

---

1) Arrange the eggplant on a thick layer of paper towels. Sprinkle the eggplant generously on both sides with salt, cover with more paper towels, and let drain for about 30 minutes while you prepare the other vegetables.

2) In a large heavy pot, heat the garlic oil over medium-high heat. Add the onions, zucchini, yellow squash, bell peppers, and eggplant to the pot and cook, stirring, until softened, 7 to 10 minutes.

3) Add the tomatoes with their juices, crushing the tomatoes in the pot with a wooden spoon. Add the bay leaf, salt and pepper to taste, and the sugar. Simmer, uncovered, until the flavors are well combined and the vegetables very tender, 25 to 30 minutes.

4) Stir in the basil and adjust the seasonings. Serve immediately or at room temperature, or let cool and refrigerate, covered, up to 3 days.

Vegetable-Citrus Couscous

SERVES 4 TO 6

No-cook couscous is a great recent addition to the American pantry, but it can be too dense when served plain. Adding vegetables for texture and citrus and cinnamon for flavor lightens up the whole dish.

1) In a skillet, heat 1 tablespoon of the oil over medium-high heat. Add half of the garlic, the scallions, zucchini, carrots, and bell peppers and cook, stirring, until softened but still firm, about 3 minutes. Transfer to a bowl and wipe out the pan.

2) Heat the remaining 2 tablespoons of oil over high heat, add the remaining garlic and the mushrooms, and cook, stirring, until the liquid has been cooked off and the mushrooms are softened and beginning to brown around the edges. Transfer to a bowl and set aside.

3) In a medium saucepan with a tight-fitting lid, bring the juices, stock, butter, cinnamon, and 1 teaspoon salt to a boil. Stir in the couscous, cover, and turn off the heat. Let rest 10 minutes to absorb the liquid, then gently fold in the scallions, peppers, mushrooms, and cucumber. Keep tightly covered until ready to serve. Before serving, fluff with a fork and season to taste with salt and pepper.

3 tablespoons olive oil

2 garlic cloves, minced

1/2 cup chopped scallions

1/2 cup diced zucchini

1/2 cup diced carrots

1/2 cup diced red bell pepper

1 cup sliced cremini, button, or shiitake mushrooms, or a combination

2 tablespoons freshly squeezed lime juice

2 tablespoons freshly squeezed lemon juice

1/4 cup freshly squeezed orange juice

2 1/2 cups Chicken Stock (page 307), low-sodium canned broth, or water

3 tablespoons unsalted butter

1 teaspoon ground cinnamon

Kosher salt

2 cups instant couscous

1/2 cup peeled, seeded, and diced cucumber

Freshly ground black pepper

Spiced Hummus

Remember when hummus was a health food? Now, just like yogurt and granola, hummus has hit the big time; it's everywhere! Of course, there is nothing truly new about chickpeas: the ancient Romans ate roasted chickpeas at fairs and performances, just as we eat popcorn. However, our highly seasoned hummus is uniquely appealing as a side dish. It's especially easy to prepare, can be served hot or at room temperature, and tastes great with Mediterranean-seasoned stews.

Three 19-ounce cans chickpeas (garbanzos)

1 cup tahini (sesame paste)

1 tablespoon ground cumin (preferably freshly ground)

6 tablespoons freshly squeezed lemon juice

1/4 cup finely chopped fresh parsley

1 teaspoon finely minced fresh ginger

1/2 teaspoon freshly ground black pepper

Kosher salt to taste

3/4 cup Garlic Oil and Puree (page 292), or 3/4 cup olive oil mixed with 3 minced large cloves garlic

1/2 teaspoon cayenne pepper, or to taste

1) Drain the chickpeas in a colander, reserving 1/2 cup of the liquid. Rinse the chickpeas well, put them in a food processor, and puree just until smooth, adding some of the reserved liquid if necessary.

2) Add the remaining ingredients and pulse just until combined. Do not overprocess; the mixture will become too thin. Adjust the seasonings, transfer to a serving bowl and set aside until ready to serve.

3) Serve at room temperature as a dip or side dish.

Brown Basmati Pilaf

SERVES 4

At the foot of the Himalayas in northern India, where basmati has been cultivated for centuries, the aromatic, delicate rice is eaten not as an everyday staple but as a festive food for special holidays. Premium basmati is more precious (and expensive) than other rices because it must be aged for a year after harvest to develop its unique flavors. Texmati rice, developed in this country, is a cross between our long-grain rice and basmati; it makes a fine substitute. Remember that brown rice, consisting of the whole rice grain, always takes longer to cook than white.

1) In a heavy-bottomed saucepan with a tight-fitting lid, heat the oil over medium-high heat. Add the carrot, celery, onion, and garlic and cook, stirring, until softened, about 8 minutes. Do not let the vegetables brown; reduce the heat if necessary.

2) Add the rice and stir until completely coated with oil. Add the stock and bring to a boil. Cover, reduce the heat to the lowest possible level, and cook without stirring until all the liquid is absorbed and the rice is tender, 25 to 30 minutes.

3) Dot with butter and keep covered until ready to serve. Just before serving, sprinkle with parsley and mix in gently with a fork. Season to taste with salt, pepper, and orange juice.

1 tablespoon olive oil

1 large carrot, chopped

3 stalks celery, chopped

1 medium onion, chopped

4 garlic cloves, minced

1 cup brown basmati rice

2 1/2 cups Chicken Stock (page 307), Fish Stock (page 310), or water

1 tablespoon coid unsalted butter, cut into pieces

1 tablespoon chopped fresh parsley, chives, or basil

Kosher salt and freshly ground black pepper

Juice of 1 orange

Soft Polenta

We never stop being amazed at how easily dry cornmeal is transformed to a fragrant, sunny mixture alive with the fresh scent of corn. Our grandparents, to whom polenta was a filling staple in hard times, would be amazed to see it on so many restaurant menus. From American cornmeal mush to Italian polenta, Hungarian zamishka, and Romanian mamaliga, this dish goes everywhere and can be dressed up or down with more or less butter and cheese.

You'll need a sturdy whisk to make this fluffy side dish. It's one of our most versatile and popular grains: everybody loves the way it drinks up savory sauces, but we also like it plain, with plenty of freshly ground black pepper and a shower of chopped parsley. Try it instead of pasta with tomato sauce, ladle on some Roasted Vegetable–White Bean Chili (pages 120–21), or top it with a simple sauté of mushrooms and greens for a satisfying vegetarian dinner. The microwave oven is a godsend for polenta lovers: you can make big batches on the stove and reheat it as needed in the microwave.

2 cups water

2 cups whole milk

1 pound imported polenta (not instant polenta or American cornmeal)

Boiling water

1 cup freshly grated Rick's House Cheese Mix (page 298)

5 tablespoons cold unsalted butter, cut into pieces

1 cup heavy cream (optional)

1 1/2 teaspoons kosher salt

1/2 teaspoon freshly ground black pepper

1) In a large heavy saucepan, bring the water and milk to a boil. Gradually whisk in the polenta, then reduce the heat to low. Cook until tender, 20 to 25 minutes, whisking constantly to prevent sticking and clumping. As needed, add boiling water 1/2 cup at a time to keep the polenta moist.

2) When the polenta is cooked through and creamy (not grainy), raise the heat to medium and whisk in the cheese, butter, cream, salt, and pepper. Adjust the seasonings and serve immediately.

Pumpkin Polenta

A New World side dish with old-fashioned richness and holiday flavor, this combines the distinctly American flavors of pumpkin and corn with luxurious results. Once you've mastered the basic polenta technique, there's no limit to the ingredients and seasonings that can be added. This is one of our favorite variations. See the recipe for Curried Pumpkin Soup with Apple and Toasted Pumpkin Seeds (pages 40–41) for a discussion of pumpkin puree.

1)   In a large heavy saucepan, bring 2 cups of the stock and 2 cups of the cream to a boil. Gradually whisk in the polenta, then reduce the heat to low. Cook until tender, 25 to 30 minutes, whisking constantly to prevent sticking and clumping. As needed, add the remaining stock 1/2 cup at a time to keep the polenta moist.

2)   When the polenta is cooked through and creamy (not grainy), raise the heat to medium and quickly mix in the pumpkin, nutmeg, cinnamon, remaining 2 tablespoons cream (or less, to taste), butter, cheese, and salt and pepper to taste. Serve immediately, sprinkled with parsley.

4 cups hot Chicken Stock (page 307) or low-sodium canned broth

1 cup plus 2 tablespoons heavy cream

1 cup imported polenta (not instant polenta or American cornmeal)

1 cup fresh or canned pumpkin puree (not pie filling)

1/4 teaspoon freshly grated nutmeg

1/4 teaspoon ground cinnamon

2 tablespoons cold unsalted butter, cut into pieces

1 cup freshly grated Rick's House Cheese Mix (page 298)

Kosher salt and freshly ground black pepper

Chopped fresh parsley

Mustard Spaetzle

Spaetzle (pronounced "shpetzle"), tiny dumplings that are somewhere between gnoc-chi and fresh egg noodles in texture, are the traditional accompaniment for Coq au Riesling (pages 142–43) and other Alsatian dishes that have luscious cream and wine sauces. Since spaetzle belong to the huge international family of dumplings, they go with many differently flavored stews, from a Provençal daube of lamb to the tradi-tional Belgian beef stew with beer, carbonnade flamande, to Breton fish cotriade made with hard apple cider. The mustard and nutmeg in the batter warm the flavors of any dish but can be omitted or altered to suit the flavors of your recipe. If you are going to serve the spaetzle immediately, you can simply toss them in melted butter, salt, and pepper when they are cooked and skip the sauce altogether. When making this dish as a side for Coq au Riesling, make the spaetzle while the chicken is mari-nating and reheat them when the chicken is almost done.

For the spaetzle:

2 large eggs

6 tablespoons milk

$1/4$ teaspoon kosher salt

$1/8$ teaspoon freshly ground black pepper

$1/2$ teaspoon dry mustard

Pinch of freshly grated nutmeg

$3/4$ cup all-purpose flour

1 tablespoon olive oil

1) Make the spaetzle: in a mixing bowl, whisk together the eggs and milk. In a separate large bowl, stir together the salt, pepper, mustard, nutmeg, and flour.

2) Gradually whisk the egg mixture into the flour mixture until you have a smooth, thick batter. Let rest 15 minutes.

3) Meanwhile, bring a large pot of salted water to a boil over high heat. The water should come no more than three-quarters of the way up the sides of the pot.

4) Reduce the heat to a simmer and add the oil. Rest a colander over the simmering water (the water should not be bubbling up into the colander) and pour one-fourth of the batter into it. With a rubber spatula, press and wipe the batter through the holes. Let the water return to a simmer, then repeat with the remaining batter.

5) Remove the colander, cover the pot, and cook the spaetzle at a steady simmer. They will rise to the surface of the water as they cook. Start tasting the spaetzle after 5 to 8 minutes. When fluffy and no longer raw-tasting, they are cooked.

6) Meanwhile, fill a large pot or bowl with ice cubes and cover with cold water. When the spaetzle are cooked, remove with a slotted spoon and drop in the ice bath to stop the cooking. When cool to the touch, remove to a baking sheet. (The spaetzle can be prepared up to 1 day in advance.)

7) When ready to serve, melt the butter in a skillet over medium heat. Add the spaetzle and cook, stirring, 1 minute. Add the Dijon mustard, cream, and stock, bring to a simmer, and cook, stirring, until heated through. Add salt and pepper to taste and serve immediately.

For the sauce:

2 tablespoons unsalted butter

1 teaspoon Dijon mustard

2 tablespoons heavy cream

1/4 cup Chicken Stock (page 307) or low-sodium canned broth

Kosher salt and freshly ground black pepper

Parsnip-Celeriac Puree

SERVES 6 TO 8

Although celeriac is often labeled "celery root" in markets, it is not the root of the celery we know; its above-ground shoots are small, dark green, and tough. Celeriac is grown for the special flavor of its large, bumpy, yellowish brown root. When cooked and pureed, it takes on a smooth texture and a light flavor with hints of celery and artichoke. Whenever we feel we're getting stuck in the potato rut, a batch of this fresh-tasting puree reminds us that all root vegetables were not created equal. Celeriac is available all winter long; buy a firm root with no cracks.

6 large parsnips, cut into 1-inch chunks

$1/2$ bulb celeriac (celery root), cut into 1-inch chunks and tossed with lemon juice

$1/2$ cup heavy cream

8 tablespoons (1 stick) unsalted butter

1 teaspoon light brown sugar

2 pinches freshly grated nutmeg

$1/2$ teaspoon ground cinnamon

Kosher salt and freshly ground white pepper

1) Put the parsnips and celeriac in a saucepan, cover with cold salted water, and bring to a boil over medium-high heat. Reduce to a simmer and cook until fork-tender, about 20 minutes.

2) Meanwhile, in a saucepan, combine the cream, butter, brown sugar, nutmeg, and cinnamon. Bring to a simmer and mix to combine. Keep warm.

3) When the vegetables are cooked, drain and return them to the pot. Over medium heat, shake them for about 30 seconds to dry them out. Transfer to a mixing bowl or a mixer with a paddle attachment. Mash or mix, gradually adding the hot cream mixture, until smooth and silky.

4) Season to taste with salt and pepper and serve. (The puree can be made up to 2 days in advance.)

Sicilian Tuna with Braised Fennel, Tomato, and Capers
on a bed of Vegetable-Citrus Couscous

Lemon-Sage Roast Chicken with
Sausage-Mushroom-Potato Stuffing

Stuffed Artichokes with
Toasted Nuts, Lemon, and Tomato

*Pork Chops with Barley Ragoût,
Apple Cabbage Compote, and Mustard Sauce*

Tramonto's Escar...
Sausage, and White Be... Stew

Cassoulet

Orange-Ricotta Gnocchi with Broccoli Rabe

Pot-au-Feu

Sweet Potato–Apple Puree

SERVES 4 TO 6; CAN BE DOUBLED

The mild flavor of roast pork, chicken, or turkey demands the contrast of a sweet, tart, creamy puree like this one.

1) Put the potatoes in a saucepan, cover with cold salted water, and bring to a boil over medium-high heat. Reduce to a simmer and cook until fork-tender, about 20 minutes.

2) Meanwhile, in a saucepan, combine the apples, cream, butter, and brown sugar. Bring to a simmer and mix to combine. Keep warm.

3) When the potatoes are cooked, drain and return them to the pot. Over medium heat, shake them for about 30 seconds to dry them out. Transfer to a mixing bowl or a mixer with a paddle attachment. Mash or mix, gradually adding the hot cream mixture, until smooth and silky. Season to taste with salt and pepper.

4) Serve immediately or let cool and refrigerate up to 3 days. (The puree can be made up to 2 days in advance.)

6 large sweet potatoes, peeled and cut into 1-inch chunks

2 Granny Smith apples, peeled, cored, and diced

2 cups heavy cream

8 tablespoons (1 stick) unsalted butter

1 tablespoon light or dark brown sugar

Kosher salt and freshly ground black pepper

Pesto Mashed Potatoes

SERVES 6

Fragrant, oily basil pesto and steaming floury potatoes are a natural combination, as in the classic Genoese dish of pesto with pasta, potatoes, and string beans. As a side dish, this is quite luxurious. The potatoes and pesto must be combined at the last minute in order to extract the maximum flavor from the basil and to preserve the bright green color; if mixed ahead of time, both will diminish. If you like, set aside a few tablespoons of pesto to add to a Vegetable–Goat Cheese Sandwich (page 86) or Grilled Shrimp with Aiolis (pages 28–29) later in the week.

For the potatoes:

1 pound Yukon Gold potatoes, peeled and cubed

2 pounds Idaho potatoes, peeled and cubed

For the pesto:

1¹/₂ cups packed basil leaves

2 medium garlic cloves

1 tablespoon pine nuts, toasted in a skillet just until golden

¹/₄ cup freshly grated Parmesan or Romano cheese, or a combination

¹/₂ teaspoon kosher salt

¹/₄ cup extra-virgin olive oil

1) Put the potatoes in a saucepan, cover with cold salted water, and bring to a boil over high heat. Reduce to a simmer and cook about 25 minutes, until fork-tender.

2) Meanwhile, make the pesto: combine the basil, garlic, pine nuts, cheese, and salt in a blender or food processor. Pulse ingredients until coarsely chopped, then drizzle in the olive oil and run until almost smooth.

3) To finish the dish, heat the butter and cream in a saucepan over low heat until the butter is melted. Keep warm.

4) When the potatoes are cooked, drain and return them to the pot. Over medium heat, shake them for about 30 seconds to dry them out. (You can hold the potatoes at this point for up to 30 minutes; do not mash with the pesto and hot cream until the last possible moment.)

5) Transfer the potatoes to a mixing bowl or a mixer with a paddle attachment. Add the pesto and mash together until smooth, adding the hot cream mixture a little at a time until the desired consistency is reached.

6) Add salt and white pepper to taste and serve.

Roasted Garlic Mashed Potatoes

SERVES 4 TO 6

You may already have learned this important lesson by trial and error, but it's worth repeating: do not use your food processor for mashing potatoes. The result is as starchy as wallpaper paste and tastes about the same.

1 whole head garlic, with the skin

2 teaspoons olive oil

6 medium potatoes, preferably Yukon Gold

³/4 cup heavy cream or whole milk

6 tablespoons (³/4 stick) unsalted butter

Kosher salt and freshly ground black pepper

1) Preheat the oven or a toaster oven to 400°F. With a very sharp knife, cut off the top ¹/8 inch from the garlic head. Rub with the oil, wrap tightly in aluminum foil, and bake until very soft, about 40 minutes. When cool enough to handle, rub off as much of the skin as possible, then squeeze out the flesh by holding the head upside down and pressing the center down with your thumbs, as though you were trying to turn the head inside out. Pick out any bits of skin or fiber and set the flesh aside until ready to use.

2) About an hour before serving, put a large pot of salted water on to boil. Peel the potatoes if you like (you don't have to) and cut them into quarters. Boil them until very tender, almost falling apart, about 20 minutes.

3) Meanwhile, in a small saucepan, combine the cream and roasted garlic. Bring to a simmer over medium heat.

4) When the potatoes are cooked, drain off the water and put the pot back on the stove. Shake the pot over medium heat for 1 minute to dry out the potatoes. Transfer to a mixing bowl or a mixer with a paddle attachment. Mash or mix, gradually adding the hot cream mixture, until smooth.

5) Mix in the butter and season to taste with salt and pepper. Serve immediately or cover tightly and keep warm in the oven until ready to serve.

210

Potato-Onion Ragoût

You can never have too many recipes for easy potato dishes that taste great with a number of different main courses. Once this dish is assembled, it cooks itself slowly over low heat without much more attention from you; in fact, it's best if you practically forget about it, since stirring will interfere with the success of the dish.

1) In a heavy saucepan with a tight-fitting lid, combine the onion, garlic, and potatoes and toss together. Gently press them down into the bottom of the pan. Pour the stock over, and sprinkle with nutmeg, adding water if necessary to cover the vegetables.

2) Bring to a boil, then reduce the heat to low, cover, and simmer gently until the vegetables are very tender, about 1 hour. Stir only a couple of times, being careful not to break up the potatoes. Add boiling water if necessary, but keep in mind that the final product should not be too wet. The goal is to have the vegetables absorb the liquid.

3) Season to taste with salt and pepper. Sprinkle with the parsley and serve immediately.

1 large onion, halved and very thinly sliced

2 garlic cloves, minced

$1^1/2$ pounds small red-skinned potatoes, sliced $^1/_4$ inch thick

Pinch of freshly grated nutmeg

$1^1/2$ cups Chicken Stock (page 307), Vegetable Stock (page 311), or low-sodium canned broth

Kosher salt and freshly ground black pepper

$^1/_2$ cup finely chopped fresh parsley, chives, or a combination

Blue Cheese Double-Baked Potatoes

SERVES 4

The name of this dish tells you all you need to know.

4 large Idaho potatoes, pierced with a fork

^{1}/$_2$ cup heavy cream

3 tablespoons Roquefort, Maytag, or other blue cheese, at room temperature

2 tablespoons unsalted butter

1 tablespoon chopped fresh chives

2 tablespoons freshly grated Parmesan cheese

^{1}/$_4$ teaspoon freshly ground black pepper

1) Preheat the oven to 425°F.

2) Space the potatoes out on a baking sheet and bake until tender all the way through, about 1 hour. Let cool 15 minutes.

3) Cut an X in the top of each potato and squeeze the potatoes gently to loosen the flesh. Scoop the centers out, leaving about a ^{1}/$_4$-inch wall all the way around.

4) Lower the oven temperature to 400°F.

5) In a saucepan, combine the cream and Roquefort over medium heat, stirring to blend. When incorporated and heated through, turn off the heat and quickly mix in the potato pulp. Mix in the butter, chives, Parmesan, and pepper. Use this mixture to restuff the potatoes. (The potatoes can be made up to this point and held, covered, at room temperature for up to 2 hours.)

6) Put the potatoes back on the baking sheet and bake 15 to 20 minutes, until heated through and browned.

Potato Galettes

It's hard to believe that the French have been eating potatoes for less than two hundred years, considering how many ways French chefs have invented to cook them. Crisp potato cakes, called galettes, *make ideal beds for dishes involving particularly delectable sauces. Make sure to keep the* galettes *around 1/2 inch thick in the pan; any thicker, and the galettes may be raw inside when the crust is crisp.*

3 Idaho potatoes, peeled
2 garlic cloves, finely minced
2 shallots, minced
Kosher salt and freshly ground black pepper
4 tablespoons (1/2 stick) unsalted butter or corn oil

1) Coarsely grate the potatoes on a box grater or in a food processor. Do not rinse; the potato starch will hold the *galettes* together.

2) In a mixing bowl, combine the potatoes, garlic, and shallots. Add salt and pepper to taste.

3) Preheat the oven to 250°F and put an ovenproof platter inside to heat.

4) Melt 1 tablespoon of the butter in a small nonstick skillet over medium-high heat. Lift one-fourth (or one-sixth) of the potato mixture out of the bowl and squeeze to remove any liquid. Place in the center of the skillet and press down with the back of a wide spatula to form a cake about 1/2 inch thick.

5) Reduce the heat to medium and cook until golden brown on the bottom, about 5 minutes, pressing and shaping the *galette* from the top and sides with the spatula as it cooks. With the spatula, flip the *galette* and cook on the other side until golden brown and cooked through. Sprinkle with salt and remove to the heated platter. Repeat with the remaining butter and potato mixture.

6) Serve as soon as possible after cooking.

Rosemary Roasted Potatoes

You'll probably want to go ahead and double this recipe: the leftovers are delicious reheated, cold, or at room temperature. Roasted potatoes go with almost anything and are especially useful when you need a starchy vegetable to turn a salad or hearty soup into dinner.

$1^1/_2$ pounds small red-skinned potatoes, quartered

2 teaspoons finely chopped fresh rosemary

2 tablespoons Garlic Oil and Puree (page 292), or 2 tablespoons olive oil mixed with 1 minced garlic clove

$^1/_2$ teaspoon kosher salt

Freshly ground black pepper to taste

1) Preheat the oven to 425°F.

2) Combine all the ingredients in a mixing bowl and toss until the potatoes are well coated with oil and rosemary. Turn out onto a baking sheet.

3) Roast 15 minutes, then stir the potatoes to ensure even browning and lower the oven temperature to 375°F. Continue roasting 10 to 15 minutes more, until golden brown and tender.

4) Serve immediately or refrigerate, covered, up to 2 days.

Pommes à l'Huile

French Potato Salad

SERVES 6

If you are a fan of potato salad or extra-virgin olive oil, you'll love pommes à l'huile, *a simple but perfect and satisfying dish. Doused while still warm with fruity olive oil, the potatoes, shallots, and herbs meld into a fragrant mixture that is wonderful right away but also keeps improving in the refrigerator. Warm, it's great with meat dishes and sausages in winter (see page 150 for what Hemingway had to say on the matter), but it is also perfect summer picnic fare—with no mayonnaise to worry about. If you can find buttery French olive oil, the flavors will be complete.*

1) Make the dressing: in a bowl, whisk together the mustard and vinegar. Gradually whisk in the oil and season to taste with salt and pepper.

2) Put the potatoes in a saucepan and cover them with cold salted water. Cover and bring to a boil, then boil, uncovered, until tender all the way through, 12 to 15 minutes.

3) When the potatoes are cool enough to handle but still hot, slice them 1/4 inch thick. Toss with the shallots, parsley, and chives, then add the dressing and toss well.

4) Add salt and pepper to taste and serve immediately. (Or cover and refrigerate up to 2 days. Bring to room temperature before serving.)

For the dressing:

1 tablespoon Dijon mustard

1 tablespoon red wine vinegar

2/3 cup extra-virgin olive oil

Kosher salt and freshly ground black pepper

For the salad:

3 pounds small boiling potatoes, peeled or unpeeled

1/2 cup finely chopped shallots

1/3 cup finely chopped fresh parsley

2 tablespoons chopped fresh chives

Garlicky Potato Gratin

SERVES 8

Slicing the potatoes very, very thin is the key to this classic French side dish—that and a good nonstick pan. Potato gratin is a fundamental dish to the French kitchen—made with cheese in Savoy and the Jura, anchovies and tomatoes in Provence, and always with cream, butter, and garlic. You'll be amply rewarded for your labor at the end. The thin slicing helps the potatoes cook through and also give off the starch that binds the dish together into a creamy, molten mass. If your oven is large enough, you can cook the gratin in the same oven as the lamb shanks and vegetables in the recipe on pages 181–83—or make it the day before and warm in the oven just before serving.

$^1/_2$ cup olive oil

2 large garlic cloves, minced

6 medium Idaho potatoes, peeled and very thinly sliced

3 large shallots, finely chopped

$^1/_4$ cup all-purpose flour

4 tablespoons ($^1/_2$ stick) unsalted butter

Kosher salt and freshly ground black pepper

$^1/_2$ cup heavy cream

2 tablespoons freshly grated Parmesan cheese

2 tablespoons chopped fresh parsley

1)   Preheat the oven to 350°F. Butter a 9-inch nonstick cake pan or baking dish.

2)   Combine the olive oil and garlic and set aside to steep.

3)   Cover the bottom of the pan with a layer of potato slices, about one-sixth of the slices. Sprinkle with one-sixth of the shallots, one-sixth of the garlic-oil mixture, and one-sixth of the flour. Dot with one-sixth of the butter, then season with a little salt and pepper. Repeat 5 times until all the ingredients have been used.

4)   Gently pour the cream over the gratin and press down gently on the potatoes to help distribute the cream evenly throughout.

5) Cover with foil, place on a baking sheet (in case the cream boils over), and bake 30 minutes. Remove the foil and bake, uncovered, an additional 30 minutes, until the potatoes are golden and tender. Let rest at least 15 minutes before serving.

6) When ready to serve, preheat the broiler.

7) Place an flameproof plate on top of the gratin and flip the gratin over so that it rests on the plate. Sprinkle with Parmesan cheese and broil 1 to 2 minutes, until the top is browned and bubbly. Sprinkle with parsley and serve.

Cheese Plates

Celery and Olives with Shaved Parmigiano-Reggiano

Spanish Manchego with Apple Butter and Crostini

Warm Goat Cheese with Poached Dried Fruit, Toasted Almonds, and Greens

Gorgonzola, Fresh Figs, and Sautéed Walnuts

Camembert and Caramelized Orange Slices with Parsley Salad

Pont l'Évêque with Medjool Dates and Endive

Celery and Olives with Shaved Parmigiano-Reggiano

SERVES 4

The cheese of the region of Parma was already famous in the fourteenth century when a character in Boccaccio's Decameron *dreams of "a mountain made of grated cheese, where the people do nothing but cook pasta and ravioli, and roll it down the slopes so that it arrives at the bottom coated with fragrant cheese." The name of the cheese has been jealously guarded over the centuries, and today the outside of each 60-pound wheel is completely covered with the stamp "Parmigiano-Reggiano." You should always be able to see the stamp on the rind of the piece you buy.*

There is some confusion these days about the cheese called grana Padano, which is being sold as an alternative to Parmigiano-Reggiano. Grana simply means "gratable"; there are many granas in Italy, and the famous ones made around the city of Padua are grana Padano. This cheese also has a protected name and is an excellent product. It is not aged quite as long as Parmigiano-Reggiano—you can tell by the large salt crystals, which make the Parmigiano more crumbly—but if you find a good one, feel free to use it for grating on pasta, pizza, and so on. Here, however, nothing but the smooth nuttiness of Parmigiano will do: it tastes wonderful before or after dinner. Serve with a seeded semolina baguette.

2 stalks celery

Kosher salt

16 whole brine-cured black olives, such as Niçoise or Gaeta

16 whole brine-cured green olives, such as Atalanti or Cerignola

2 ounces Parmesan cheese, in one piece, at room temperature

1) Using the side of a box grater with one long opening, slice the celery crosswise into small horseshoe-shaped slices. Divide among 4 small serving plates, spreading the celery slices to cover the well of each plate. Sprinkle with a little salt.

2) Divide the olives among the plates, scattering them around.

3) With a vegetable peeler, shave curls of Parmesan over each plate.

4) Drizzle each plate with olive oil, then grind pepper on top. Sprinkle with parsley and serve.

Extra-virgin olive oil
Freshly ground black pepper
1 teaspoon chopped fresh parsley

Spanish Manchego with Apple Butter and Crostini

SERVES 4

Manchego comes to us from the same region of Spain that produced Cervantes: La Mancha. Made entirely from Manchega sheep's milk, it is the most popular aged cheese in Spain. Its strong flavor develops during a nine- to twelve-month aging process. Look for Manchegos that are encased in brown, not black, wax. Apple butter is a wonderfully aromatic project for a fall afternoon. You'll have plenty left over from this recipe.

---

8 ounces aged Spanish Manchego
   cheese

For the apple butter:

2¹/2 pounds apples (not too sweet or
   too tart), peeled, cored, and cut
   into chunks

1 cup dark brown sugar

1 teaspoon ground cinnamon

1/2 teaspoon ground allspice

For the crostini:

1 small baguette (preferably sourdough), sliced ¹/4 inch thick (about
   12 slices)

2 tablespoons Garlic Oil and Puree
   (page 292), or 2 tablespoons extra-
   virgin olive oil mixed with 1 minced
   garlic clove (optional)

---

1) Bring the cheese to room temperature, removing it from the refrigerator 4 hours before serving.

2) Make the apple butter: put the apple pieces in a heavy-bottomed pot with a lid, cover, and cook over low heat, stirring occasionally, until very soft and cooked down, 1 to 2 hours. Add the brown sugar, cinnamon, and allspice, stir well, and continue cooking until very thick, about 30 minutes more, stirring to break up any pieces. To test for doneness, place a small spoonful on a plate and set aside 20 minutes. If a ring of water forms, the apple butter is not quite done. Continue cooking over low heat until no ring forms.

3) Make the crostini: preheat the oven to 350°F.

4) In a mixing bowl, toss the baguette slices with the garlic oil and spread out on a baking sheet. Bake until lightly browned and crisp, about 10 minutes.

5) To finish the dish, core and quarter the Granny Smith apple, then slice thinly and toss with the lemon juice.

6) Cut the cheese into 8 wedges and place 2 wedges on each serving plate. With a soup spoon, scoop up about 2 tablespoons of apple butter and rest the spoon with the apple butter in it on the plate. Repeat with 3 more spoons.

7) Divide the apple slices among the plates, then scatter the pecans and raisins around the plates. Place 3 crostini on the rim of each plate and serve.

To finish the dish:

1 Granny Smith apple

1 teaspoon freshly squeezed lemon juice

24 pecan halves, lightly toasted (see page xxxiii)

16 golden raisins

Warm Goat Cheese with Poached Dried Fruit, Toasted Almonds, and Greens

SERVES 4

This plate was designed around the intense flavor of aged goat cheese, not the soft, crumbly, fresh white kind. Goat cheeses are made by some American producers, and French ones are known as bucheron *or* bûches de chèvre. Bûche *simply means "log," and that is the usual shape, although round aged* crottins *are also available. A good one will have a grayish exterior rind with some white bloom; the inside is chalky white. The outside may have thin ridges, as some cheeses are aged while wrapped tightly in straw. Serve with toasted semolina bread with sesame seeds. You can make the poached fruit up to 2 days in advance.*

For the poached fruit:

2 cups water

1 cup sugar

1/2 cup whole dried apricots

1/4 cup raisins

1/4 cup dried cherries or dried cranberries

1/2 cup whole prunes

1/2 vanilla bean, split lengthwise

1 strip lemon zest, 1 inch wide

To finish the dish:

8 ounces ripened goat cheese with a rind, such as Boucheron or Coach Farm Aged, preferably in 1 log

1) Make the poached fruit: combine all the ingredients for the poached fruit in a saucepan and bring to a boil. Turn off the heat and let cool. Use immediately or cover and refrigerate until ready to serve; bring to room temperature before serving.

2) Preheat the oven to 400°F. Line a baking dish with aluminum foil.

3) Cut a 1 1/2-inch-thick slice off the log. Lay it flat, then cut into quarters to form thick, chunky wedges. Transfer to the baking dish and repeat with the remaining cheese. Bake 3 to 5 minutes, until warmed through and slightly melted.

4)   In a mixing bowl, whisk together the vinegar, oil, and salt and pepper to taste. Add the greens and almonds and toss quickly to coat. Divide among the serving plates.

5)   With a spatula, gently place the warm cheese on top of the greens, dividing it among the plates.

6)   With a slotted spoon, place a spoonful of poached fruit next to the greens. With a spoon, drizzle a little bit of the syrup over each plate. Serve immediately.

2 tablespoons red wine vinegar

1/4 cup extra-virgin olive oil

Kosher salt and freshly ground black pepper

4 cups mixed salad greens (mesclun) or a mixture of at least 3 lettuces such as red leaf, romaine, endive, radicchio, arugula, frisée, watercress, and Boston

1/4 cup whole almonds, lightly toasted (see page xxxiii)

Gorgonzola, Fresh Figs, and Sautéed Walnuts

Gorgonzola is produced near Milan, in the northern Italian region of Lombardy. Made entirely from cow's milk (unlike Roquefort, the world's other famous blue cheese, which is made from sheep's milk), true Gorgonzola is begun with "evening milk" from the second milking of the day, which is heated and left to cool overnight, and completed with warm "morning milk" the next day. It is the temperature contrast between the two that produces the characteristic blue-green mold.

There is some variation among Gorgonzolas, but all are yellowish, buttery, and smooth when ripe. The cheeses are ripened by the producers, so all you have to do is make sure the piece you buy has not become overripe and slimy. It is more interesting to buy a whole cheese, because you will be able to see the cheese turn more blue after you cut it, exposing it to the air. If you cannot find a good Gorgonzola, Wisconsin Maytag blue cheeses are also made from cow's milk. Serve with Seeded Multigrain Rolls with Golden Raisins (page 75) or warm raisin-walnut bread from the bakery.

8 ounces Gorgonzola or Maytag blue cheese, in one piece

4 ripe fresh figs, halved

4 small bunches ripe sweet grapes, such as Muscatel, Champagne, or Red Flame

2 tablespoons unsalted butter

24 fresh walnut halves

Kosher salt and freshly ground black pepper

1) Bring the cheese to room temperature, removing it from the refrigerator 4 hours in advance. Do not unwrap.

2) When ready to serve, unwrap the cheese, cut into chunks, and divide among the serving plates.

3) Arrange the figs and grapes on the plates.

4) At the last minute, melt the butter in a skillet over medium heat. Add the walnuts and cook, stirring, until lightly toasted and fragrant. Turn off the heat and sprinkle with salt and a little bit of pepper to taste. Divide among the plates and serve immediately.

Camembert and Caramelized Orange Slices with Parsley Salad

SERVES 4

Camembert is the great cheese of Normandy, the northern region of France that is most celebrated for its cream and butter. Creamy, soft, and pungent when fully ripe, Camembert is no trendy newcomer to the market; it has been famous for a thousand years and more. However, Camembert, like Brie, is not an adequately protected name, and there are now American and less eminent French cheeses that call themselves Camembert, some even made with ultra-pasteurized milk that changes the nature of the cheese completely. True (or veritable) Camembert is a raw-milk cheese with a downy-white, brown-flecked rind. It is made in one size only: the 8-ounce round, each one made from almost a gallon of milk. If you cannot find a veritable Camembert or a Camembert de Normandie, look for a genuine Brie cheese, always labeled Brie de Meaux. The cheeses are closely related. (They also have a cousin, Gale's favorite cheese: Brillat-Savarin, named for the celebrated author of The Physiology of Taste.*)*

In choosing Camembert and similar cheeses, it's always best to buy a whole cheese. The size, the rind, and the fat content all affect the ripening, and once the cheese is cut into—by your grocer, for example—the ripening process is altered forever. The cheese should be plump in the middle, not sunken, and should smell fresh, not ammo-niated. This type of cheese ripens from the outside edges to the center, so if possible, press the cheese before buying; when ripe, it will be soft all the way through. You can buy an underripe cheese and ripen it in a cool place in your kitchen or cellar, but never buy an overripe one. When the cheese is ripe, you can refrigerate it until you are ready to serve, but try to serve as soon as possible. If you do not plan to finish the cheese at one sitting, cut off what you will use and keep the remainder refrigerated. Chilling and warming the cheese repeatedly is what destroys the texture. Serve this plate with Seeded Multigrain Rolls with Golden Raisins (page 75) or a warm baguette.

1 ripe 8-ounce wheel Camembert, Brie, or other soft ripened cow's milk cheese with a rind

2 large navel oranges

1/2 cup coarse sugar

2 tablespoons cider vinegar

1/4 cup extra-virgin olive oil

Kosher salt and freshly ground black pepper

4 cups mixed salad greens (mesclun) or a mixture of at least 3 lettuces such as red leaf, romaine, endive, radicchio, arugula, frisée, watercress, and Boston

1/4 cup loosely packed whole parsley leaves

1) Bring the cheese up to room temperature, removing it from the refrigerator at least 4 hours in advance and leaving it in the wrapper. When ready to serve, unwrap, cut into 4 wedges and place each in the center of a serving plate.

2) Cut a slice off the top and bottom of each orange to expose the flesh. With a very sharp knife, following the contours of the orange, remove the peel and white pith completely. Do not be concerned if some of the flesh comes off with the peel.

3) Preheat the broiler.

4) Slice the oranges 1/4 inch thick, cutting across the grain so that the slices have a star pattern. Spread the sugar on a plate.

5) In a mixing bowl, whisk together the vinegar, oil, and salt and pepper to taste. Add the greens and parsley and toss quickly to coat. Divide among the serving plates, placing the greens on one side of the cheese wedges.

6) Working quickly, dip one flat side of each orange slice in the sugar to coat. Arrange the slices on a broiler pan, sugar side up. Immediately place in the broiler, not too close to the heat. Broil just to melt and caramelize the sugar, 2 to 3 minutes. Place 2 slices on each plate, on the other side of the cheese wedges. Serve immediately.

Pont l'Évêque with Medjool Dates and Endive

SERVES 4

Creamy ripened cheeses like Alsatian muenster and Pont l'Évêque from Normandy get their creaminess not from butterfat, like many runny cheeses, but from moisture. The rinds are washed throughout the aging process, and the water is absorbed into the cheese. The cheeses often develop a chewy orange or yellowish rind and an extremely pungent odor—although the flavor is not stronger than that of other ripe cheeses. Pont l'Évêque is formed in small squares; always buy a whole, plump one.

Dates should be fat and sweet, not hard and dry. Medjool dates are especially large, sweet, and succulent.

1) Bring the cheese to room temperature, removing it from the refrigerator at least 4 hours before serving. When ready to serve, cut into wedges and arrange on serving plates.

2) In a mixing bowl, toss the endive with the walnut oil, orange juice, and salt and pepper to taste. Divide among the serving plates.

3) Place 2 dates on each plate, sprinkle the endive salad with chervil, and serve.

8 ounces Pont l'Évêque cheese

2 Belgian endive, sliced into $^1/_2$-inch lengths

1 tablespoon walnut oil

2 teaspoons freshly squeezed orange juice

Kosher salt and freshly ground black pepper

8 whole Medjool dates

Pickled chervil leaves

Desserts

Roasted Fruits with Cinnamon–Red Wine Glaze and Toasted Almonds

Individual Caramelized Apple Tarts

Tarte Flambée aux Pommes
(Alsatian Apple Pizza)

Plum Crostata

The Best Banana Cream Pie

Aunt Jimmy's Streusel Apple Crisp

Tangerine Angel Food Cake with Tangerine Glaze

Sticky Toffee Pudding with Butterscotch Sauce

Blueberry Bread-and-Butter Pudding

Raspberry Rice Pudding

Summer Berry Pudding

Triple-Chocolate Custard

Double-Chocolate Mousse Mud Pie

Chocolate Sour Cream Marble Cake

Fromage Blanc Cheesecake with Toffee Crust and Strawberry-Lime Salsa

Roasted Fruits with Cinnamon–Red Wine Glaze and Toasted Almonds

Poaching fruit in wine is a French dessert tradition, but we've found that oven-roasting brings out more sweetness and taste—without adding any fat at all. The deep, exotic flavors of the sauce come from common ingredients like honey, brown sugar, and cinnamon, combined with the unexpected fruitiness of red wine. Almonds add crunch to this simple dessert, but if you're in a real rush, skip them and simply spoon the compote over frozen yogurt. Your guests will swoon. Stored in the refrigerator, this will last for at least a week.

2 ripe plums

2 ripe peaches

2 ripe pears, peeled

2 tablespoons honey

2 tablespoons light brown sugar

2 tablespoons light-bodied red wine, such as Beaujolais

$^1/_2$ teaspoon ground cinnamon

$^3/_4$ cup sliced almonds

$^1/_4$ cup granulated sugar

1 large egg white

1) Preheat the oven to 400°F.

2) Quarter the fruit and remove all the seeds and pits.

3) Combine the honey, brown sugar, wine, and cinnamon in a 9-inch baking dish. Add the fruit and toss to coat.

4) Bake until tender, 20 to 30 minutes. When the fruit is done, remove it and lower the oven temperature to 350°F.

5) Meanwhile, toss the almonds and granulated sugar together, then add the egg white and mix well to coat. Lightly grease a baking sheet and spread the almond mixture on it.

6) Bake the almonds, turning them with a spatula every 5 minutes, until golden brown and caramelized, 10 to 12 minutes.

7) Serve the fruit warm or at room temperature, with the almonds sprinkled on top.

TRY TO FIND A QUALITY HUNGARIAN TAKAJI ASZU 5 PUTTONYOS TO HIGHLIGHT THE FRUIT OF THIS DESSERT, OR DRINK A FORTIFIED RED THAT HARMONIZES WITH THE COOKING WINE.

Individual Caramelized Apple Tarts

SERVES 6

These juicy tarts are unbelievably easy to make, unbelievably impressive, and unbelievably good: an irresistible combination. We've rewritten the classic French tarte Tatin to make it quick and simple, using a quintessentially American piece of equipment: the muffin tin. Tarte Tatin is different from an apple tart in several ways: it is cooked upside down and then turned out for serving, the sugars are caramelized to a deep topaz brown, and the apples are cut in big chunks, not thin slices. This beautiful dessert looks like a baked apple encased in amber. Frozen or refrigerated puff pastry in sheets is available in most supermarkets and gourmet stores, and it's usually of very good quality.

12 tablespoons (1^1/2 sticks) unsalted butter

1^1/2 cups sugar

3 tablespoons brandy

1 tablespoon freshly squeezed lemon juice

6 Granny Smith or Golden Delicious apples, peeled, cored, and halved

One 9 x 12-inch sheet puff pastry, kept moist by covering with plastic wrap

1) Preheat the oven to 350°F. Lightly grease 6 cups of an extra-large muffin pan.

2) Melt the butter in a small skillet over medium heat. When the butter is completely melted, stir in the sugar and reduce the heat to low. Simmer, stirring occasionally, until the mixture turns brown and caramelizes, about 15 minutes.

3) Add the brandy and lemon juice (be careful; the mixture will bubble up when you add the liquid) and stir to combine. Simmer about 2 minutes to blend the flavors.

4) Divide the caramel among the muffin cups and place 2 apple halves in each cup.

5) Bake until the apples start to become tender, about 30 minutes.

6) Meanwhile, cut the puff pastry into 6 rounds slightly larger than the muffin cups.

7) Remove the apples from the oven, lightly press a pastry round on top of each cup, and continue baking until the pastry is golden brown and flaky, about 25 minutes more. Let cool in the pan at least 45 minutes to allow the caramel to set.

8) When ready to serve, reheat in a 450°F oven for 10 minutes to loosen the caramel. Turn out upside down onto a baking sheet and transfer immediately to individual plates. Note that the tarts should be served with the pastry on the bottom.

A YOUNG SAUTERNES IS THE PERFECT MATCH.

Tarte Flambée aux Pommes

Alsatian Apple Pizza

MAKES 2 MEDIUM PIZZAS OR 4 SMALL ONES; SERVES 8

One wonderful Alsatian specialty that has never made it to Paris brasseries is flammekueche or tarte flambée, a thin crisp dough round topped with milky cream cheese, matchsticks of bacon, and rings of onion. Quickly baked in a wood-burning oven, tarte flambée looks a lot like pizza to the American eye. The traditional way to top off a dinner of tarte flambée is with this unique dessert, which lies somewhere between a pizza and an apple tart.

1 recipe Semolina Pizza Crust (page 60), made with light olive oil instead of extra-virgin and with $^1/_4$ teaspoon freshly grated nutmeg added to the dough along with the salt

8 tablespoons (1 stick) unsalted butter

$^1/_4$ cup light brown sugar

$^1/_2$ vanilla bean, split, or $^1/_4$ teaspoon vanilla extract

2 tablespoons Calvados or another apple brandy or Cognac

Grated zest of $^1/_2$ lemon

Juice of $^1/_2$ lemon

4 large Granny Smith apples, peeled, cored, and thinly sliced

2 tablespoons granulated sugar

1 teaspoon ground cinnamon

1) Preheat the oven to 450°F.

2) On a lightly floured surface, pat or roll the pizza dough out into rounds about $^1/_4$ inch thick. Transfer onto pizza pans or baking sheets and let rest 10 minutes.

3) Meanwhile, melt the butter in a skillet over medium-high heat. When it foams, add the brown sugar and stir to combine, cooking until the mixture is caramelized and nutty brown. Reduce the heat to medium and stir in the vanilla bean, Calvados, lemon zest, lemon juice, and apple slices. Cook, stirring, until the apples are tender and glazed with sauce, about 10 minutes.

4) Lift the apples out of the pan and divide among the dough rounds, spreading the apples out evenly with a spatula. Reserve the cooking liquid in the skillet.

5) Combine the granulated sugar and cinnamon in a small bowl. Brush the edges of the dough rounds with water, then sprinkle with the cinnamon sugar.

6) Bake until the crust is lightly browned and crisp on the bottom, 12 to 15 minutes.

7) Meanwhile, reduce the apple cooking liquid to a thick glaze over medium heat. Pour over the apples as the pizzas come out of the oven. Let cool slightly, slice, and serve.

CHILL THE LATE-HARVEST ALSATIAN GEWURZTRAMINER KNOWN AS VENDANGE TARDIVE.

Plum Crostata

Under the name of tarte aux quetsches, *plum tart is a favorite dessert all over Alsace, especially in the fall when the purply-blue* quetsch *(pronounced "kwetch") plums come into season. A heavenly eau-de-vie is also made from the ripe fruits, which we know as Italian prune plums. This crostata is easier to make than any tart, since no custard is required: just sound fruit and good jam. The recipe can be doubled; it can also be made in any shape you like and with any soft fruits: peaches and berries are especially good.*

For the dough:

2 cups all-purpose flour

$^1/_2$ cup sugar

Finely chopped zest of 1 lemon

1 cup (2 sticks) cold unsalted butter, cut into pieces

1 large egg plus 1 large egg yolk, whisked together

For the filling:

2 tablespoons raspberry jam

6 to 8 ripe but firm plums, pitted and cut into wedges

1 cup raspberries, fresh or frozen

1 tablespoon honey

2 tablespoons whole milk

1 tablespoon coarse, turbinado, or "raw" sugar

1) Make the dough: in the bowl of a mixer, blend the flour, sugar, and lemon zest at low speed. Add the butter and continue blending at low speed until the mixture is coarse and sandy-looking. Add the egg mixture and blend just until the mixture comes together. Form into a ball, wrap with plastic wrap, and refrigerate at least 1 hour.

2) Preheat the oven to 375°F. Line a baking sheet with parchment paper.

3) On a floured surface, roll the dough out to a rough circle about 14 inches in diameter. Transfer it to the baking sheet. All around the edge of the dough, fold in the outer $^1/_2$ inch to form a rough, "rustic" edge for the tart.

4) Using a rubber spatula, gently spread the jam over the bottom of the tart. Then arrange the plum wedges in concentric circles over the jam. Dot with the raspberries and drizzle with the honey.

5) With a pastry brush, brush the tart edge with the milk. Sprinkle with the coarse sugar.

6) Bake until the fruit is tender and the underside of the tart is lightly browned, 25 to 30 minutes.

BELGIAN WHITE BEER, WITH ITS ORANGEY FLAVOR, WOULD DRINK WELL WITH THIS BRIGHT, FRUITY DESSERT.

MATCH WITH AN EXOTIC BLACK MUSCAT FROM CALIFORNIA OR AUSTRALIA.

The Best Banana Cream Pie

If you've only tasted diner versions of banana cream pie, you must make this recipe before another day passes. Please don't argue; you simply have to taste the delicate, vanilla-scented cream spooned inside a brittle, buttery crust, with nuggets of fresh cold banana in every bite. Life is too short not to experience a homemade banana cream pie—or two. Gale's mother, Myrna, was famous for her flaky pie crusts, and this is her recipe, with a bit of vinegar to ensure a tender crust.

This recipe makes two pies, but you can easily make just one: make two pie crusts but cut the filling ingredients in half. Refrigerate or freeze the remaining crust (make it through step 3 and refrigerate, wrapped tightly) for another day. How about using it for a savory purpose like the Caramelized Onion Tart on pages 18–19?

For Myrna's Pie Crust:

4 1/2 cups sifted all-purpose flour

2 teaspoons kosher salt

2 teaspoons sugar (optional)

1 1/2 cups (3 sticks) cold unsalted butter, cut into pieces

1/2 cup ice water

2 teaspoons red wine vinegar

For the filling:

8 cups whole milk

1/4 teaspoon kosher salt

1 vanilla bean, split lengthwise

24 large egg yolks

2 2/3 cups sugar

1 cup cornstarch

1) Make the pie crust: in the bowl of a mixer fitted with a paddle attachment, combine the flour, salt, and sugar. Mix 1 minute. Add the butter and mix just until the mixture resembles coarse crumbs.

2) Stir the water and vinegar together, then gradually add to the flour mixture. Mix at medium speed just until a dough forms. Do not overmix; the mixture may still have bits of butter.

3) Divide the dough in half and shape into round, flat discs on sheets of wax paper. Wrap separately and refrigerate 30 minutes.

4) Lightly flour your rolling pin. On a lightly floured surface, roll one dough disc out into a large round about 1/8 inch thick. Place

a pie plate upside down on top and trim around it with a sharp knife, leaving about 2 inches extra dough all the way around.

5) Roll the dough onto your rolling pin, then unroll it into the pie plate, or fold it into quarters, transfer to the pie plate, and unfold. Gently press the crust into place, turning under any excess dough to create a thicker edge. Pinch the edge with your fingers to create a decorative edge. Repeat with the other dough disc, then refrigerate the crusts, covered, 30 minutes.

6) Preheat the oven to 375°F.

7) Line each crust with a sheet of regular-weight aluminum foil, then pour in dried beans or pie weights to fill it to the edge. Bake the crusts 25 to 30 minutes, just until dry and set, then remove the foil and beans.

8) Bake another 10 to 15 minutes, checking frequently to prevent overbaking, until just golden brown. Remove from the oven immediately and let cool on wire racks.

9) Make the filling: combine the milk, salt, and vanilla bean in a nonreactive saucepan and heat over medium heat, stirring occasionally. As soon as the mixture begins to boil, turn off the heat.

10) Whisk the egg yolks and sugar together until thick and pale yellow, then gradually whisk in the cornstarch. Gradually whisk in half of the hot milk mixture.

11) Pour the yolk-milk mixture into the saucepan with the rest of the milk and cook over medium heat, whisking frequently, until the mixture begins to thicken and boil. Reduce the heat to medium and cook, whisking, 3 to 5 minutes more, until the mixture no longer tastes starchy. It should become very thick, like a set custard. When it is cooked, turn off the heat.

6 tablespoons ($^3/_4$ stick) cold unsalted butter, cut into pieces
6 ripe bananas, sliced $^1/_4$ inch thick
Whipped cream for serving (optional)

12) Stir in the butter until it is melted, then fold in the bananas. Pour the filling into the prebaked pie shells.

13) Push the bananas below the surface to prevent them from browning, then smooth the tops. Cover with plastic wrap, gently pressing the plastic wrap against the surface to prevent a skin from forming.

14) Refrigerate at least 7 hours or overnight. Serve topped with whipped cream.

TRY A BOTRYTIS-INFECTED VOUVRAY MOELLEUX FROM FRANCE'S LOIRE VALLEY.

Aunt Jimmy's Streusel Apple Crisp

SERVES 4 TO 6

This dessert is a Gand family tradition, a specialty of Gale's Aunt Sylvia—always called Jimmy since the long-ago day when she got a very, very short haircut. This is a great way to use up apples in the fall, even the wrinkled ones that are still in the bottom drawer of the refrigerator months later. It is an infinitely multipliable recipe, so you can make up large batches of topping for the freezer. For a quick dessert, just thaw, sprinkle over cut-up apples, and bake.

1) Preheat the oven to 400°F. Butter a deep 2-quart baking dish.

2) Place the apples in the baking dish. They should be at least 2¹/2 inches deep; add more if necessary.

3) In a bowl, stir together the flour, sugars, cinnamon, and nutmeg. Using a pastry blender or the paddle attachment of a mixer, cut in the butter to make a crumbly, sandy mixture. Sprinkle the topping over the apples.

4) Bake for 30 minutes, until apples are tender and the topping is browned.

5) Serve warm with heavy cream or ice cream.

4 to 6 large McIntosh or other tart, crisp apples, peeled, cored, and thickly sliced

¹/2 cup all-purpose flour

¹/4 cup dark brown sugar

1 tablespoon granulated sugar

¹/4 teaspoon ground cinnamon

Pinch of freshly grated nutmeg

4 tablespoons (¹/2 stick) cold unsalted butter, cut into pieces

Heavy cream or vanilla ice cream

A DARK, RICH BRITISH OLD ALE WILL HAVE ENOUGH FRUIT TO MARRY WELL
WITH THIS AUTUMNAL DESSERT.

TRY A GERMAN RIESLING BEERENAUSLESE FROM THE MOSEL.

Tangerine Angel Food Cake with Tangerine Glaze

ONE 10-INCH ANGEL FOOD CAKE; SERVES 8

We find that more and more of our customers are watching their fat grams—but none of them can resist our cakes. Here's our favorite solution. No one with a forkful of this fluffy, moist, tangerine-scented cake has ever felt dessert-deprived. If you don't have tangerines at hand, any sweet orange with a deeply colored rind will do.

Gale has had an angel food cake for her birthday for as many years as she can remember. Now that she is a professional baker, only her intrepid best friend Karen Katz, who tested the recipes for this book, will make one for her! Creating birthday and holiday traditions around baking is a great way to make cooking a part of your life.

For the cake:
1¹/₂ cups egg whites, at room temperature
1¹/₄ teaspoons cream of tartar
¹/₂ teaspoon kosher salt
1¹/₂ cups sugar
1¹/₈ cups sifted cake flour
1 teaspoon vanilla extract
Grated zest of 1 tangerine

For the glaze:
¹/₄ cup freshly squeezed tangerine juice
1 tablespoon egg whites
8 ounces confectioners' sugar

1) Preheat the oven to 375°F.

2) Make the cake: In a large mixing bowl, whip the egg whites till white and foamy. Add the cream of tartar and salt and continue whipping until soft, droopy peaks form. Still whipping, add 1 cup of the sugar in a thin stream and whip until stiff and glossy.

3) With a sifter, sift the remaining ¹/₂ cup sugar and the flour together 3 times to aerate and lighten the mixture. Work quickly so the egg white does not deflate. (Or sift through a strainer onto a sheet of wax paper.) Fold into the egg whites one-third at a time.

4) Fold in the vanilla and tangerine zest.

5) Gently spoon the mixture into an ungreased tube pan. Smooth the top and bake 30 to 35 minutes, until golden brown.

6) Turn the pan upside down and hang it around the neck of a wine bottle to cool to room temperature.

7) Slide a butter knife around the sides of the pan and put a serving plate on top. Turn over and knock the cake out onto the plate. (The browned crust of the cake will stick to the pan.)

8) When the cake has cooled thoroughly, make the glaze: Whisk together the tangerine juice and egg whites, then add the confectioners' sugar and stir until smooth. Drizzle the glaze evenly over the cake. Let set in a cool place.

AN AUSTRIAN SCHEUREBE BEERENAUSLESE MARRIES BEAUTIFULLY WITH THE TANGERINE.

Sticky Toffee Pudding with Butterscotch Sauce

SERVES 8 TO 10

British sweets have the most wonderful names, like Crundle Pudding, Gooseberry Fool, Blackberry Crumble, Lardy Cakes, and Plum Heavies. Toffee pudding is a Lake District classic, and the term sticky is the highest praise such a pudding can receive. This is a very moist date cake that is baked, infused with butterscotch sauce, and then baked again to caramelize the sugar into a bubbly coating.

For the cake:

12 ounces dates, pitted and roughly chopped

2¹/₂ cups water

2 teaspoons baking soda

3¹/₄ cups sifted all-purpose flour

2 teaspoons baking powder

8 tablespoons (1 stick) cold unsalted butter, cut into pieces

1²/₃ cups granulated sugar

4 large eggs

2 teaspoons vanilla extract

For the sauce:

2¹/₄ cups light brown sugar

7 tablespoons unsalted butter

1 cup half-and-half

1 teaspoon brandy

¹/₄ teaspoon vanilla extract

1 cup cold heavy cream (optional)

1) Preheat the oven to 350°F. Line a 13 x 9-inch baking pan with parchment or wax paper.

2) Combine the dates and water in a saucepan and bring to a boil. Turn off the heat and gradually stir in the baking soda (it will foam up) and set aside.

3) In a bowl, combine the flour and baking powder.

4) In the bowl of a mixer, cream the butter until fluffy. Add the sugar and cream together until fluffy. Without stopping the mixer, add 2 of the eggs and mix until combined. Add the remaining 2 eggs and vanilla and mix until combined. Add about one-third of the flour mixture and one-third of the dates and mix until combined. Repeat until all the flour mixture and dates are incorporated into the batter.

5) Pour into the baking pan and bake about 40 minutes, until firm and set in the center.

6) Let cool in the pan. When cool, turn out of the pan onto a baking sheet and peel off the parchment paper. (The recipe can be made through this step up to 2 days in advance.)

7) When ready to serve, preheat the oven to 400°F.

8) Make the sauce: Combine the brown sugar, butter, half-and-half, and brandy in a saucepan and bring to a boil. Boil 3 minutes, until combined. Remove from the heat and stir in the vanilla.

9) Pour the sauce evenly over the top of the cake. Bake until the sauce is bubbly and cake is heated through, about 5 minutes.

10) Meanwhile, whip the heavy cream into soft peaks with the mixer. Cut the cake into squares and serve with whipped cream.

A MUSCAT DE BEAUMES-DE-VENISE MARRIES WELL WITH THIS DISH.

Blueberry Bread-and-Butter Pudding

SERVES 6 TO 8

This special dessert is typical of our approach to classic desserts: we look at it and think, how can we make this great dish even better? This creamy, fruit-spiked pudding brings new meaning to the word luscious. Even if you've never had real homemade bread pudding, you'll recognize this immediately as the ultimate in simple, delicious home cooking. You might also recognize it as a dessert version of French toast. In France that dish is called pain perdu—lost bread—*because it is made from slightly stale loaves. It is always served as dessert.*

---

1 loaf Brioche (pages 82–83) or day-old challah, crust removed

2 cups whole milk

2 cups heavy cream

Pinch of kosher salt

1 vanilla bean, split, or 1 teaspoon vanilla extract

6 large eggs

1 cup granulated sugar

1 pint blueberries, picked over and washed

Confectioners' sugar

1) Cut the bread into 1-inch cubes and set aside in a bowl.

2) In a saucepan, bring the milk, cream, salt, and vanilla bean just to a boil. (If using vanilla extract, add it after the mixture has come to a boil.) Turn off the heat and set aside to allow the vanilla to infuse.

3) In a mixing bowl, whisk together the eggs and sugar. Still whisking, add the hot cream mixture in a thin stream until combined.

4) Strain the mixture through a fine sieve into the bowl containing the bread cubes. Mix gently. Cover and refrigerate to let the bread soak up the custard, at least 30 minutes or as long as overnight.

5) Preheat the oven to 300°F.

6) Sprinkle the blueberries evenly in the bottom of 6 small baking dishes or ramekins—or 1 medium baking dish. Divide the bread cubes among the dishes and spoon any remaining custard over them.

7) Arrange the baking dishes in a roasting pan. Make a water bath: add enough hot water to come halfway up the sides of the dishes.

8) Bake until set and light golden brown on top, 30 to 45 minutes.

9) Sprinkle with confectioners' sugar and serve.

TRY A LIGHT, REFRESHING MOSCATO D'ASTI FROM PIEDMONT.

Raspberry Rice Pudding

We always had a hard time choosing between two favorite creamy desserts: rice pudding and crème brûlée. Fortunately, it occurred to us that they could easily be combined into a single sublime dessert! Tender raspberries make a much nicer addition to a delicate, soft-as-snow rice pudding than the usual chewy raisins.

^{2}/$_3$ cup whole milk
^{2}/$_3$ cup water
^{1}/$_2$ cup arborio rice
1^3/$_4$ cups heavy cream
^{1}/$_4$ cup half-and-half
^{1}/$_2$ vanilla bean, split lengthwise
6 large egg yolks
^{1}/$_3$ cup sugar
1 pint ripe raspberries
Coarse sugar for caramelizing
   (optional)

1) In a small, heavy saucepan with a lid, bring the milk and water to a simmer over medium heat. Add the rice, stir, and cover. Reduce the heat to very low, so the mixture stays at a bare simmer. Cook, stirring occasionally, until all the liquid is absorbed and the rice is very soft, 18 to 25 minutes.

2) Meanwhile, make the custard: heat the cream, half-and-half, and vanilla bean in a saucepan over medium heat, stirring occasionally. As soon as the mixture begins to boil, turn off the heat. Let it sit so that the flavors infuse.

3) Whisk the egg yolks and sugar together until combined. Gradually whisk in half of the hot cream mixture. Add the remaining hot cream mixture and whisk to combine. Strain the mixture through a fine sieve or chinois into a clean bowl.

4) Preheat the oven to 300°F.

5) Divide the cooked rice among 6 to 8 ramekins or spread it evenly in 1 baking dish. Arrange the raspberries on top of the rice.

6) Ladle the custard evenly over the rice and berries. Make a water bath: arrange the dish or dishes in a roasting pan and pour hot tap water around them until it comes halfway up the sides.

7) Bake 30 to 40 minutes until it sets. Let cool on a rack 10 minutes, then cover tightly with plastic wrap. Refrigerate until well chilled. (The recipe can be made through this step up to 2 days in advance.)

8) Serve plain or, when ready to serve, preheat the broiler to very hot. Sprinkle a coat of coarse sugar over each pudding (it will stick to the condensation on the pudding's surface), then tip the pudding to shake off the excess sugar. This gives you the right amount of sugar for caramelizing.

9) Place the dishes in a roasting pan and broil, not too near the heat, just until melted and caramelized, 2 to 3 minutes. Serve immediately.

MATCH WITH A DEMI-SEC OR LIGHT ROSÉ CHAMPAGNE.

Summer Berry Pudding

SERVES 8 TO 10

When living and cooking in England, we were fascinated by the English love of bread. Fried bread with breakfast, baked beans on toast for lunch, sandwiches for tea, bread stuffing in roast chicken for dinner, followed by brown-bread ice cream for dessert would not be an unusual day's menu. English white and wheat loaves have wonderful flavor and texture that we grew to love as well.

This is a pudding in the English, not the American, sense of the word: an extravagantly delicious dessert that may or may not involve cream or custard. This simple pudding has no added fat or sugar, just plenty of summertime ripe berry flavor. The natural pectins in the fruit help it hold together. The result is an intense purply-red mass of fruit; snowy whipped cream is the perfect foil.

10 to 15 thin slices white bread, crusts removed

$^1/_2$ cup thawed frozen apple juice concentrate

$1^1/_2$ cups raspberries

$1^1/_2$ cups red currants

2 cups strawberries, hulled

$^1/_2$ cup cranberries

1 cup blueberries

1 teaspoon unflavored gelatin

2 tablespoons cold water

1 cup cold heavy cream (optional)

1) The day before you plan to serve the pudding, line a mixing bowl with plastic wrap. Line the plastic wrap with the bread slices, trimming the pieces so that they fit together neatly. Save enough bread to cover the top of the pudding.

2) In a saucepan, combine the apple juice concentrate and all the berries. Bring the mixture to a boil and cook until the strawberries begin to soften, about 1 minute. Immediately turn off the heat.

3) Stirring, dissolve the gelatin in the water, then add the mixture to the berries and stir to combine.

4) Spoon the berry mixture into the bread-lined bowl. Cover with remaining bread slices. Cover the bowl with plastic wrap and chill overnight.

5) When ready to serve, whip the cream until soft peaks form.

6) Remove the pudding from the refrigerator and remove the plastic wrap on top of the bowl. Carefully turn the pudding out onto a platter and serve in spoonfuls with whipped cream on top.

COMPLEMENT WITH A DELICATE MOSCATO D'ASTI.

Triple-Chocolate Custard

SERVES 6 TO 8

Chocolate from South America first made its way to Europe in the form of cocoa, and there was a tremendous fad when the drink was introduced to France in the seventeenth century. The Marquise de Sevigne, the most famously witty letter writer of her era, wrote to her daughter in 1671: "If you are not feeling well, if you have not slept, chocolate will revive you. But you have no chocolate pot! I think of that again and again! How will you manage?"

Cocoa, bittersweet chocolate, and white chocolate make this pudding deep and velvety. Dutch cocoa is richer and darker than plain cocoa; it has been treated to reduce the natural acidity of the cocoa, allowing the chocolate flavor to come through more strongly without bitterness. White chocolate, of course, is not really chocolate at all, but in chip form it provides a wonderful sweet counterpart to the dark chocolate.

$1^1/_2$ cups sugar

$^3/_4$ cup cocoa powder (preferably Dutch-process)

$^1/_2$ cup cornstarch

Heaping $^1/_8$ teaspoon kosher salt

3 cups whole milk

3 cups half-and-half

3 ounces bittersweet chocolate

2 tablespoons vanilla extract

3 ounces white chocolate, chopped

1) In a mixing bowl, whisk together the sugar, cocoa, cornstarch, and salt. In a thin stream, whisk in the milk until smooth. In a thin stream, whisk in the half-and-half until smooth.

2) Strain the mixture through a fine sieve or chinois into a saucepan. Over medium heat, whisking the mixture constantly, bring to a boil. Boil gently 2 minutes. Turn off the heat and stir in the bittersweet chocolate and vanilla.

3) Fill a large bowl with ice cubes, rest the saucepan on top, and add cold water to cover the ice cubes. Let the mixture cool, stirring frequently, about 15 minutes.

4) Fold in the white chocolate and pour the mixture into 1-cup ramekins, cups, or mugs.

5) Refrigerate until well chilled. (The recipe can be made through this step up to 2 days in advance.) Serve cold.

DARK CHOCOLATE AND WINE DO NOT HARMONIZE; DRINK ESPRESSO COFFEE WITH THIS INTENSE DESSERT.

Double-Chocolate Mousse Mud Pie

To some of us, chocolate mousse is simply the only French dessert there is—a true chocolate lover will never tire of it. In France the mousse is traditionally made with whipped egg whites but no cream, which makes for a darker mousse; most American recipes add whipped cream for a milk-chocolate effect. This sophisticated "mud pie" includes both.

It takes time to create the scrumptious layers of this pie, but you'll find it's worth every minute. Even people who claim to be able to resist chocolate desserts will succumb to its multiple charms—a fluffy chocolate whip atop a dense mousse atop a crunchy, nutty dark chocolate crust.

For the crust:
2 cups finely ground Oreo® cookies
¹/₂ cup chopped cashew nuts
2 tablespoons unsalted butter, melted

For the dense chocolate mousse:
12 ounces semisweet chocolate
8 tablespoons (1 stick) unsalted butter
5 large eggs, separated
²/₃ cup malt powder
2¹/₂ tablespoons sugar

For the light chocolate mousse:
4 ounces semisweet chocolate
2 ounces unsweetened chocolate

1) Make the crust: combine all the ingredients in a bowl and toss until thoroughly combined. Press the mixture into the bottom of a 10-inch springform pan and refrigerate.

2) Make the dense mousse: melt the semisweet chocolate and butter together in the top of a double boiler over medium-low heat. Let cool slightly, then whisk in the egg yolks. Whisk in the malt powder. Keep warm.

3) In the bowl of a mixer, whip the egg whites until they form soft, droopy peaks. Still whipping, add the sugar in a thin stream and whip until the whites are stiff and glossy. Fold into the chocolate mixture.

4) Pour into the springform pan and smooth the top with a rubber spatula. Refrigerate.

5) Make the light mousse: Melt the chocolates together in the top half of a double boiler over medium-low heat. Let cool slightly.

6) In the bowl of a mixer, whip the egg whites until they form soft, droopy peaks. Still whipping, add the sugar in a thin stream and whip until the whites are thick and glossy. One-third at a time, fold the egg whites into the chocolate mixture. (You may need to whisk, not fold, the first third if the mixture is very thick.)

7) With the mixer, whip the cream until it forms soft peaks. Fold it into the mousse.

8) Pour the light mousse over the dense mousse and smooth the top with a rubber spatula. Chill until set, at least 3 hours or up to 1 day.

9) Run a hot damp cloth around the springform pan wall and remove. Slice with a knife dipped in hot water and serve with warm chocolate sauce if desired.

$1/2$ cup large egg whites (from about 3 eggs)
$1/4$ cup sugar
$1/2$ cup heavy cream

A VELVETY OR LATE-BOTTLED VINTAGE PORT WILL WORK WELL
WITH THE RICH CHOCOLATE.

Chocolate Sour Cream Marble Cake

The buttery flavor of the vanilla batter makes this cake delightfully different from the usual bland marble cake—and so do its fragrant chocolate-coffee swirl, its rich sour cream tang, and its moist, tender crumb. This improved all-American classic is wonderful plain but becomes truly heavenly when served with banana-walnut ice cream. The recipe can also be baked in one 9-inch tube pan; add about 10 minutes to the baking time.

8 tablespoons (1 stick) unsalted butter

1^1/$_4$ cups sugar

2 large eggs, separated

^{1}/$_2$ teaspoon vanilla extract

1^1/$_4$ cups all-purpose flour

2 teaspoons baking powder

^{1}/$_2$ cup sour cream

2 tablespoons half-and-half

^{1}/$_4$ cup cocoa powder (preferably Dutch-process)

^{1}/$_4$ cup strong brewed coffee

Pinch of baking soda

1) Preheat the oven to 350°F. Grease and flour 6 miniature Bundt pans.

2) In the bowl of a mixer, cream the butter and 1 cup of the sugar together until fluffy. Add the egg yolks and vanilla and mix well to combine.

3) In another bowl, sift together the flour and baking powder.

4) At low speed, mix about one-third of the flour mixture, one-third of the sour cream, and one-third of the half-and-half into the butter mixture. Repeat two more times and mix well to combine.

5) In a clean, dry bowl, whip the egg whites until droopy peaks form. Still whipping, slowly add the remaining ^{1}/$_4$ cup sugar and whip until stiff and glossy. Fold the egg whites into the batter.

6) In a bowl, combine the cocoa, coffee, and baking soda. Ladle out 2 cups of the batter and stir into the cocoa mixture.

7) Spoon in the batter into the Bundt pans in this order—2 spoonfuls of vanilla batter, then 1 of chocolate—until each pan is three-quarters full. Swirl a butter knife through each pan in a snaking "S" pattern to create the marble effect.

8) Bake for 25 to 30 minutes, until firm to the touch or until a tester inserted into the middle of a Bundt cake comes out clean.

9) Let cool in the pan for 20 minutes, then turn out.

A DARK IMPERIAL STOUT WITH THE FLAVOR OF TREACLE, COFFEE, AND DRIED FRUIT WOULD WORK HERE, OR A RICH, CREAMY SWISS SAMICHLAUS.

TRY A FORTIFIED SWEET RED WINE LIKE BANYULS FROM THE SOUTHWEST OF FRANCE.

Fromage Blanc Cheesecake with Toffee Crust and Strawberry-Lime Salsa

ONE 10-INCH CAKE; SERVES 10

This is a wonderful special-occasion dessert: a grown-up rendition of the classic cheesecake with graham cracker crust. Fromage blanc, or "white cheese," is a close French cousin of our American cream cheese, so it's a natural for perfect cheesecake. Fromage blanc is miraculously smooth and creamy, with almost no fat and true cream flavor. Sprinkled with sugar and fruit, it is served as dessert in France—especially to children.

Our filling is basic, but that's where the simplicity stops. The crust is a creatively crunchy mixture of almond toffee, white chocolate, and graham cracker crumbs. It contrasts beautifully with a tangy citrus and berry salsa, and the perfume of mint freshens all the flavors. Against the cool background of the creamy filling, all the elements get up and dance together, but if you're in a rush, omit the strawberries and serve the cake slices on a puree of all-fruit strawberry preserves and lime juice. We guarantee you'll hear no complaints. Fromage blanc is available in many gourmet shops, and toasted almond toffee is available at candy stores. To chop the chocolate and toffee, chill them in the freezer for half an hour, then feed them in chunks into your food processor with the motor running.

For the crust:

- **4 tablespoons ($^1/_2$ stick) unsalted butter**
- **$^3/_4$ cup graham cracker crumbs**
- **$^3/_4$ cup finely chopped white chocolate**
- **$^3/_4$ cup finely chopped toasted-almond toffee**

1) Make the crust: melt the butter in a medium saucepan. Add the remaining crust ingredients and combine until well coated with butter. Press into the bottom of a 10-inch springform pan.

2) Make the filling: in the top half of a double boiler over medium-low heat, combine 1 cup of the sugar and the *fromage blanc*. Whisk until the sugar has dissolved, about 2 minutes.

3) Add the gelatin to the *fromage blanc* mixture. Stir gently until gelatin has dissolved, about 2 minutes. Turn off the heat under the double boiler but leave it on the stove.

4) In the bowl of a mixer, whip the egg yolks with the remaining 1/2 cup of sugar until thick and pale. Fold into the *fromage blanc* mixture.

5) With the mixer, whip the cream until stiff peaks form. Fold the cream into the *fromage blanc* mixture.

6) Spoon the filling into the crust, smooth the top, and chill until set, about 2 hours.

7) Make the salsa: cut the strawberries into quarters or eighths, depending on their size. Mix with the strawberry puree, then squeeze the lime over and stir to combine. Refrigerate until ready to serve.

8) To serve, spoon the salsa onto a plate and place a slice of cake next to it. Sprinkle with mint.

For the filling:

1 cup sugar

1 pound *fromage blanc* or cream cheese

1 envelope (7 grams) unflavored gelatin mixed with 1/3 cup cool water

3 large egg yolks

1 1/2 cups heavy cream

6 fresh mint leaves, julienned

For the salsa:

1 pint ripe strawberries, washed and hulled

1/3 cup pureed fresh ripe strawberries or all-fruit strawberry preserves

1 lime, quartered

COMPLEMENT THIS WITH AN ALSATIAN VENDANGE TARDIVE, LATE-HARVEST PINOT GRIS, OR RIESLING.

Cookies

Chocolate-Almond Biscotti

Crisp Oatmeal-Raisin Cookies

Elsie's Poppyseed Shortbread

Malted Chocolate Chip Cookies

Myrna's Hungarian Pecan Cookies

Molasses Crisps

Big Chewy Peanut Butter Cookies

Espresso Tuiles

Cranberry Coconut Bars

Chocolate-Dipped Coconut Macaroons

Chocolate-Almond Biscotti

MAKES ABOUT 24 BISCOTTI

In Italian, biscotti *means "cooked twice," and that's just how you make them—bake once, then slice and bake again. (This is also the original source for our word* biscuit; *in French,* bis cuit *means "cooked twice"). The two-part cooking process is what accounts for biscotti's unique crunch. For a light but intensely chocolatey dessert, serve these with espresso and the best fresh fruit you can find at the market.*

Dutch-process cocoa powder is richer and darker than the regular product, but any good-quality cocoa will do, especially if the jar is reasonably fresh.

²/₃ cup whole almonds

2 cups all-purpose flour

1 cup sugar

¹/₃ cup cocoa powder (preferably Dutch-process)

1 teaspoon baking soda

¹/₄ teaspoon kosher salt

2 large eggs

2 large egg whites

³/₄ teaspoon vanilla extract

¹/₂ cup semisweet chocolate chips

1 large egg, beaten

1) Preheat the oven to 350°F.

2) Spread the almonds on a baking sheet and toast briefly, about 10 minutes, shaking the pan once or twice. Set aside to cool.

3) In the bowl of a mixer, combine the flour, sugar, cocoa powder, baking soda, and salt. In another bowl, whisk together the eggs, egg whites, and vanilla extract. Blending at low speed, slowly add the egg mixture to the flour mixture. Do not completely mix.

4) In another bowl, toss the cooled almonds and chocolate chips together. Add to the dough and blend just until combined. If your mixer is not very powerful, you may need to finish mixing the dough by turning it onto a floured surface and kneading it by hand. Knead it just until combined, or the dough will become sticky.

5) Reheat the oven to 350°F and lightly grease a baking sheet.

6) Divide the dough in half. On a well-floured surface, using your hands, roll out the dough into 2 logs 2 inches in diameter. Place the logs on the baking sheet and brush them with the beaten egg.

7) Bake until firm, 30 to 35 minutes.

8) Let cool 5 to 10 minutes but no longer; the logs should still be warm, or you won't be able to cut them. With a serrated knife, cut the logs at an angle into slices $1/2$ inch thick.

9) Reheat the oven to 350°F. Grease the baking sheet again.

10) Spread the biscotti out on the baking sheet, then toast in the oven 15 to 20 minutes.

11) Let cool on wire racks and store in an airtight container.

Crisp Oatmeal-Raisin Cookies

MAKES ABOUT 4 DOZEN COOKIES

This is a crisp, not doughy or chewy, oatmeal cookie. It's all about the buttery flavor, so if you are able to hunt down some "gourmet" butter from France or a local dairy, do use it here. Serving suggestion: a glass of very cold milk.

$1^1/_2$ cups (3 sticks) unsalted butter

1 cup light brown sugar

$1^1/_8$ cups granulated sugar

1 large egg

$1^1/_2$ teaspoons vanilla extract

3 cups rolled oats (not instant oatmeal)

$1^1/_2$ cups all-purpose flour

$^3/_4$ teaspoon kosher salt

$2^1/_2$ teaspoons baking soda

$1^1/_2$ cups raisins

1) Preheat the oven to 350°F.

2) In the bowl of a mixer, cream the butter until fluffy. Add the sugars and cream together until light and fluffy. Add the egg and vanilla and mix well.

3) In a separate bowl, stir together the oats, flour, salt, and baking soda.

4) With the mixer running, slowly add the oat mixture to the butter mixture and beat just until combined.

5) Add the raisins and mix just until combined.

6) Drop by tablespoonfuls onto the baking sheets, leaving at least 2 inches between the cookies.

7) Bake 8 to 10 minutes, until browned and crispy around the edges.

8) Let cool on wire racks and store in an airtight container.

Elsie's Poppyseed Shortbread

Gale's Hungarian grandmother, Elsie, was the cookie queen of the family. She grew up and learned to cook in the great baking tradition of Austria and Hungary, in which poppyseeds are a frequently used, delicate flavoring. Buttery shortbread offers an ideal background. Perfect simplicity is rarely achieved in life, except where shortbread is involved. Like pie crust and pound cake, shortbread is a matter of putting a few tried and true ingredients together and then not fussing over it too much. This recipe uses only four ingredients, so the butter should be especially fresh and tasty.

1) Preheat the oven to 350°F. Line a baking sheet (preferably one with sides) with parchment paper.

2) In the bowl of a mixer, cream the butter until fluffy. Add 1/2 cup of the sugar and cream together until light and fluffy.

3) Slowly add the flour and mix just until combined. Just as the mixture is getting smooth, mix in the poppyseeds.

4) On a well-floured surface, roll out the dough to about 3/4-inch thickness. Transfer it to the baking sheet and continue rolling, pushing the dough out toward the edges of the pan until 1/4 inch thick.

5) Prick the dough all over with a fork, then sprinkle with 1/2 tablespoon sugar.

6) Bake for 25 to 30 minutes, rotating the pan after 10 minutes. Shake the pan up and down, not side to side, as you rotate it to settle the dough.

7) When the surface is golden, remove from the oven and sprinkle immediately with the remaining 1/2 tablespoon sugar. Cut immediately into bars with a knife or pizza cutter and let cool in the pan. Store in an airtight container.

1 cup (2 sticks) cold unsalted butter,
cut into pieces
1/2 cup plus 1 tablespoon sugar
2 1/2 cups all-purpose flour
2 tablespoons poppyseeds

Malted Chocolate Chip Cookies

Another chocolate chip cookie recipe? Absolutely. Malt powder adds a milky richness that we love, and the finished cookies are chewier than the ordinary kind.

2 cups all-purpose flour

1 teaspoon baking soda

1 teaspoon salt

1 cup (2 sticks) cold unsalted butter, cut into pieces

$^3/_4$ cup light brown sugar

$^3/_4$ cup granulated sugar

1 teaspoon vanilla extract

2 large eggs

$^1/_2$ cup malt powder

2 cups semisweet chocolate chips

1) Preheat the oven to 350°F. Lightly grease two baking sheets.

2) Sift together the flour, baking soda, and salt and set aside.

3) In the bowl of a mixer, cream the butter until fluffy. Add the sugars and cream with the butter. The mixture will look a bit grainy. Add the vanilla and eggs, and beat together until fluffy. Add the malt powder and mix at low speed just until combined.

4) One-third at a time, add the flour mixture, beating after each addition just until combined. Gently mix in the chocolate chips.

5) Drop by tablespoonfuls onto the baking sheets.

6) Bake 8 to 10 minutes, depending on how crispy you like your cookies. The cookies will be flat.

7) Let cool on wire racks and store in an airtight container.

Myrna's Hungarian Pecan Cookies

MAKES ABOUT 4 DOZEN SMALL COOKIES

In baking, ground nuts provide flour, flavor, and fat all at once. Here they also act as the binder for the cookies. Gale's mother, Myrna, used to make hundreds of these during the holidays. Her secret for the best cookies: they must be rolled in the powdered sugar while still warm, so work quickly. (As Gale knows from experience, kids love to help with this task.)

1) Preheat the oven to 350°F. Lightly grease 2 baking sheets.

2) In the bowl of a mixer, combine the butter and vanilla. Add 1/2 cup of the sugar, then slowly add the flour and pecans and mix just until combined. Use your hands to roll the dough into balls about 3/4 inch in diameter, and arrange them on the baking sheets.

3) Bake 15 to 20 minutes, until golden brown. Meanwhile, spread the remaining confectioners' sugar out on a plate.

4) When the cookies are done, remove from the oven, let cool 3 to 5 minutes, and then roll each cookie in the sugar until coated, letting each rest in the sugar for a minute to absorb it. Let cool completely on wire racks, then store in airtight containers.

1 cup (2 sticks) unsalted butter, softened
1 teaspoon vanilla extract
2 1/2 cups confectioners' sugar
2 1/4 cups all-purpose flour
1 cup finely chopped pecans

Molasses Crisps

MAKES ABOUT 6 DOZEN COOKIES; CAN BE HALVED

Spicy gingerbread in crisp cookie form, these can be made more or less fiery by adjusting the amount of ginger to your taste. The flavor of molasses is one that our American forebears were very familiar with, but it isn't used much today. However, its deep caramel taste has a place at the table—and in the cookie jar. These crisps can be made in any size, from thumbnail to saucer.

1¹/₂ cups (3 sticks) unsalted butter

2 cups sugar

2 large eggs

¹/₂ cup molasses

¹/₂ teaspoon salt

1 teaspoon ground ginger

2 teaspoons ground cinnamon

2 teaspoons baking soda

3¹/₂ cups all-purpose flour

1) In the bowl of a mixer, cream together the butter and sugar until light and fluffy. Scrape down the sides of the bowl with a rubber spatula, then beat in the eggs one by one. Beat until the mixture is light and lemon-colored. Add the molasses and mix until combined. Scrape down the sides of the bowl.

2) In a separate bowl, stir together the salt, ginger, cinnamon, and baking soda. Add this to the butter mixture and mix until combined.

3) One-third at a time, add the flour to the butter mixture and mix just until combined.

4) Divide the dough in half, then wrap in plastic and chill at least 2 hours or overnight.

5) Preheat the oven to 350°F. Lightly grease 2 baking sheets.

6) Roll the dough into balls ¹/₂ to 2 inches in diameter and arrange them in well-spaced rows on the baking sheets.

7) Bake 10 to 12 minutes, just until crisp. The cookies will be thin and flat.

8) Let cool on the baking sheets 2 minutes, then transfer to wire racks. When cool, store in an airtight container.

Tuscan Arugula Pizza

*Camembert and Caramelized Orange Slices
with Parsley Salad*

Roasted Fruits with
Cinnamon–Red Wine Glaze and Toasted Almonds

Plum Crostata

Double-Chocolate Mousse Mud Pie

Profiteroles with
Warm Glossy Chocolate Sauce

*Chocolate-Almond Biscotti and
Crisp Oatmeal-Raisin Cookies*

Big Chewy Peanut Butter Cookies

People always say that peanut butter cookies are great for kids, but we suspect that grown-ups like them just as much. After all, this is a pretty serious cookie, with a salty-sweet flavor and crumbly richness that could even be called sophisticated.

1) Preheat the oven to 350°F. Lightly grease 2 baking sheets.

2) Sift together the flour, baking soda, and salt.

3) In the bowl of a mixer, cream the butter until fluffy. Add the sugars and cream with the butter. The mixture will look a bit grainy. Add the eggs, vanilla, and peanut butter and beat until fluffy.

4) Mixing at low speed, slowly add the dry ingredients and mix just until combined. If using, mix in the chocolate chips by hand.

5) Drop by tablespoonfuls onto the baking sheets. Bake for 10 to 12 minutes, until golden brown.

6) Let cool on wire racks and store in an airtight container.

2 cups all-purpose flour

$1/2$ teaspoon baking soda

$1/4$ teaspoon salt

8 tablespoons (1 stick) cold unsalted butter, cut into pieces

$1^1/4$ cups light brown sugar

$1^1/4$ cups granulated sugar

3 large eggs

2 teaspoons vanilla extract

1 cup chunky or creamy peanut butter

1 cup milk chocolate chips or peanuts (optional)

Espresso Tuiles

An elegant black-coffee lace cookie, with peaks and valleys for interesting texture and crunch. The clear, dark brown of the cookie glows like stained glass; Vanilla Ice Cream (pages 278–79) sets them off beautifully. These look much more difficult to make than they actually are. When spacing the batter on the baking sheet, remember that the tuiles spread out as they bake.

¹/₄ teaspoon salt

¹/₂ cup light brown sugar

¹/₂ cup light corn syrup

¹/₂ cup plus 2 tablespoons all-purpose flour

6 tablespoons (³/₄ stick) unsalted butter, melted

¹/₄ teaspoon pure vanilla extract

¹/₄ cup fresh decaffeinated espresso beans, crushed in a mortar or coarse-ground in a grinder

¹/₂ cup chopped pecans

1) Preheat the oven to 350°F. Line a baking sheet with parchment paper.

2) In the bowl of a mixer, combine the salt, brown sugar, and corn syrup. Add the flour, butter, and vanilla extract and mix well. Add the espresso and pecans and mix just to combine.

3) Drop tablespoonfuls of batter onto the baking sheet, leaving plenty of room between for the tuiles to spread out as they bake.

4) Bake 8 to 10 minutes, until the edges are browned. When done, the tuiles will be bubbly and flat.

5) While the tuiles are baking, crumple up a piece of parchment paper so that you have a crumpled, textured surface to drape the hot tuiles on.

6) When the tuiles are baked and still hot, lift them (still on the parchment paper) off the baking sheet. One by one, peel the tuiles off the parchment paper and drape them over the crumpled piece to cool.

7) When cool, store carefully in an airtight container.

Cranberry Coconut Bars

MAKES 12 BARS

Sweet, tart, chewy, nutty—these are cookies taken to extremes. If you've grown fond of the orange-cranberry combination, imagine adding crunchy pecans and tender coconut to the mix, and you'll understand why these are so popular at our Vanilla Bean Bakery.

1) Make the crust: preheat the oven to 350°F.

2) In a mixing bowl, combine the butter, brown sugar, and salt and mix well. Gradually add the flour, mixing to combine. Stir in the pecans. Press the mixture into the bottom of an ungreased 9-inch square baking pan. Bake 15 to 20 minutes, until browned.

3) Meanwhile, make the filling: in the bowl of a mixer, combine the sugar, flour, and baking powder and mix well. Add the eggs, milk, vanilla, and orange zest and mix well. Fold in the cranberries, coconut, and pecans.

4) When the crust is baked, remove from the oven and spread the filling over it. Return to the oven and bake an additional 30 minutes.

5) Cool in the pan on a wire rack. Cut into bars for serving.

For the crust:

6 tablespoons (³/₄ stick) cold unsalted butter, cut into pieces
¹/₂ cup light brown sugar
¹/₂ teaspoon kosher salt
1 cup all-purpose flour
¹/₂ cup finely chopped pecans

For the filling:

1 cup granulated sugar
2 tablespoons all-purpose flour
¹/₂ teaspoon baking powder
2 large eggs, beaten
1 tablespoon whole or 2% low-fat milk
1 tablespoon vanilla extract
1 tablespoon grated orange zest
1 cup coarsely chopped cranberries
¹/₂ cup sweetened shredded dried coconut
¹/₂ cup coarsely chopped pecans

Chocolate-Dipped Coconut Macaroons

These are lightened with stiffly whipped egg white, but they resemble a big, chewy Passover macaroon more than a classic French meringue. Macaroons are a traditional Jewish holiday dessert at Passover, when no flour or yeast can be eaten. Lumps of tender coconut, lightly bound together with a bit of egg white and coated with dark chocolate, are too good to eat only once a year. The white chocolate drizzle makes them more spectacular but can certainly be omitted. We feel that bigger is better as far as macaroons are concerned, but you can make them smaller if you like.

¹/₄ cup cake flour or fine matzo meal

1 cup sugar

¹/₄ teaspoon kosher salt

4 large egg whites

1 teaspoon vanilla extract

4 cups sweetened shredded dried coconut

10 ounces bittersweet chocolate

3 ounces white chocolate (optional)

1)   Preheat the oven to 350°F.

2)   Sift together the flour, sugar, and salt. Line a baking sheet with parchment paper.

3)   Whip the egg whites until stiff peaks form, then fold in the flour mixture. Fold in the vanilla and coconut.

4)   For large cookies, drop the batter onto the baking sheet by tablespoonfuls or pipe into mounds through a pastry bag fitted with a plain tip. For small cookies, drop by teaspoonfuls or use a smaller tip.

5)   Bake 15 to 20 minutes, until golden. Let cool on wire racks.

6)   Line the baking sheet with fresh parchment paper.

7) Melt the dark chocolate in a double boiler or microwave, stirring very frequently to prevent burning. Dip a macaroon into the chocolate to coat the top half, then place on the baking sheet to cool. Repeat with remaining macaroons.

8) Melt the white chocolate in a double boiler or microwave, stirring very frequently to prevent burning. Use the tines of a fork to drizzle or spatter the chocolate-covered cookies. Let cool or refrigerate until the chocolate firms up.

9) Store in airtight containers, with wax paper between cookie layers to prevent sticking.

Ice Cream and Cool Drinks

Vanilla Ice Cream and Variations

Profiteroles with Warm Glossy Chocolate Sauce

Caramelized Banana Split with Orange-Glazed Walnuts

Coffee-Toffee Ice Cream with Cinnamon Prune Compote

Gale's Root Beer Float

The Best Chocolate Malted

Bob's Favorite Pink Grapefruit Granita

Passionfruit Lemonade

Raspberry Lemonade

Mint Lemonade

Ginger Limeade

Strawberry-Banana Whip

Raspberry-Lime Yogurt Smash

Vanilla Ice Cream and Variations

MAKES 2 QUARTS; CAN BE HALVED

Homemade ice cream is an inexpensive luxury, and an easy one. In this recipe we use lots of fresh cream, not milk, which makes a dense and satisfying mixture. The key to great flavor is using whole vanilla beans. If you are lucky enough to be choosing among vanilla beans from around the world, here's a quick flavor guide: Mexican beans are creamy, with spicy overtones. Madagascar beans are even more creamy, but Indonesian ones have a sweet, woody flavor. Tahitian vanilla is very fruity, with a strong flavor of ripe cherries. Most extracts are made by blending the four into the basic vanilla flavor we recognize; whole beans have more individuality.

4 cups half-and-half
4 cups heavy cream
1 vanilla bean, split lengthwise
18 large egg yolks
1$^{1}/_{2}$ cups sugar

1) Put a large mixing bowl in the freezer to chill.

2) In a saucepan over medium heat, bring the half-and-half, cream, and vanilla to a simmer, stirring occasionally to make sure the mixture doesn't burn or stick to the bottom of the pan.

3) Meanwhile, whisk together the egg yolks and sugar.

4) When the cream mixture reaches a fast simmer (do not let it boil), turn off the heat. In a thin stream, whisk half of it into the egg yolk mixture. Then pour the egg-cream mixture into the saucepan containing the rest of the cream mixture.

5) Cook over medium heat, stirring constantly with a wooden spoon. At 160°F, the mixture will give off a puff of steam. When the mixture reaches 180°F, it will be thickened and creamy, like eggnog,. If you don't have a thermometer, test it by dipping a wooden spoon into the mixture. Run your finger down the back of the spoon. If the stripe remains clear, the mixture is ready; if the edges blur, it is not quite thick enough yet. When it is ready, quickly remove from the heat.

6) Meanwhile, remove the bowl from the freezer, put 4 handfuls of ice cubes in the bottom, and add cold water to cover. Rest a smaller bowl in the ice water.

7) Strain the cream mixture through a fine sieve or chinois (to remove the vanilla bean pieces) into the smaller bowl. Chill 3 hours, then freeze according to the directions for your ice cream maker.

For Chocolate Ice Cream:
Reduce the sugar to 3/4 cup. Add 14 ounces of semisweet chocolate at the end of step 4.

For White Chocolate Ice Cream:
Reduce the sugar to 3/4 cup. Add 14 ounces of white chocolate at the end of step 4.

For Cinnamon Ice Cream:
Add 2 cinnamon sticks and 1 1/2 teaspoons of ground cinnamon in step 2.

For Coffee Ice Cream:
Add 1/4 cup finely ground decaffeinated coffee beans (freshly ground if possible) in step 2.

For Banana–Toasted Walnut Ice Cream:
Puree 3 very ripe bananas in a food processor and add at the end of step 5. After straining in step 7, discard any banana puree that doesn't pass through the strainer. As the ice cream comes out of the ice cream maker, fold in 1 cup toasted walnut pieces.

Profiteroles with Warm Glossy Chocolate Sauce

At the small but bustling right-bank Paris brasserie called Flo, families, friends, lovers, businessmen, and tourists all rub shoulders. (They have no choice, since the tables are so close together.) Everyone wants to eat at Flo, one of the most popular and atmospheric restaurants in all of Paris. It has thrived despite its out-of-the-way location (on the eighteenth-century site of the royal stables) for well over a century. Sarah Bernhardt ordered her dinners in from Flo when she was acting in the neighborhood, and the current decor dates back almost to her era: Flo was last redecorated in 1913.

It seems entirely possible that Flo's profiterole recipe hasn't changed since then: why would they tamper with perfection? Plenty of homemade chocolate sauce is the key.

For the puffs:

2 cups cold water

16 tablespoons (2 sticks) unsalted butter

1 teaspoon kosher salt

1 tablespoon sugar

2 cups flour

10 large eggs

1 teaspoon cold water

About 3 cups Vanilla Ice Cream (pages 278–79)

1) Make the puffs: preheat the oven to 425°F. Line a large baking sheet with parchment paper.

2) In a large saucepan, bring the water, butter, salt, and sugar to a rolling boil over medium-high heat. Stirring with a wooden spoon, add all the flour at once and stir hard until the mixture forms a ball. Cook for 1 minute, stirring constantly to keep the mixture from sticking.

3) Scrape the mixture into the bowl of a mixer with the paddle attachment and mix at medium speed. One by one, add 9 of the eggs, stopping the mixer occasionally to scrape down the sides of the bowl. Mix until the dough is smooth and glossy.

4) Using a pastry bag, pipe the dough into 18 mounds, each about 3 inches across, on the baking sheet. Or use a spoon to scoop and shape the dough into mounds. Whisk the remaining egg with water until beaten, then use a pastry brush to brush it on each mound.

5) Bake for 15 minutes, then lower the oven temperature to 350°F and bake for another 20 to 25 minutes, until the puffs are golden brown.

6) Let cool on wire racks. (The puffs can be made 1 day ahead and stored, tightly covered.)

7) Make the sauce: in the top half of a double boiler, combine the 2 chocolates over simmering water. Stir constantly until melted, then whisk in the corn syrup and water. Whisk until smooth and shiny.

8) When ready to serve, cut the puffs horizontally in half with a sharp knife and remove the ice cream from the freezer to soften.

9) To assemble the profiteroles, place a scoop of ice cream inside each puff and arrange them on serving plates. Pour the warm chocolate sauce over and around the puffs, or pass it at the table in a pitcher.

For the sauce:

3 ounces unsweetened chocolate
7 ounces semisweet chocolate
$^3/_8$ cup light corn syrup
$^1/_2$ cup hot water

Caramelized Banana Split
with Orange-Glazed Walnuts

SERVES 4

Here's an elaborated childhood dessert with upscale details: a crackly caramel crust on the bananas, dark chocolate sauce instead of hot fudge, and a bright-flavored orange glaze coating the walnuts.

For the walnuts:
³/₄ cup sugar
¹/₃ cup water
Pinch of ground cinnamon
Grated zest of ¹/₄ orange
2 cups walnut halves

For the sundae:
¹/₂ cup coarse sugar
4 small ripe bananas, peeled and split lengthwise
8 scoops Vanilla Ice Cream (pages 278–79)
1 recipe Warm Glossy Chocolate Sauce (see Profiteroles with Warm Glossy Chocolate Sauce, pages 280–81)
4 sprigs fresh mint

1) Make the walnuts: in a saucepan, combine the sugar, water, cinnamon, and orange zest and bring to a boil. Add the walnuts and simmer, stirring, as the water evaporates. The glaze will be shiny and transparent at first, then turn opaque as the water cooks off. The finished nuts will be completely coated with sugar crystals.

2) Preheat the broiler until very hot.

3) Spread the sugar on a plate and dip the cut faces of the bananas in it. Arrange the bananas, sugar-coated side up, on a broiler pan. Broil, not too close to the heat, until browned and the sugar is caramelized.

4) Put 2 scoops of the ice cream in each serving bowl or stemmed glass and top with chocolate sauce. Tuck the bananas into the bowl, sticking up like rabbit ears (if you like). Sprinkle with the glazed walnuts and garnish each bowl with a mint sprig.

Coffee-Toffee Ice Cream
with Cinnamon Prune Compote

SERVES 4 TO 6

This grown-up sundae pours the classic prune-Armagnac flavor combination over espresso ice cream. With sweet crunchy toffee on top, the composition in flavor and texture is complete.

1) Make the toffee: lightly grease a small baking sheet or roasting pan. Combine the sugar and water in a heavy saucepan and bring to a boil. Reduce the heat and cook gently (do not stir) until golden amber. Stir in the butter. When the butter is incorporated, pour the mixture into the greased pan and set aside to cool at least 30 minutes, until hardened. Break into pieces with your hands and chop into chunks by pulsing in the food processor. Don't be concerned if they are not uniform in size.

2) As the ice cream comes out of the ice cream maker, fold the toffee pieces into it, or fold the toffee into softened store-bought ice cream. Freeze.

3) Meanwhile, make the compote: combine all the remaining ingredients in a saucepan and simmer until the prunes are plump and softened, about 10 to 15 minutes. Cover and set aside until ready to serve.

4) When ready to serve, warm the compote over low heat. Scoop ice cream into individual serving bowls and top with 2 prunes and a few spoonfuls of sauce.

2 cups sugar

$^1/_2$ cup water

6 tablespoons ($^3/_4$ stick) unsalted butter

$^1/_2$ recipe Coffee Ice Cream (see Vanilla Ice Cream and Variations, pages 278–79) or 1 quart store-bought ice cream

For the compote:

16 pitted whole prunes

$^1/_4$ cup Armagnac, Cognac, or other brandy

1 cup freshly squeezed orange juice

$^1/_4$ teaspoon ground cinnamon

Gale's Root Beer Float

When we moved from Chicago to England in 1990, we had no idea that we were leaving root beer behind. Gale had always loved it, and it didn't occur to us that root beer is an entirely American phenomenon. Root beer was originally brewed from a variety of barks for medicinal purposes: like cola, it eventually crossed over from medicine to refreshment. But not in Europe, where root beer's dominant flavor, sassafras, is still entirely associated with cough syrup. If we wanted root beer, we had to order it from the States—or make it ourselves. That's when the seed of Gale's Root Beer was planted.

The recipe for homemade root beer (which was extremely popular in America as recently as the 1940s) no longer includes sassafras, which has since been allegedly found to be carcinogenic. Gale uses birch bark, cinnamon bark, star anise, ginger root, and vanilla beans to flavor her root beer, which she brews in 150-gallon batches. Root beer is brewed like tea, not like beer: there's no fermentation involved. A deeply flavored syrup is prepared and then combined with carbonated water. Maple-molasses and cinnamon-ginger-vanilla are just two of the variations she has come up with so far. It's so easy to experiment with new flavors that Gale's predicting a root beer revolution in the near future. For now, if you want to try Gale's original, you can order it by phone (see page 323).

Miniature root beer floats are always part of our most popular dessert at Brasserie T: the Blue Plate Special, small tastings of many different desserts. We know that's not as practical for home kitchens as it is in a restaurant, but just serving two kinds of homemade cookies and a fresh, creamy root beer–vanilla ice cream float seems to make everyone very happy. Remember to pour the root beer over the ice cream so they have a chance to mix.

Place 2 scoops of ice cream in each of 4 tall soda glasses. Pour the root beer over the ice cream. Serve with elbow straws.

2 cups Vanilla Ice Cream (pages 278–79) or store-bought ice cream

One 30-ounce bottle Gale's Cinnamon-Ginger-Vanilla Root Beer, well chilled, or another root beer of your choice

The Best Chocolate Malted

MAKES 2

Very, very, very thick. Serve very, very, very cold.

1 cup Vanilla Ice Cream (pages 278–79) or store-bought premium ice cream

2 tablespoons Warm Glossy Chocolate Sauce (see Profiteroles with Warm Glossy Chocolate Sauce, pages 280–81)

2 teaspoons malt powder

1 cup chilled heavy cream

Combine all the ingredients in a blender and blend until smooth.

Bob's Favorite Pink Grapefruit Granita

SERVES 4 TO 6

Granitas are pure, fresh, and easy, and we find just looking at a mound of pale pink, icy granita decorated with a cool mint sprig soothing and refreshing. Served after a rich or overwhelming meal, granitas wake you up and cool you down. Our friend Bob Payton loved this one best of all, and anyone who is a sorbet fan will probably agree. Pink grapefruits are slightly sweeter than yellow ones, and the color is incomparable. This technique works with many kinds of fruit juices or even with dark, sweet coffee: just remember to keep the ice cubes small.

4 cups freshly squeezed pink grapefruit juice
Juice of 1 lime
2 cups water
1 cup sugar

1) Combine the grapefruit juice and the lime juice in a large bowl.

2) In a saucepan, boil the water and sugar until the sugar is dissolved. Let cool slightly and add to the juice mixture. Stir to combine.

3) Pour into ice cube trays to a depth of no more than 1/2 inch. Freeze overnight, along with the dishes you plan to serve the granita in.

4) When ready to serve, unmold the cubes into a food processor fitted with the metal blade. Process, pulsing, just until crushed and serve immediately in chilled dishes.

Cool Drinks

Beer and wine shouldn't be the only options for drinking with a meal, especially when kids or cars are involved. At Brasserie T we find that a lot of our customers, for one reason or another, aren't drinking. But there's something not quite festive about ice water. In addition to Gale's Root Beer on tap, we've come up with some other options: fresh lime and lemonades, infused with aromatic spices and fruit. Frozen unsweetened lemon juice is available in some supermarkets and makes the whole process easy. Of course, for the best flavor, fresh juice is preferable. We've also thrown in a couple of bright-tasting blender drinks that are breakfast favorites at the Vanilla Bean Bakery. Cheers!

Passionfruit Lemonade

SERVES 12

9 cups water

2 cups freshly squeezed lemon juice (about 12 lemons)

2 cups superfine sugar

$^{1}/_{2}$ cup passionfruit or mango juice (available at Latin and some health-food markets)

In a pitcher, whisk all the ingredients together until the sugar dissolves. Serve over ice.

Raspberry Lemonade

SERVES 12

$^{3}/_{4}$ cup fresh or thawed frozen raspberries

9 cups water

2 cups freshly squeezed lemon juice (about 12 lemons)

2 cups superfine sugar

Puree the raspberries in a blender and strain through a fine sieve into a pitcher. Add the remaining ingredients and whisk together until the sugar dissolves. Serve over ice.

Mint Lemonade

SERVES 12

12 large fresh mint sprigs
9 cups water
2 cups freshly squeezed lemon juice (about 12 lemons)
2 cups superfine sugar

Put the mint in a 3 to 4 quart pitcher and crush lightly with a wooden spoon to release the flavor. Add the remaining ingredients and stir together until the sugar dissolves. Serve over ice.

Ginger Limeade

SERVES 12

9 cups water
2 cups freshly squeezed lime juice (about 20 limes)
2 cups superfine sugar
10 thin slices peeled fresh ginger

In a pitcher, whisk together all the ingredients until the sugar dissolves. Let steep at least 1 hour to bring out the ginger flavor. Serve over ice.

Strawberry-Banana Whip

SERVES 2

8 strawberries, hulled and halved
1 banana, cut into 1-inch chunks
1 cup freshly squeezed orange juice
1 tablespoon freshly squeezed lime juice

Combine all the ingredients in a blender and blend until smooth. Chill or serve immediately.

Raspberry-Lime Yogurt Smash

SERVES 2

2 tablespoons freshly squeezed lime juice
$1/2$ cup frozen raspberries in syrup or fresh raspberries
$1/2$ cup freshly squeezed orange juice
1 cup vanilla or plain yogurt
2 tablespoons honey, or 3 tablespoons if using fresh raspberries

Combine all the ingredients in a blender and blend until smooth. Chill or serve immediately.

Brasserie Basics

Garlic Oil and Puree

Herb Oil

Mushroom Mix

Herb Mix

Bouquet Garni

Rick's House Cheese Mix

Mayonnaise

Spicy Aioli

Roasted Garlic Aioli

Roasted Eggplant

Slow-Roasted Tomatoes

Roasted Red Peppers

Caramelized Onions

Seasoned Breadcrumbs

Chicken Stock

Veal, Lamb, or Beef Stock

Fish Stock

Vegetable Stock

Barbecue Sauce

Garlic Oil and Puree

This indispensable mixture is used in many, many of our dishes. Once you make it, you'll never be without it. You'll use the oil as a flavoring and cooking medium, especially on our pizzas and pastas. If you keep topping up with fresh oil as you use it, each batch will last a month in the refrigerator. The puree at the bottom can be dipped out to use whenever a recipe calls for minced garlic: figure 1 teaspoon of puree per clove.

2 large whole heads of garlic
3 cups pure olive oil
1 cup canola oil

1) Separate the cloves of garlic and trim off the stem ends.

2) Crush the cloves with the flat side of a heavy knife, pressing hard to separate the skins from the flesh. Peel the cloves and discard the skins.

3) In a food processor or blender, or in a container using a hand blender, combine the garlic and oils. Puree 2 minutes, until minced.

4) Before using, let the garlic pieces settle to the bottom of the container.

5) Cover tightly and store in the refrigerator, topping up with oil as necessary.

Herb Oil

We use infused oils instead of sauces when we want to add flavor and aroma to a dish without making it heavier or richer. Herb oils, citrus oils, and spice oils are all widely available now, each with its own very strong character: taste and smell them before using so you can control their effects in your cooking. The bright green colors and flavors of this mixed-herb oil make it a versatile favorite, great for drizzling on almost anything: soups, pizzas, roasts (especially Roast Pork Loin with Armagnac-Prune Stuffing, pages 171–73), and as a final touch of freshness on salads. Feel free to adjust the ingredients and proportions to your taste, but be careful when adding stronger herbs like rosemary and sage: they can have a very pungent quality.

1)   Bring a saucepan of water to a boil. Fill a large bowl with ice cubes and cover with cold water.

2)   Blanch the herbs in the boiling water just until wilted, then remove with a slotted spoon and plunge into the ice water to stop the cooking.

3)   Blot the herbs dry on paper towels, then transfer to a blender. Add olive oil to cover and blend until smooth. Transfer to a jar and mix in the remaining oil.

4)   Store in the refrigerator in an airtight container. After 2 days, discard it.

3 sprigs fresh basil, leaves only
6 sprigs fresh parsley, leaves only
1 sprig fresh mint, leaves only
6 sprigs fresh cilantro, leaves only
6 fresh chives
2 cups extra-virgin olive oil

Mushroom Mix

MAKES ABOUT 5 CUPS

As our friend Jack Czarnecki says in his Cook's Book of Mushrooms, "Mushrooms know no national boundaries." Neither does garlic, and this simple sauté that puts them together is a key element in our French, Italian, and American dishes. A main component of a classic French kitchen is an elegant, finely diced mushroom mixture called duxelles: this is our heartier version, with lots of substance and unmistakable woodsy flavor. We chose this mix for its flavors and textures, but also because these varieties are widely available all across the country. Don't be afraid to experiment with the mushrooms at your supermarket: chanterelles, trumpet mushrooms, porcini, and others can add excitingly different flavors to your food.

Mushrooms should never be washed: their open pores absorb water and become spongy. Just brush them clean and wipe with a damp paper towel. Cooking them quickly over very high heat brings out the liquids and concentrates the flavors, but be careful not to overcook them. If you're not familiar with these mushrooms, here's a crash course:

Shiitake is a domestically cultivated Asian mushroom with distinctive smoky taste and a dry texture that can stand up to strong spices and sauces. Look for firm caps, and always discard the stems before cooking.

Cremini is a more robust variety of the cultivated domestic mushroom, with a true mushroom flavor and a firm texture.

Domestic, white, or button mushrooms are mild and very moist with a light mushroom flavor.

Oyster refers to a whole category of mushrooms with wavy shapes that make them look like sea creatures. They are versatile and mild, with a great texture, but should be cooked only very briefly.

1) Wipe all the mushrooms clean with a damp cloth but do not rinse them.

2) Remove and discard the stems of the shiitakes. Trim off the stem ends of the other mushrooms.

3) Slice the shiitake, cremini, and button mushrooms 1/4 inch thick. With your hands, gently pull the oyster mushrooms apart into bite-size pieces.

4) In a skillet, heat the oil over high heat. When the pan is very hot, add the garlic and shallot and cook, stirring, just until softened, about 1 minute.

5) Add the shiitakes and stir. Add the creminis and stir. Add the buttons and stir. Add the oysters and cook the mixture, stirring, just until the mushrooms have released their liquid and begun to brown, about 3 to 5 minutes. Do not lower the heat; you want to get rid of the liquid and cook the mushrooms quickly. Do not overcook; the mushrooms will continue to cook after you remove them from the pan.

6) Remove from the heat and use immediately, or transfer to a bowl and let cool to room temperature. Cover tightly and refrigerate up to 1 day.

8 ounces shiitake mushrooms

8 ounces cremini mushrooms

8 ounces white button mushrooms

4 ounces oyster or another exotic mushroom

2 tablespoons light olive oil

2 garlic cloves, minced

1 shallot, minced

Kosher salt and freshly ground black pepper

Herb Mix

A sprinkle of fresh herbs can make more of a difference in the finishing of a dish than any single ingredient did in cooking it. The flavor helps keep your palate fresh and ready for the next bite, and the fragrance accents the all-important aromas of your food—using fresh herbs regularly will make a real impression on your cooking. This is just a basic mix of soft, leafy herbs; add and subtract, using chervil, tarragon, mint, chives, basil, cilantro, whatever you like best. However, herb mixes that include the stronger, stiffer herbs like marjoram, rosemary, thyme, oregano, and sage will have a different character—more pungent and powerful—so use them carefully.

The amounts given here are just a guideline for shopping. The main point is to have equal amounts of each so that no single herb can dominate. Feel free to use this mixture whenever a recipe calls for chopped parsley, basil, or chives; we often do. Have fun with it.

2 ounces fresh flat-leaf parsley leaves
2 ounces fresh chives
2 ounces fresh basil leaves

1) Chop the parsley: with one hand, gather the leaves together in a tight bunch. With the other hand, use a long, sharp knife to slice the bunch into fine shreds. Then, with one hand holding the knife handle and the other on top of the knife blade, use a rocking motion to reduce the leaves to small bits.

2) Chop the chives: holding the chives bunched together in one hand, use the knife to slice them into short lengths. Or snip them with sharp scissors.

3) Chop the basil: stack the leaves into a pile, then roll tightly into a cylinder. Use the knife to thinly slice the cylinder crosswise into fine shreds.

4) Combine the herbs in an airtight container and shake to combine. Cover and refrigerate 1 day.

Bouquet Garni

The subtle aromatics of this basic mixture are fundamental to our soups and stews. This is a very green, herbal mixture that can be adjusted to suit your taste. The bouquet garni is always discarded before serving.

Bundle the herbs together and tie tightly with kitchen twine.

1 sprig fresh thyme
1 sprig fresh rosemary
1 bay leaf
6 sprigs fresh parsley
4 chives, or $^1/_4$ leek

Rick's House Cheese Mix

We love the delicate nuttiness of Parmigiano-Reggiano, especially when balanced by the sharp gaminess of pecorino Romano. Our last touch on almost any dish, this is too good to save just for pasta. If the cheese is bought in blocks, grated by hand (never buy pregrated cheese), and properly stored, you will notice a world of difference in the flavor. The important thing to remember is not to reduce the cheese to a powder, which will cause it to become stale quickly.

4 ounces Parmigiano-Reggiano cheese

4 ounces pecorino Romano cheese

1) Using a box grater, hand grater, or the food processor, grate the cheeses into fine shreds; do not reduce them to a powder. If using a food processor, feed both cheeses through the coarse grating blade, then attach the metal blade and pulse just until grated.

2) In an airtight jar, combine the grated cheeses and shake to combine. Cover tightly and refrigerate up to 3 weeks.

Mayonnaise

Supermarket mayonnaise is fine for many purposes, but if you've never tasted the real thing (or its many delectable variations), you're missing out on a great pleasure. Homemade mayonnaise tastes like a fresh sauce, not like a condiment: think of the flavor gap between a jar of maraschino cherries and a handful of ripe ones. And when you move on to homemade Roasted Garlic Aioli (page 301), it will be only a matter of time before you go wild and start floating delicious croutons of Spicy Aioli (page 300) in your soups.

Using a whole egg makes the mixture lighter, fluffier, more stable, and easier to make. Just be patient at the beginning when adding the oil: take a break from pouring every so often to give the mixture a chance to emulsify as you go. As always when working with raw eggs, buy them fresh and keep them in the refrigerator until the last moment. Fresh mayonnaise should be eaten within 3 days.

1) In a food processor, mixer, or blender, combine the egg and lemon juice. Blend for 10 seconds at medium speed. Still blending, pour in the oil in a very thin stream and process until the mixture is thick and creamy.

2) Add the salt and pepper and pulse just to combine. Use immediately, or let the mayonnaise firm up in the refrigerator for 30 minutes, or scrape it into an airtight container and refrigerate up to 3 days.

1 large egg

1 tablespoon freshly squeezed lemon juice

1 cup light olive oil

¼ teaspoon kosher salt

⅛ teaspoon freshly ground black pepper

Spicy Aioli

MAKES 1 CUP

1 cup Mayonnaise, homemade
(page 299) or store-bought

1 tablespoon freshly squeezed lemon
juice

1 small garlic clove, finely minced

1 teaspoon hot paprika

$^{1}/_{4}$ teaspoon cayenne pepper, or to
taste

$^{1}/_{4}$ teaspoon ground cumin

Kosher salt and freshly ground black
pepper

In a bowl, whisk the mayonnaise and lemon juice together until well blended. Mix in the remaining ingredients, making sure no clumps of spices remain. Scrape into an airtight container, cover, and refrigerate up to 3 days.

Roasted Garlic Aioli

MAKES 1 CUP

1) Preheat the oven or a toaster oven to 400°F.

2) Cut the top ¼ inch off the garlic head and rub the head lightly to remove excess skin.

3) Put the garlic head on a sheet of aluminum foil, add the oil, salt, and pepper, and rub to coat. Wrap the garlic tightly and bake until very soft and sweet, about 40 minutes.

4) When cool enough to handle, squeeze out the cloves by turning the head upside down and pressing down on the center with your thumbs, as though you were trying to turn the head inside out.

5) Remove any bits of skin and fiber from the flesh and place in a blender or food processor.

6) Add the mayonnaise and parsley and process until smooth.

7) Scrape into an airtight container, cover, and refrigerate up to 3 days.

1 whole head garlic, with the skin
1 teaspoon light olive oil
1 teaspoon kosher salt
½ teaspoon freshly ground black pepper
1 cup Mayonnaise, homemade (page 299) or store-bought
1 tablespoon chopped fresh parsley

Roasted Eggplant

Well-roasted eggplant is firm and nutty, with a meaty bite that no other vegetable can supply to dishes like earthy Roasted Eggplant–Wild Rice Risotto (pages 112–13) or Caramelized Onion Pizza (page 62). Use firm, heavy, smooth-skinned eggplants that are small to medium in size; the size is more important than the variety. Large ones are too mature and may be bitter.

4 to 6 eggplants, any variety, small to medium size

Kosher salt

Freshly ground black pepper

2 tablespoons Garlic Oil and Puree (page 292), or 2 tablespoons olive oil mixed with 1 minced garlic clove

1) Preheat the oven to 450°F.

2) Cut the stems off the eggplant and discard. Cut off the bottom $1/2$ inch of each eggplant and discard.

3) Slice the eggplants in half lengthwise. With the tip of a knife, score the flesh in a diamond pattern, cutting almost all the way through the flesh. Rub the cut surfaces with salt and pepper. Drain cut side down 15 minutes.

4) Arrange the eggplant halves on a baking sheet, cut side up. Brush with garlic oil. Roast 15 minutes, turn over, and bake 15 to 20 minutes more, until cooked through but still firm.

5) Let cool, then cut for the recipe. Use immediately, or cover tightly and refrigerate up to 2 days.

Slow-Roasted Tomatoes

These are the perfect midpoint between chewy sun-dried tomatoes and plump ripe red ones. Meaty and soft, slow-roasted tomatoes have the taste and texture of a slightly concentrated fresh tomato, with no cooked taste. They are stunning when made with ripe tomatoes but will do wonders for even medium-ripe winter tomatoes. Plum tomatoes have lots of meat and low moisture, so they are our choice for this process. A cup or so is wonderful in pasta, on pizza, or by itself as an intense tomato salad.

1) Preheat the oven to 200°F.

2) Cut tomatoes in half lengthwise and remove the seeds and gel.

3) On a baking sheet, toss the tomato halves with the oil, garlic, and salt and pepper to taste. Arrange them cut side up and scatter the thyme on top.

4) Bake about 4 to 6 hours, depending on the ripeness of the tomatoes, until sweet and concentrated but still plump and juicy. They should not be dried out or tough. The goal is to have the tomatoes slowly cook and release their liquids.

5) Let cool in the pan. Use immediately or transfer to a container and cover with the pan juices and a little extra olive oil. Cover and refrigerate up to 3 days.

3 pounds ripe plum tomatoes
^{1}/$_2$ cup extra-virgin olive oil
4 medium garlic cloves, minced
Sea salt or kosher salt and freshly ground black pepper
6 sprigs fresh thyme

Roasted Red Peppers

Anyone who has roasted peppers in the house is automatically transformed into a great cook: healthy, deep-flavored pastas, pizzas, sandwiches, antipasti, and soups appear as if by magic. Red peppers are the best candidate for the flame-roasting method, which produces results of unbeatable silkiness and sweetness. You needn't splurge on glossy imported peppers for this purpose, as variations in shape and color won't make much difference to the finished product. What will make a difference is too much water: don't rinse the charred peppers to get the seeds and scraps of skin off, or you will lose all the flavorful oils as well.

Red bell peppers
Olive oil

1) Skewer a whole pepper on the end of a long fork. Hold the pepper directly over the flame of a gas burner, turning to roast all the sides. (If you have an electric stove, use a very hot cast-iron skillet or griddle, or a broiler.) When the skin is completely black and charred, transfer the pepper to a thick plastic bag and close the top. Steam for 5 to 8 minutes.

2) When cool enough to handle, use your hands or a knife to gently pull and scrape off the skin and stem.

3) Cut the pepper into quarters and lightly rinse if necessary.

4) Use immediately or cover with olive oil and refrigerate, tightly covered, up to 3 days.

Caramelized Onions

These have a rich sweetness all their own, with a completely different character from raw or sautéed onions. The starches and carbohydrates in the onions must be slowly converted into sugar; if you rush the process, they will scorch. Cook over very low heat and do not stir constantly; give the onions a chance to caramelize and turn a deep topaz brown. Nonstick pans will not work well for this procedure. Use the soft, sweet result—it's almost a chutney—on pizzas, in soups and stews (especially our French Onion Soup with Gruyère and Country Mustard, pages 34–35), on sandwiches, or on top of steamed or sautéed vegetables.

3 tablespoons unsalted butter

2 large yellow onions, halved and thinly sliced

1) In a large skillet, melt the butter over medium heat.

2) Add the onions, reduce the heat to low, and cook, uncovered, stirring occasionally, until soft and sweet, about 25 minutes. The onions will be limp and caramel-colored; do not let them burn.

3) Cover tightly and refrigerate up to 2 days.

Seasoned Breadcrumbs

MAKES ABOUT 4 CUPS

The perfect balance of crunch, herbs, spices, and salt makes a big difference to any dish with breadcrumbs. This version goes into our Individual Veal Meat Loaves with Tomato-Basil Sauce (pages 148–49), on top of Cassoulet (pages 168–70) to form a fragrant golden crunch, and into the coating for thin, crisp scallops of Veal Milanese with Red Wine Sauce, Artichokes, and Cremini Mushrooms (pages 176–77). Or just sprinkle it on top of pasta for a savory change from grated cheese, as frugal Italians have done for hundreds of years.

1 loaf Brioche (pages 82–83) or sourdough bread

¹/₂ cup freshly grated Parmesan cheese

¹/₄ cup dried oregano

¹/₄ cup dried basil

¹/₄ cup chopped fresh parsley

1 tablespoon extra-virgin olive oil

¹/₂ teaspoon red pepper flakes (optional)

¹/₂ teaspoon kosher salt

Freshly ground black pepper

1) Preheat the oven to 300°F.

2) Cut the bread into 1-inch cubes. Arrange on a baking sheet and bake about 45 minutes, until golden brown. Set aside to cool for at least 20 minutes.

3) When cool and dry, put the cubes in a food processor and pulse until reduced to small crumbs. Add the rest of the ingredients and pulse to combine.

4) Cover tightly and store in a cool, dry place.

Chicken Stock

We know you've heard this before, but we can't say it too many times: your cooking is only as good as the raw materials you put into it. That's the best reason for making your own stock, and the same rule applies to the stock as well. Use fresh bones or fresh chicken (well rinsed to remove impurities), good-tasting water (some tap water is highly chlorinated or rusty), pure kosher salt, and plenty of vegetables, and your stock will never fail you. Just be very careful not to let the mixture boil after the initial boil is achieved, or the stock will turn cloudy. Even cloudy stock, however, is perfectly usable.

1) Rinse the chicken bones under cold water for 5 to 10 minutes to remove impurities, then put them in a large stockpot. Add the water and set the pot over high heat. Bring to a boil, then skim off any foam that comes to the top.

2) Add the rest of the ingredients, cover, and let the mixture come to a boil. Skim again, removing any more foam that comes to the top. Reduce the heat so that the liquid stays at a bare simmer. Do not boil or the stock will be cloudy.

3) Simmer, uncovered, 2 hours, skimming off any foam and scum that rises to the top.

4) When stock is golden and lightly flavorful, strain into another pot. Use immediately, or cool the stock by immersing the pot in a sink full of ice water. When cool, pour into containers or ice-cube trays and freeze as soon as possible. Two ice cubes is the equivalent of about 1/4 cup stock. Frozen, the stock lasts up to 2 months.

4 pounds chicken bones (preferably raw; backs and necks are fine), or one 4-pound chicken, cut up, skin and fat removed

8 quarts water, preferably filtered or spring water

2 large carrots, chopped

2 large stalks celery, chopped

2 medium onions, chopped

1 bulb fennel, diced

1 large whole head of garlic, halved horizontally, with the skin

2 bay leaves

1 tablespoon kosher salt

1 teaspoon black peppercorns

3 sprigs fresh thyme

3 sprigs fresh rosemary

Veal, Lamb, or Beef Stock

MAKES ABOUT 6 CUPS

This recipe makes a more concentrated, flavorful broth than the chicken stock above. The bones must cook for at least 3½ hours to extract all the flavor from the marrow, so the initial liquid is very much reduced in the final result. If the stock tastes very strong, dilute with boiling water for use in soups. Again, remember not to let the mixture boil.

6 pounds veal, lamb, or beef bones, including some knuckles, cut into 3-inch pieces

2 tablespoons light olive oil

1 cup tomato paste

8 ripe plum tomatoes, diced

2 large onions, chopped

2 large carrots, chopped

2 large stalks celery, chopped

1 bulb fennel, diced (for veal or lamb stock only)

2 whole heads garlic, halved horizontally, with the skin

8 quarts cold water, preferably filtered or spring water

10 bay leaves

1 tablespoon dried thyme

1 tablespoon dried oregano

1 tablespoon dried tarragon (optional)

¹/₂ cup chopped fresh parsley

1¹/₂ teaspoons black peppercorns

1 tablespoon kosher salt

2 cups dry red wine

1) Preheat the oven to 425°F.

2) Rinse the bones under cold running water for 5 to 10 minutes to remove any impurities.

3) In a large roasting pan, place the bones in the pan. Roast about 30 to 40 minutes, until browned. Add the tomato paste and toss to coat, then return to the oven to roast 10 minutes more. Add the tomatoes, onions, carrots, celery, fennel if using, and garlic and toss to mix. Return to the oven and roast until the vegetables and bones are well browned, about 30 minutes more. Keep tossing and checking.

4) Remove from the oven and transfer the bones and vegetables to a large stockpot. Set the roasting pan with the juices aside.

5) Pour the water over the bones and vegetables, then add the bay leaves, thyme, oregano, tarragon, parsley, peppercorns, and salt. Cover and bring just to a boil over high heat.

6) Meanwhile, put the roasting pan on top of the stove and reheat the pan juices over medium heat, adding a little water if necessary to moisten. When the juices are hot, pour the wine into the pan and stir, scraping with a wooden spoon to bring up the browned bits from the bottom of the pan. When the bottom of the pan is clean, pour the mixture into the stockpot. Stir well.

7) When the mixture just comes to a boil, uncover and reduce the heat so that the liquid stays at a simmer. Do not boil or the stock will be cloudy. Skim off any scum that has risen to the top with a slotted spoon.

8) Simmer, uncovered, about 4 hours, skimming as necessary.

9) When the stock is reduced and flavorful, strain into another pot. If you want to get a more concentrated stock (demi-glace), reduce by half. Use immediately, or cool the stock by immersing the pot in a sink full of ice water. When cool, pour into containers or ice-cube trays and freeze as soon as possible. Two ice cubes is the equivalent of about 1/4 cup stock. Frozen, the stock lasts up to 2 months.

Fish Stock

A light, well-flavored fish stock makes a tremendous difference in your seafood soups, stews, and pastas. Commercial clam juice is fine for what it is, but it isn't a true stock. Our recipe has plenty of vegetables, herbs, and citrus that brighten the flavors of any dish. Note that the cooking time is much shorter than for other stocks.

2 pounds fresh raw fish bones, including heads, from light-fleshed fish such as snapper, sea bass, grouper, flounder, halibut, or cod (do not use bones from salmon, bluefish, mackerel, swordfish, or other oily fish)

2 tablespoons olive oil

4 quarts cold water, preferably filtered or spring water

2 large onions, chopped

2 large carrots, chopped

2 large stalks celery, chopped

1 orange, scrubbed and halved

1 lemon, scrubbed and halved

7 bay leaves

$^1/_2$ cup chopped fresh parsley

1 teaspoon dried thyme

1 teaspoon dried tarragon

$^3/_4$ teaspoon black peppercorns

2 teaspoons kosher salt

1) Rinse the bones under cold running water for 5 to 10 minutes to remove any impurities, then put them in a large stockpot with olive oil and sweat 10 minutes.

2) Add the remaining ingredients, and cook 10 minutes more. Cover, and bring just to a boil over high heat.

3) Uncover and reduce the heat so that the liquid stays at a bare simmer. Do not boil or the stock will be cloudy. Skim off any scum that has risen to the top with a slotted spoon and simmer 10 minutes.

4) Raise the heat to medium and cook 30 minutes more.

5) When the stock is reduced and lightly flavorful, strain into another pot. Use immediately, or cool the stock by immersing the pot in a sink full of ice water. When cool, pour into containers or ice-cube trays and freeze as soon as possible. Two ice cubes is the equivalent of about $^1/_4$ cup stock. Frozen, the stock lasts up to 2 months.

Vegetable Stock

Vegetarians and vegetable lovers are often directed to use water instead of stock in soups and stews, without mention of how much this will affect the flavor of the finished product. Using water certainly will not ruin a well-seasoned dish, but a dimension of flavor is always lost. Here's a better solution, with great taste and rich color.

1) In a large stockpot, heat the oil over high heat. Add the onion, carrot, celery, and garlic and cook, stirring, until the vegetables are softened and the onion is translucent, about 3 to 5 minutes.

2) Add the remaining ingredients in order, cover, and bring to a boil over high heat.

3) When the mixture comes to a boil, uncover and reduce the heat so that the liquid stays at a bare simmer. Skim off any scum that has risen to the top with a slotted spoon and simmer about 1³/4 hours.

4) When the stock is reduced and lightly flavorful, strain into another pot. Use immediately, or cool the stock by immersing the pot in a sink full of ice water. When cool, pour into containers or ice-cube trays and freeze as soon as possible. Two ice cubes is the equivalent of about ¹/4 cup stock. Frozen, the stock lasts up to 2 months.

1 tablespoon light olive oil

1 large onion, halved and thinly sliced

1 large carrot, chopped

1 large stalk celery, chopped

3 whole heads garlic, halved horizontally, with the skin

2 ripe medium tomatoes, diced

2 ears corn, kernels and cobs included but kernels cut off the cobs, or one 10-ounce package frozen corn kernels

8 ounces cremini mushrooms or shiitake mushroom stems, ends trimmed off

6 bay leaves

1 tablespoon chopped fresh parsley

1 teaspoon chopped fresh oregano

1 teaspoon chopped fresh basil

1 teaspoon chopped fresh thyme

1 teaspoon chopped fresh chives

1 teaspoon black peppercorns

1 teaspoon kosher salt

Barbecue Sauce

MAKES ABOUT 1 QUART

There are thousands of competing sauces out there, but making a batch at home reminds you what barbecue sauce is supposed to taste like: fresh and bright, not super-sweetened and overcooked. We experimented with this sauce for months before getting it just right, with the perfect balance of sweet and hot. But it's no magic formula, just the one we like best because of the extra citrus juices that bring out the other flavors. This sauce has lots of ingredients and lots of flavor but requires very little effort: just simmer the mixture in a saucepan, let cool, and refrigerate it for up to a month. Use as a barbecue sauce on beef, ribs, or chicken; as a marinade, thinned with oil; or as a condiment on sandwiches and burgers.

2 tablespoons olive oil

1 small onion, minced

2 garlic cloves, minced

$^1/_4$ cup freshly squeezed lemon juice

$^1/_4$ cup freshly squeezed orange juice

1 teaspoon chili powder

3 tablespoons cider vinegar

One 28-ounce can canned crushed tomatoes

$^1/_2$ cup packed light brown sugar

$^1/_4$ cup dark molasses

2 tablespoons Worcestershire sauce

$^1/_4$ cup red wine vinegar

2 tablespoons honey

1 teaspoon ground cumin

1 teaspoon freshly ground black pepper

1) Heat the olive oil in a skillet over medium heat. Add the onion and garlic and cook, stirring, until softened and translucent, about 5 minutes. Do not let them brown. Transfer to a bowl and set aside to cool.

2) In another bowl, combine the remaining ingredients and mix thoroughly. Stir in the onion and garlic, cover, and refrigerate overnight.

3) The next day, bring to a boil and simmer, uncovered, about 1 hour, until thickened. Adjust the seasonings with cayenne and salt to taste. If a smooth consistency is desired, use a hand blender to puree the sauce, or do it in batches in a blender.

4) Use immediately or let cool, cover tightly, and refrigerate up to 1 week.

1 tablespoon dried oregano

1 heaping teaspoon coarse-grain mustard

$^{1}/_{2}$ teaspoon garlic powder

1 tablespoon sweet paprika

$^{1}/_{2}$ teaspoon kosher salt

$^{1}/_{2}$ to 1 teaspoon cayenne pepper

Seasonal and Favorite Menus

Summer

Riviera Caesar Salad

Zigzag Breadsticks

*Fusilli with Chicken and Asparagus in
Thyme-Tomato-Cream Sauce*

Summer Berry Pudding

Passionfruit Lemonade

Tuscan Arugula Pizza

Grilled Shrimp with Aiolis

*Sicilian Tuna with Braised Fennel, Tomato,
and Capers*

Plum Crostata

Autumn

*Curried Pumpkin-Apple Soup with
Cinnamon Pumpkin Seeds*

*Skirt Steak Sandwiches with Roasted
Shallots and Horseradish Mayonnaise*

*Triple-Chocolate Pudding
Crisp Oatmeal-Raisin Cookies*

Escargots with Lots of Garlic

*Roquefort and Pear Salad
with Grapes and Spiced Pecans*

*Osso Buco with Saffron Risotto
and Orange Gremolata*

Aunt Jimmy's Streusel Apple Crisp

Winter

French Onion Soup with
Gruyère and Country Mustard

Cassoulet

Gale's Root Beer Float

Tangerine Angel Food Cake
with Tangerine Glaze

Steamed Mussels with Fennel, Cream,
and Pernod

Chicago Choucroute

Camembert and Caramelized Orange Slices
with Parsley Salad

Sticky Toffee Pudding with
Butterscotch Sauce

Spring

Spring Vegetable Minestrone
with White Beans and Pesto

Parmesan–Black Pepper Biscuits

Salmon Paillards with Mustard-Dill Sauce
and Creamy Cucumber Salad

Elsie's Poppyseed Shortbread

Crab Cakes and Baby Greens with Citrus
Vinaigrette and Spicy Aioli

Orecchiette with Zucchini, Chickpeas,
and Red Chile

Spring Vegetable and Rabbit Fricassee

The Best Banana Cream Pie

Brasserie Classics

Escargots with Lots of Garlic

Saucisson with Green Lentils
and Potato-Onion Ragoût

Profiteroles with Warm Glossy
Chocolate Sauce

Mediterranean Flavors

Roasted Eggplant–Wild Rice Risotto

Ricotta-Stuffed Flatbread

Portofino Bouillabaisse

Bob's Favorite Pink Grapefruit Granita

Seafood Menu

Gazpacho with Crabmeat and Croutons

Linguine with Manila Clams
and Fresh Basil

Sautéed Red Snapper with Tarragon Sauce
and Vegetable-Citrus Couscous

Blueberry Bread-and-Butter Pudding

Vegetable Menu

Caramelized Onion Tart

Roasted Stuffed Artichokes with Toasted
Nuts, Lemon, and Tomato

Farfalle with Many Mushrooms,
Tomatoes, and Fresh Herbs

Pont l'Évêque with Medjool Dates
and Endive

New Year's Eve Feast

First Course

Truffled Chicken Liver Mousse

Pizza Bianco with Porcini

Celery and Olives with Shaved
Parmigiano-Reggiano

Roasted Garlic Soup with
Polenta Croutons

Main Course

Marinated Rib-Eye Steaks
with Tobacco Onions

Blue Cheese Double-Baked Potatoes

Dessert

Caramelized Banana Split with
Orange-Glazed Walnuts

Chocolate Almond Biscotti

The Best Chocolate Malted

Valentine's Day Dinner

Chilled Asparagus, Shaved Fennel, and
Pecorino with Lemon-Basil Vinaigrette

Four-Pepper Oyster Stew

Pan-Roasted Salmon with
Coriander Seed and Wilted Spinach

Roasted Garlic Mashed Potatoes

Double-Chocolate Mousse Mud Pie

Dessert Diva Party

Warm Goat Cheese with Poached Dried
Fruit, Toasted Almonds, and Greens

Raspberry Rice Pudding

Chocolate Sour Cream Marble Cake

Coffee-Toffee Ice Cream
with Cinnamon Prune Compote

Chocolate-Dipped Coconut Macaroons

Gale's Root Beer Float

317

Appendix A

The Principles of
Pairing Food and Wine

by Marty Tiersky

The food in this book is based on the great European traditions of food and wine production. The choices of grapes, or "varietals," used to produce the wines of France and
Italy evolved together with, and as a complement to, the native cuisines of those regions.

The art of matching wine with food can be as simple as returning to the regional
source of the cuisine and seeking a traditional wine pairing. In many cases a wine made
from the same or a similar grape to the traditional match will also match the dish. This
simple formula is the foundation of my wine selections for *American Brasserie*.

Unfortunately, the choosing and drinking of wine is often made into an overcom-
plicated ritual instead of a natural, pleasurable accompaniment to a meal. A bottle of wine
should simply be considered a component of your meal, like the chicken, the vegetables, and
the bread. Try choosing wine the way you would choose the other elements of the meal.

First, choose wines that suit the occasion and the setting. A picnic or casual dinner with friends calls for different wine choices than a formal or holiday dinner. Second,
always look for wines with a balance of fresh fruit, rich flavor, and palate-refreshing acidity, whether red or white, sweet or sparkling. Consider the position in the meal: the same
pasta dish, served as a first course or as the central dish, might call for different wines.
Finally, select wines that complement the food on the table according to your palate: only
you know exactly how a combination tastes at your table.

When choosing the wines to accompany a multicourse meal, the wine, like the
food, should progress from lighter to fuller bodied. (If you are planning to serve only one
wine throughout a meal, the most realistic goal is to choose a wine that complements the
entree and preferably does not overwhelm earlier dishes.) Here is a course-by-course
breakdown of the points to remember:

Appetizers and salads should always be accompanied by young, light, crisp wines with fresh, clean flavors. Choices could include sparkling wines, vibrant whites with racy acidity, or light, fresh, fruity reds. When you are considering first-course wines, the preparations and ingredients are less important than the need to keep the palate fresh and not satiated.

Soups are complex foods, as the many flavors in the broth are often different from other elements of the soup: meats, pastas, vegetables, and so on. Match the wine to the solid elements of the soup rather than to its liquid. Pureed or cream soups are usually complemented by correspondingly rich wines with a good balance of acidity. If you are serving soup as a main course, serve a more complex and robust wine than you would otherwise choose.

Pasta and risotti can be very elegant and impressive dishes, but expensive wines are not usually called for. Look to the sauce and the ingredients of the dish when choosing a wine. Light, simple pastas with vegetables or seafood require light, fresh whites. Pastas with cream sauces and risotti will demand a white wine with more fullness and richness. Light tomato sauces, whether made with meat, poultry, or seafood, are best with light- to medium-bodied reds. Pasta and risotto made with hearty fowl or game demand hearty red wines.

The entree is the focal point of the meal. Therefore the wine choice should be more complex and distinctive than preceding wines. Here, saucing is perhaps the single most important factor in food and wine pairing. The sauce's base, richness, level of spicing, texture, and many other factors all give direction for wine choices. Where wine is used in the construction of a sauce, choose a similar wine to drink with the dish.

When serving entrees with neutral foundations like chicken, mild fish, and some cuts of veal, the saucing, cooking method, and the most dominant accompaniment should be your primary considerations. For example, when choosing a wine for a complicated entree like a traditional Thanksgiving turkey dinner, match the wine to the strong-flavored side dishes rather than the neutral turkey. Other rules of thumb: with **simple or rustic dishes**, look for straightforward, balanced, flavorful wines. When cooking with precious ingredients, choose a more complex and important wine.

With **seafood** the texture of the fish must be considered. For example, flaky fish require lighter wines than fish with rich, dense flesh. Meaty tuna and salmon often pair best with reds with soft tannins. Steamed, sautéed, and grilled preparations of the same fish require an escalating range of delicate to hearty wines. Rich, elegant whites are usually the answer for shellfish. Seafood sauced with intense stock reductions or tomato sauces often call for red wines.

Chicken is the ultimate neutral ingredient, so wine choices are completely dictated by the preparation and the side dishes. Cold chicken and chicken cooked with cream sauces are best with white wines, but with more distinctly flavored chicken dishes, medium-bodied reds with ripe fruit flavors are the best choice. When serving **duck, squab, and other game birds,** richer red wines normally apply, unless, for example, the saucing dictates a fruity white to accommodate a sweet or particularly spicy sauce. Grilled preparations or strongly marinated poultry require stronger red wines than sautéed or simply roasted birds.

Lean white meats such as veal, rabbit, and pork normally point to richer white and red wines to contrast the leanness of the meat, but also consider the sauce and the side dishes here. Rustic preparations like ragoûts and stews call for straightforward, balanced wines, as do sausages. When serving **red meats,** your choice should always be a red wine. The best bottles of red can be dusted off for the most simple preparations of beef and lamb: roasts, steaks, and chops.

Wine and **cheese** are foods with a natural affinity. This subject could be discussed in great detail, but the simplest approach is to complement a cheese with a wine produced from the same native region. The result will be a seamless pairing.

Sweet **dessert** wines can provide a wonderful finish to a meal. Always choose dessert wines with a good balance of fruit and acidity, with no cloying character. For the most pleasing match, the wine should always be sweeter than the dessert.

Pizza and sandwiches are simple and unpretentious dishes best served with your favorite fresh, crisp whites or light, fruity reds.

Finally, the considerations you make when matching flavors, textures, and ingredients in composing a meal are the same for wine as they are for food: complement, contrast, and balance. Wine is food. Enjoy it.

Appendix B

Where to Find Brasseries in France

In Paris:

Balzar
49, rue des Écoles
75006
1 43 54 13 67

Bofinger
7, rue de la Bastille
75004
1 42 72 87 82

Chez Jenny
39, boulevard du Temple
75011
1 42 74 75 75

La Coupole
102, boulevard du
Montparnasse
75014
1 43 20 14 20

Brasserie Flo
7, cour des Petites Écuries
75010
1 47 70 13 59

Brasserie de l'Île Saint-Louis
55, quai de Bourbon
75004
1 43 54 02 59

Julien
16, rue du Fauborg
Saint-Denis
75010
1 47 70 12 06

Lipp
151, boulevard
Saint-Germain
75006
1 45 48 53 91

Mollard
115, rue Saint-Lazare
75008
1 43 87 55 62

Au Pied de Cochon
6, rue Coquillière
75001
1 42 36 11 75

Brasserie Stella
133, avenue Victor Hugo
75016
1 47 27 60 54

Terminus Nord
23, rue de Dunkerque
75010
1 42 85 05 15

Le Train Bleu
place Louis Armand
75012
1 43 43 09 06

Le Vaudeville
29, rue Vivienne
75002
1 40 20 04 62

Le Zimmer
1 place du Chatelet
75001
1 42 36 74 03

And Beyond:

L'Ami Schutz
1, Ponts-Couverts
67000 Strasbourg
88 32 76 98

Brasserie André
71, rue de Bethune
59000 Lille
20 54 75 51

Le Bibent
5, place du Capitole
31000 Toulouse
61 23 89 03

La Cigale
4, place Graslin
44000 Nantes
40 69 76 41

Brasserie du Commerce
31, rue des Granges
25000 Besancon
81 81 33 11

Les Deux Garçons
53, cours Mirabeau
13100 Aix-en-Provence
42 26 00 51

L'Excelsior
50 rue Poincaré
54000 Nancy
83 35 24 57

Buffet de la Gare
3, place du General de Gaulle
57000 Metz
87 66 52 13

Brasserie Georges
30, cours de Verdun
69002 Lyons
72 56 54 54

Maison Kammerzell
16, place de la Cathédrale
67000 Strasbourg
88 32 42 14

Grand Café des Négociants
1, place Francisque-Regaud
69002 Lyons
78 42 50 05

Café de la Paix
54, rue Chaudrier
17000 La Rochelle
46 41 39 79

Appendix C

Mail-Order Sources

For chocolate truffles, provençal breadcrumbs, cookies, biscuit mix, flavored oils and vinegars, and Gale's Root Beer:

Gale by Mail
888-218-FOOD

For imported cheese, oil, pasta, grains, chocolate:

European Imports Ltd.
1334 W. Fulton Street
Chicago, IL 60607
312-227-0600

For fresh seafood:

The Seafood Merchants
900 Forest Edge Drive,
Corporate Wood
Vernon Hills, IL 60061
312-634-0900

For smoked seafood:

Homarus of Illinois
126 Touby Court
Des Plaines, IL 60018
847-298-2800

For wild game, wild mushrooms, foie gras:

Wild-Game
2315 W. Huron Street
Chicago, IL 60612
312-278-1661

For fresh and specialty produce:

Geo. Cornille & Sons Produce
60 S. Water Market
Chicago, IL 60608
312-226-1015

For fresh herbs:

The Herb Farm
32804 Issaquah-Fall City Road
Fall City, WA 98024
800-866-HERB

For spices and vanilla beans:

Penzey's Spice House
1921 S. West Avenue
Waukesha, WI 53186
414-574-0277

For fresh mozzarella, mascarpone, and ricotta cheeses:

The Mozzarella Company
2944 Elm Street
Dallas, TX 75226
800-798-2954

For all kinds of gourmet and imported products:

Dean & Deluca
800-221-7714
or
Balducci's
800-BALDUCCI'S
or
Williams-Sonoma
415-421-4242

For kitchen equipment:

The Chef's Catalog
3215 Commercial Avenue
Northbrook, IL 60062-1900
800-338-3232
or
Williams-Sonoma
415-421-4242

Bibliography

Aidells, Bruce, and Dennis Kelly. *Real Beer and Good Eats*. New York: Alfred A Knopf, 1993.

Beard, James. *James Beard's American Cookery*. New York: Little, Brown & Co., 1972.

Bentley, James. *Alsace*. Harmondsworth, UK: Penguin Books, 1978.

Chamberlain, Samuel. *Clementine in the Kitchen*. Boston: David R. Godine, 1988.

Child, Julia. *The Way to Cook*. New York: Alfred A. Knopf, 1989.

———, and Simone Beck. *Mastering the Art of French Cooking*. Vol. I. New York: Alfred A. Knopf, 1961.

Colwin, Laurie. *Home Cooking*. New York: HarperCollins, 1993.

———. *More Home Cooking*. New York: HarperCollins, 1995.

David, Elizabeth. *English Bread and Yeast Cookery*. Newton, MA: Biscuit Books, Inc., 1994.

de Groot, Roy Andries. *The Auberge of the Flowering Hearth*. Hopewell, NJ: The Ecco Press, 1983.

Grausman, Richard. *At Home with the French Classics*. New York: Workman Publishing Co., 1988.

Hazan, Marcella. *Essentials of Classic Italian Cooking*. New York: Alfred A. Knopf, 1992.

Hell-Girod, Ginette. *L'Esprit des Brasseries*. Paris: Editions de Chene, 1995.

Jackson, Michael. *Michael Jackson's Beer Companion*. Philadelphia: Running Press, 1993.

Lang, Jenifer Harvey, ed. *Larousse Gastronomique*. New York: Crown Publishers, 1988.

Lukins, Sheila, and Julee Rosso. *The New Basics Cookbook*. New York: Workman Publishing Co., 1989.

Olney, Richard. *Lulu's Provençal Table*. New York: HarperCollins, 1994.

Restaurants of Paris. New York: Alfred A. Knopf, 1994

Rombauer, Irma S., and Marion
    Rombauer Becker. *Joy of
    Cooking*. New York: Scribner,
    1995.

Root, Waverley. *The Food of
    France*. New York: Vintage
    Books, 1966.

———. *The Food of Italy*. New
    York: Vintage Books, 1971.

Toussaint-Samat, Maguelonne.
    History of Food. Trans.
    Anthea Bell. London:
    Blackwell Publishers Ltd.,
    1992.

Visser, Margaret. *Much Depends
    on Dinner*. New York: Collier
    Books, 1988.

Wechsberg, Joseph. *Blue Trout and
    Black Truffles*. Chicago:
    Academy Chicago Publishers,
    1985.

Wells, Patricia. *Bistro Cooking*.
    New York: Workman
    Publishing Co., 1989.

Index